THE SECOND AMENDMENT MANIFESTO

What Every American Should Know
about Their Constitutional
Right to Own Guns

JOHN PAINE

By John Paine (secondamendmentmanifesto.com)

Copyright © 2020 John Paine

All rights reserved. This book or any portion thereof may not be reproduced or used in any manner whatsoever without the express written permission of the publisher except for the use of brief quotations in a book review. The scanning, uploading, and distribution of this book via the internet or via any other means without the permission of the publisher is illegal and punishable by law. Please purchase only authorized electronic editions of this book. Don't participate in or encourage electronic piracy of copyrighted materials.

This book is a general educational historical and political information product and is intended for mentally sound, physically healthy adults aged 18 and over; and is solely for information and educational purposes and does not constitute legal, medical, or military advice.

Cover designed by Richard Ljoenes (richardljoenes.com)
Book designed by Victoria Wolf (wolfdesignandmarketing.com)
Edited by Mary Adams-Legge
Published by American Arms LLC (secondamendmentmanifesto.com)

ISBN 978-1-7360835-0-5 (paperback)

This book is dedicated to the patriots, pioneers, and partisans who created the United States, who risked their lives, fortunes, and freedoms to leave us a better world than they enjoyed, and to the free men and women who've fought tyranny in all its forms throughout the ages.

Contents

Free Summaries, Checklists, and Guides vii

Foreword ix

Why You Should Read This Book 1

The Two-Thousand Year History of the Right to Bear Arms
(In 15 Minutes) 5

Guns, Money, and Religion: The Bloody War that
Created the English Right to Bear Arms 15

America's Love Affair with Guns Is Older than America 35

Everything You Know About the American Revolution Is Wrong 41

Why Does the United States Have a Bill of Rights? 63

What the Second Amendment Was *Really* Meant to Protect 77

Are Guns Only for People in the Military?
Here's What the Founders Wanted 95

"You Only Have the Right to Own a Musket" and
Other Second Amendment Myths, Debunked 119

3 Things You Can Do Right Now to Defend Your Second Amendment Rights 143

The Civilian's Guide to Buying (and Safely Using) Guns,
Ammo, and Other "Military" Arms 155

The Fight Ahead 213

Would You Do Me a Favor? 217

Glossary: What "They" Don't Want You to Know
About Your Second Amendment Rights 219

References 241

Free Summaries, Checklists, and Guides

Thank you for reading *The Second Amendment Manifesto*.

To help you understand, appreciate, and preserve your Second Amendment rights as effectively as possible, I've put together several free resources for you to enjoy, including:

- A savable, shareable, printable reference guide with all of this book's key takeaways, organized by chapter.
- A list of the best books, websites, and other resources for understanding the Constitution, Bill of Rights, Second Amendment, gun rights, and the safe and effective use of firearms.
- A list of all of the most important gun-related gear, including product recommendations for firearms, ear and eye protection, ammunition, holsters, medical equipment, and more.

To get instant access to all of those free bonuses, go here now:
⇒ secondamendmentmanifesto.com/bonus

Also, if you have any questions, concerns, or feedback, just send me an email at john@secondamendmentmanifesto.com and I'll do my best to help! I read and respond to every message.

Foreword

Unlike many books on history, politics, or government, this one isn't a soggy and scholastic slog through cherry-picked facts and figures used like a drunkard uses a lamppost—for support rather than illumination.

Instead, it's a panoramic and penetrating analysis of the origin, meaning, and significance of the Second Amendment. Most importantly, this book demonstrates why the Second Amendment still matters. As you'll learn, it has always been about more than serving in a militia, hunting, or merely toting around firearms—it's entwined in the age-old struggle between the commoners and tyrants; between those who desire freedom and those who enslave; between good and evil.

You'll also appreciate that John is upfront about his agenda: He wants you to understand your Second Amendment rights so you can defend them from those who wish to take them away. That's it. To do this, however, he doesn't give short shrift to the "other side." In fact, by the end of this book, you'll know the strongest arguments for *and* against gun ownership, so you can make up your own mind about what role guns should play in our modern society.

I've also known and worked with John for years and can say without reservation that he's one of the most meticulous researchers I've ever known. When there are needles in the haystacks, he uncovers them, and he then presents his findings in an entertaining, enlightening, and inspiring way.

So, read this book and reflect on its teachings. We've reached a high noon in the perennial clash between individual liberty and state supremacy, and you can have a hand in what happens next. Will we preserve this fundamental right to bear arms, and with it the only effective method of defending against despotism and lawlessness, or will we abandon the Second Amendment and throw fat in the fire?

Also, to get the most out of this book, consult the glossary frequently—it's a gem. By learning the precise meanings of the words related to the Second Amendment, guns, and the mechanics of government found in this book, you'll gain a much deeper understanding of your rights as an American (and how to protect them!).

Happy reading. I hope you enjoy and benefit from the journey as much as I did.

—Sean Patrick, bestselling author of *The Know Your Bill of Rights Book*

1
Why You Should Read This Book

"No free man shall ever be debarred the use of arms."
—Thomas Jefferson, third President of the United States and author of the Declaration of Independence and the first draft of the Virginia Constitution, 1776.

"Hell, yes, we're going to take your AR-15, your AK-47."
—Beto O'Rourke, Democratic Texas congressman, September 12, 2019.

Have you ever wondered why the Second Amendment exists, and what it really means?

Have you ever felt confused about why a certain gun law gets passed in one state, but not in another?

Have you ever asked yourself why other countries *don't* look at gun ownership as a right or trust civilians to own many of the same guns as the police and military, yet we do?

If so, this book is for you.

Keep reading, and you'll learn why the Founding Fathers of the United States created the Second Amendment, what it was really meant to protect, and why it's still worth preserving over two centuries later.

Whether you're already a dyed-in-the-wool supporter of the Second Amendment, lukewarm toward the idea of owning guns, or even strongly anti-gun, you'll get something out of this book.

Instead of trying to convince you to support gun ownership or making fun of gun control advocates, this book takes a different approach.

First, you'll take a trip back in time to ancient Greece and Rome, medieval Europe, and enlightenment England, so you can understand the timeless moral and practical origins of the right to bear arms.

Next, you'll journey to the New World and learn the crucial role weapons played in the development of early American society, and how this legacy still affects us today.

You'll then learn what the American Revolutionary War was really about (it wasn't taxes), and how this logically and inevitably led to the creation of the Bill of Rights and the Second Amendment.

Then, you'll learn why the wise, iconoclastic, farsighted rebels we now call the Founding Fathers wrote the Second Amendment. Not only will you learn about the pragmatic reasons they wanted to protect the right of Americans to own guns, you'll learn the philosophical, moral, and ethical principles that guided their hands as they drafted it into the Bill of Rights.

Then, you'll learn the answer to the most important question of all: What role should the Second Amendment play in modern society? You'll learn why the Founding Fathers wanted civilians—not just the police and military—to own guns, what kind of guns they wanted Americans to own, and the reason Americans have a right to own guns now and in the future.

Finally, you'll learn what you can do to protect your Second Amendment rights. You'll learn how you can impact what laws do and don't get passed, what organizations are worth supporting, and how to buy and safely use and store a gun, if you wish to exercise your Second Amendment rights.

By the end, you'll know more about the Second Amendment than most of your fellow Americans ever will—and a *lot* more than most politicians, lobbyists, and lawmakers.

Not only will you understand the current legal issues surrounding the gun debate—whether new gun laws are unconstitutional or not—but you'll grasp the moral, philosophical, and historical lessons and principles that have made America the most free, prosperous, and powerful nation in history.

Chapter 1

The Second Amendment is something all free men and women should be able to get behind, regardless of their political persuasion or country of origin. Although the right to bear arms was codified as a keystone of the American government, this right transcends and predates American culture by centuries. At bottom, it represents a simple but profound idea: you were born with the rights to life, liberty, property, and the pursuit of happiness, you have the right to defend these precious possessions, and thus you have the right to own the tools you need to defend them—guns.

Before we continue, though, allow me to offer a home truth:

Now more than ever, it's time to throw your hat in the ring and educate yourself about the debate over guns in America. If you're pro-gun, it's no longer enough to sit on the sidelines and grumble about gun laws, console yourself that you own a gun, and put a rattlesnake sticker on your car. If you're on the fence about guns or anti-gun, you're doing a disservice to your country, community, and yourself if you mindlessly repeat the platitudes you pick up from the media without digging deeper. But no matter your political leanings, you need to inform yourself.

Politicians in every state are mounting a full-frontal assault on the Second Amendment, but as Daniel Webster proclaimed over two-hundred years ago, "God grants liberty only to those who love it, and are always ready to guard and defend it." That liberty will evaporate like a raindrop in the sun if you take it for granted.

This doesn't mean grabbing a rifle and rushing into the streets. Instead, the real battleground over your Second Amendment rights begins in private conversations over the dinner table, online, and among your friends.

If you're at all concerned about the gun debate in America and want to arm yourself to join the war of words that's currently being waged over the Second Amendment . . . you need to read this book.

2

The Two-Thousand Year History of the Right to Bear Arms (In 15 Minutes)

"Arms are the only true badge of liberty. The possession of arms is the distinction of a free man from a slave."
—Andrew Fletcher, Scottish writer, politician, and patriot, 1698.

"Banning guns addresses a fundamental right of all Americans to feel safe."
—Diane Feinstein, Democratic California senator, 1993.

Like much of American history, the story of the Second Amendment begins in England.

Specifically, it starts in 17th century England, when the country was riven in two by a civil war that crippled the monarchy and created the English Bill of Rights. This document was the first in human history to explicitly protect the right to bear arms, but the right to self-preservation—to defend oneself against criminals and tyrants—is as old as civilization.

This idea has existed since the time of ancient Greece and Rome, when free men could keep swords, spears, shields, and armor at home to defend their families and their country's borders. Not only were Greeks and Romans allowed to own weapons, their fighting skills were considered one of their most important functions as citizens. The Greeks invented the concept of *civic militarism*—the idea that those who take part in government must also fight to defend it.

To the Greeks, separating arms ownership from citizenship was not only impractical, but immoral. Anyone who took part in government was allowed to own weapons and was expected to use them to fight for the state and their own safety. Virtually all of the great Greek city-states, like Athens, Sparta, Thebes, Corinth, and Argos, fielded armies of free men who carried their own weapons into battle.

Greek citizens were also permitted to use their weapons in self-defense. The Athenian luminaries Aristotle, Draco, and Demosthenes describe cases in which citizens were allowed to use weapons to defend themselves from violence. Even the ancient Mesopotamian king Hammurabi alluded to the concept of self-preservation 4,000 years ago when he had these words chiseled in stone: "If a man put out the eye of another man, his eye shall be put out." In other words: harm someone, and they have the right to harm you.

The Romans expanded and perfected this concept of "a nation-in-arms" and used it to create the most powerful, prosperous, and stable empire the world had ever seen. When Rome was a republic, soldiers were required to show up for battle carrying their own weapons and armor. Even as Rome transformed into a sprawling empire, legionaries usually purchased their weapons from the state, after which they were considered private property. Specifically, the government would give the soldier weapons, the cost of which was deducted from their paychecks over time. What's more, any weapons they found on the battlefield were theirs to keep. "When a Roman soldier joined the roll of his centuria," explains historian Michael C. Bishop, "he was not just issued with the requisite items of equipment, but was rather expected to provide them for himself... There was special provision within Roman law to allow a soldier to actually own his equipment, since normally all property belonged to a father as the head of a household."

As the right to self-preservation has always been a fixture of free society, it's been a thorn in the side of those who seek to dominate others. Tyrants only maintain their grasp on power by being able to harm their subjects without fear of reprisal, which is why they've always attempted to disarm those they wish to rule. From the Thirty Tyrants of Athens to the Soviet Union to present-day Venezuela, stripping people of weapons so they can't fight back has ever been a tool the few use to control the many.

Many cultures understood this, but the English were the first to create a law prohibiting their rulers from disarming citizens. A century later, the Americans carried this concept to full fruition in the form of the Second Amendment. Before the United States was, well, the United States, it was a collection of English colonies, and almost every law in these colonies was transplanted from England, including the right to bear arms. Even the colonists' clothing, music, customs, and accents were nearly identical to their countrymen back home (the modern stereotypical British accent didn't fully form until decades later). As French diplomat, historian, and political scientist Alexis de Tocqueville observed when struck by the similarities between the English and the Americans, there is "not a single opinion, habit, or law . . . which the point of departure cannot readily explain."

In other words, early American history *is* English history, and the Second Amendment was inspired by and based on the English right to bear arms. To understand why we have the Second Amendment, what it means, and why it's worth protecting, you first need to learn about the English right to bear arms.

The history of this right traces back to the bloody foundations of England, when it was little more than a band of seven warring kingdoms ruled by Anglo-Saxons, Scots, Welshmen, and Vikings in the ninth century. These groups raided, pillaged, and slaughtered one another, but the greatest conflict was between the Vikings and the Anglo-Saxons. The Vikings made constant lightning raids into Anglo-Saxon territory, leaving villages burned, citizens slain or sold into slavery, and wealth, food, weapons, horses, and other valuables stolen. The Anglo-Saxons gave as good as they got, but by the mid-800s, the Vikings had the whip hand.

To defend themselves against this unyielding and unpredictable threat,

Anglo-Saxons were encouraged to own swords, spears, axes, bows, and almost any other weapon they could find. Not only were these weapons needed to fend off the Vikings, but they were also invaluable tools for hunting and self-defense against criminals. At this time, all tenants of the most powerful Anglo-Saxon kingdom, Wessex, were required to carry out the three "common burdens" of public service—the *trinoda necessitas*, or "three-knotted obligation" as it was called in Latin—fighting in the militia, building fortresses, and repairing bridges. Citizens were to produce their own weapons, keep them at home, and be ready to fight when the need arose, as they did when the Vikings invaded with their largest army yet in 865 AD.

This "Great Heathen Army" descended upon the outnumbered and surrounded West Saxons and nearly captured their king, Alfred. From his hiding place in the Somerset swamplands of southwest England, King Alfred commanded his lords to summon the *fyrds*—the armed citizens that protected Wessex. Armed with their own weapons and a spirit of defiance, conviction, and pride that would soon propel England into preeminence, these citizen soldiers shattered the war-hardened Vikings at the Battle of Edington, preserving the budding Anglo-Saxon kingdom that would one day bloom into modern Britain.

Long after Viking invasions ceased to be a problem, Englishmen used their weapons to defend themselves from foes both foreign and domestic. As England faced greater enemies and began to flex its militaristic muscles on the world stage, its rulers began to pass laws to encourage and even require citizens to own and train with weapons.

In the Assize of Arms of 1181, King Henry II specified the exact weapons that freemen, knights, and peasants were to own. Specifically, "Every knight was forced to arm himself with coat of mail, and shield and lance; every freeholder with lance and hauberk [a coat of mail], every burgess and poorer freeman with lance and iron helmet." The citizens of England were to be fully prepared for war, with even the lowliest peasants carrying almost the same weapons and panoply as the highest-ranking knights.

Henry II had multiple reasons for entrusting arms to people at every level of society. He feared the growing power of his barons would not only threaten his royal prerogative as king, but the safety and freedoms of his subjects. Thus, Henry killed two birds with one stone: by reviving the fyrd system established by Alfred and giving citizens weapons, he strengthened the power of the lower classes and his kingdom as a whole, and weakened the power of the nobility.

A century later, King Henry III extended this policy by requiring all subjects aged fifteen to fifty to own a weapon other than a knife. Towns were required to build shooting ranges so citizens could practice with the longbow, which English rulers realized gave them a major advantage over their enemies. (The longbow was more or less the assault rifle of the middle ages.) King Edward I took these policies one step further and banned all other sports on Sundays except for archery, and several decades later, Englishmen were required by law to practice archery on Sundays.

These laws weren't just meant to prepare citizens for military service, but to also make them more effective at protecting themselves and their towns from criminals. In the Statute of Winchester of 1285, Edward I required citizens to take part in the "watch and ward" of the kingdom, taking turns guarding towns and roads, and assisting in the identification and capture of criminals and suspicious persons. When a criminal was identified, men joined in the "hue and cry"—calling for assistance and pursuing anyone who committed a crime, resisted arrest, or escaped custody. Although this was the first time this primitive police system was codified, it had been practiced informally for centuries. This was a serious matter, and if someone witnessed a crime and didn't help capture the culprit, they would be held partly responsible. For example, in 1322, one John Brayn was imprisoned when he witnessed a murder in Northamptonshire and failed to raise the "hue and cry."

In all of these cases, the arms in question weren't provided by, stored, or owned by the state. These were privately owned weapons that the citizens kept in their homes and practiced with as they pleased (or as mandated by law). Eventually, these arms-bearing groups of citizens became known as the *militia* and were organized under a commander known as the Lord Lieutenant. In fact, the term *militia* only came into existence starting in the

1500s, as before this point there was little distinction between a free male citizen and a militiaman—you couldn't be one without also being the other.

Other kingdoms of Europe followed much the same system for centuries. Medieval Europe was a wild, ruthless, unpredictable world, and defenseless civilians were easy prey for marauding bands of mercenaries, rogue soldiers, and invading armies. As a result, towns formed sophisticated, well-armed, skilled militias that could face off against the finest knights of the era.

In Germany, "not only every noble, but even every burgher [a middle-class citizen] in the guilds has an armoury in his house so as to appear equipped at every alarm," writes Enea Piccolomini in 1444, the future Pope Pius II. "The skill of the citizens in the use of weapons is extraordinary," he exclaimed. In many towns across the Holy Roman Empire, full citizens and their dependents were required to keep weapons and armor in their homes, and in some towns, men could be arrested for not owning a sword.

The same was true in Renaissance Italy. The great political pragmatist Machiavelli wrote extensively about the virtues of an armed citizenry, writings that would influence the opinions of America's founders. Machiavelli was a diplomat, politician, writer, and adviser to many powerful men in 16th-century Italy. Although he wrote about myriad subjects, including military science, religion, and drama, Machiavelli's name has become synonymous with amoral power politics. Critics have said his most famous book, *The Prince,* taught "evil recommendations to tyrants to help them maintain their power." He condoned killing political opponents, silencing dissenters, and doing whatever was necessary to gain and maintain power. He was brutal, cunning, and some would say wicked, but he believed these vices served a greater good—protecting the welfare of his countrymen and his state.

Thus, you would expect Machiavelli to be an ardent supporter of disarming citizens to keep them passive and compliant. Instead, he was a fervent proponent of an armed populace. He organized and led a Florentine militia and wrote page after page about the merits of private arms ownership in his *Discourses on the First Ten Books of Titus Livy*, published in 1531.

Why?

Chapter 2

After years of studying history and practicing politics, Machiavelli concluded that the most sustainable, secure way for a leader to maintain power was to encourage his citizens to be armed. Machiavelli didn't see arms ownership as a right or an obligation as the English did, but as the most effective way to defend against invasion, to keep the peace, and most importantly, to prevent rulers from turning against their people.

Machiavelli's writings illustrate how citizens across Europe resented rulers who restricted their right to own weapons, and he urged leaders not to make this mistake. "Such are the inconveniences, then, that arise from depriving your people of arms…," he wrote, "For he who lives in the aforesaid way treats ill the subjects who reside within his domain…" He also knew that allowing citizens to own weapons would help earn their trust and create a massive militia force that could defend the borders. He championed a volunteer militia army over a conscripted or standing army, because "…compulsion makes men mutinous and discontented; but both experience and courage are acquired by arming, exercising, and disciplining men properly…"

Although Machiavelli encouraged rulers to be ruthless against individual political opponents, he knew this policy would backfire if applied to the population at large. As he wrote in *Discourses*, "For if you reduce them [citizens] to poverty, 'though despoiled, they still have arms,' and, if you disarm them, 'their fury will provide them with arms.'" This was particularly true in Machiavelli's time, when muskets and cannons were replacing swords and spears. Guns allowed unskilled peasants to compete with and kill armored knights who had trained all their lives in swordsmanship and military tactics. Wars would no longer be won by mail-clad men-at-arms wielding swords and lances, but by the common man aiming a musket, which made it much more difficult for the rich and powerful to suppress the lower classes by force.

Instead of fighting this inevitable rise of firearms ownership, Machiavelli encouraged it. When sharing his recommendations for training the militia, he urged physical conditioning "and using the crossbow, longbow, and harquebus [a short matchlock musket]—the last, you know, is a new, but very useful weapon. To these exercises I would accustom all the youth in the country..."

At bottom, Machiavelli was a realist. He made political decisions based on how people actually behaved, not how he wanted them to behave, and he knew that all rulers had a tendency to slide toward tyranny. The best deterrent against a would-be tyrant, he believed, was the threat of thousands of armed citizens rising up in rebellion.

No people embodied Machiavelli's views on arms ownership better than the English. For almost 600 years—from the founding of England to the reign of Charles II—there were few changes to English arms laws, with one notable exception.

In 1328, the Statute of Northampton was passed by King Edward III. This law forbade men from carrying arms or wearing armor when interacting with judges or royal officials, in markets or fairs, and when traveling on the roads. The law said that no man shall "... come before the King's justices, or other of the King's ministers doing their office, with force and arms, nor bring no force in affray of the peace, nor to go nor ride armed by night nor by day, in fairs, markets, nor in the presence of the justices or other ministers, nor in no part elsewhere..." Some historians point to this statute as evidence that England has a lengthy history of arms control laws, but—pun intended—their argument is weak tea.

First, people serving the king or joining in the hue and cry were exempt from the law. Second, it's not clear whether the law referred to carrying weapons or wearing armor. When the statute was written, "arms" had a broader meaning than it usually does now, encompassing both weapons like swords, spears, axes, and bows, and armor like mail, helmets, gauntlets, and shields. The *Encyclopaedia Londinensis* of 1810, a "universal dictionary of arts, sciences, and literature," states that "Arms, in the understanding of the law, are extended to any thing that a man wears for his defence, or takes into his hands or useth in anger to strike or cast at another." In the same volume, the section on the Statute of Northampton says that "Under these statutes none may wear (unusual) armor publicly..."

There are other pieces of evidence that show this statute was more about preventing people from wearing armor than carrying weapons. The famous English legal commentator William Blackstone compared the Statute of Northampton to the laws of the Athenian statesman Solon, which fined people for wearing armor in the city in times of peace. A few decades later, a manual produced for justices of the peace explained the statute as saying "A man cannot excuse the wearing of such armour in public." Finally, the punishment for violators of the statute was to ". . . forfeit their armour to the King, and their bodies to prison at the King's pleasure . . .," but not to give up their weapons, which suggests the law had more to do with wearing armor than carrying weapons.

Why would the king pass a law preventing people from wearing armor? The statute was passed during a turbulent time for the English. Queen Isabella of France had just usurped the throne from her husband with the help of her lover, Roger Mortimer, war with France was imminent, and the nation's coffers were almost empty. The last thing Edward wanted was to scare or provoke his subjects, and men riding across the country dressed in their war glory would have done exactly that.

The most convincing evidence that the Statute of Northampton was *not* meant to disarm Englishmen is the way in which Edward enforced it. There is no evidence of anyone being disarmed because of the law, and one of the first recorded attempts to use the statute in this way occurred several hundred years later. In 1686, Sir John Knight was charged with violating the statute when he carried a gun into a church. Many people witnessed his actions, and there was no doubt he carried the gun, but the court acquitted him because they didn't believe the statute prohibited Knight's right to bear arms in public.

Aside from the Statute of Northampton, the only meaningful arms control laws passed in England until the reign of Charles II came from Henry VIII, the poster child of feckless monarchs. When he wasn't dragging England into needless wars or executing his wives, he made a few half-hearted attempts to regulate the carrying of crossbows and pistols. Most of these laws were ignored, loosely enforced, overturned, or rendered obsolete by the time he died.

For all intents and purposes, Englishmen were free to buy, keep, and carry whatever weapons they liked. They took great pride in their right to bear arms and saw it as an emblem of their freedom, independence, and unity as a people. From the reign of Alfred the Great to the English Civil War, Englishmen were not just allowed to own, train with, and carry weapons, but were often forced to by law. They carried these weapons when patrolling their towns, pursuing criminals, and prosecuting England's wars, and they came to view arms ownership as a permanent aspect of their status as Englishmen.

It was these citizen soldiers—not mercenary armies—that fought off the Vikings, the French, the Dutch, and the Spanish, that settled the New World, and that would one day found and fight for the United States of America.

Many other Europeans understood the importance of owning weapons, too. Machiavelli, the most ruthless political pragmatist of the Renaissance, recognized early that it's better to allow people to have weapons than attempt to disarm them and risk their wrath and rebellion. Townsfolk across the Holy Roman Empire organized themselves into stalwart militias that repelled invaders, criminals, and corrupt government agents.

As you'll learn in later chapters, the Americans would inherit this tradition of arms ownership and protect it in their constitution. Before all of that, though, the English would force their own rulers to guarantee their right to bear arms after a civil war that drenched their island with blood.

3

Guns, Money, and Religion: The Bloody War that Created the English Right to Bear Arms

"One of the ordinary modes, by which tyrants accomplish their purposes without resistance, is, by disarming the people, and making it an offense to keep arms."
—Joseph Story, Associate Supreme Court Justice of the United States of America, 1840.

"I will support legislation that prevents the sale of military-style weapons to civilians, a magazine limit, and red-flag legislation . . . The carnage these military-style weapons are able to produce when available to the wrong people is intolerable."
—Mike Turner, Republican Ohio congressman, August 6, 2019.

In 1642, King Charles I of England declared war on his political opponents—Protestant members of Parliament and their followers.

The war was the culmination of a power struggle between the king and Parliament that had been brewing for years. On the one hand, Charles sought to regain what he saw as his royal right to rule unencumbered by self-absorbed aristocrats and simple commoners. On the other hand, Parliament resented his encroachments on their powers and feared his true aim was to create an absolute monarchy modeled after Catholic France. Tensions simmered during the Thirty Years War in the 1620s, when Charles declared martial law in England. Under martial law, citizens were forced to house and feed soldiers against their will, and they were subject to military trials where the local commander was judge, jury, and sometimes, executioner.

Angered by Charles' behavior and fearful of his growing power, Parliament responded by withholding funding for the war—which only they could provide. Charles flouted them and instead raised lucre by demanding "forced loans" from many of his subjects and imprisoning those who refused to pay. This scheme wasn't enough to defray the astronomical costs of the war, however, so Charles returned to Parliament to ask for funds. Finally able to twist Charles' arm, Parliament agreed to fund the war—but only after he conceded to a set of guarantees that would put an end to the worst of his abuses.

These concessions were recorded in a document known as the *Petition of Right*, which prohibited the King from collecting taxes without the consent of Parliament, billeting soldiers in civilians' homes, declaring martial law during peacetime, and imprisoning subjects without cause. Charles I bridled at these demands, yet desperate for money, agreed. But he didn't forget. As retribution, Charles refused to summon Parliament—one of his rights as king—for a decade after the incident. He short-circuited their power over taxes by instituting outdated policies, such as heavily fining people for not attending royal ceremonies and charging fees on shipping in English rivers.

Charles also clashed with Parliament over religion. Charles and many of his supporters were Catholic, but 98 percent of England was Protestant, and they were ever wary that Charles would limit their ability to worship, give preferential treatment to Catholics, or even attempt to convert the nation to Catholicism. The king justified their fears when he waged an abortive war against the Scots after they refused to accept his repressive religious rules. The invasion of Scotland was wildly unpopular in England, for many citizens feared Charles would soon impose the same policies on them. Scores of English militiamen abandoned the army as they marched north, further embittering Charles against his own subjects. The war also plunged Charles into debt once again, so for the first time in eleven years, he summoned Parliament.

Charles demanded more money, but Parliamentarians refused until he first addressed a long list of grievances, including the way he had fleeced English subjects for funds without their approval, spurned Parliament, and tried to impose his religious doctrine on the Scots.

Chief among their complaints was Charles' monopoly on military might in England. By law, Charles was granted control over the 90,000-man English militia, the largest force on the island. He also refused to disband the army he had raised to fight the Scots, violating the Petition of Right. In response, Parliament mustered their own militia against the king's wishes, which kicked off a mad scramble for control of the arsenals of guns and gunpowder across England. The country chose sides, and the English Civil War had begun.

One of the first things Charles did was start confiscating weapons from local communities to arm his soldiers, which further turned the populace against him. Parliamentarians chose the opposite tack and encouraged citizens to join their army and bear their own arms against the king.

The war was a cataclysm the likes of which England had never seen.

For nine years, both armies tore across England, Ireland, and Scotland like murderous cyclones, consuming one million souls—the bloodiest war per capita in English history. Charles was captured and beheaded in 1649, and the Parliamentarians triumphed in the end, but it was a Pyrrhic victory for the average English citizen. They now lived under an authoritarian Parliament headed by the Puritan dictator, Oliver Cromwell, backed by a standing army that dwarfed the one Charles had led.

Cromwell used his new power and position as head of this army to harass, search, seize, and disarm his political opponents, purging Parliament of any royalist sympathizers and most Catholics. He later disbanded Parliament, angered by its reluctance to follow his policies, and ruled the kingdom by himself, adopting the title of "Lord Protector." He was king in all but name. Yet despite his desire for reforms, he only magnified Charles' mistakes and abuses.

Cromwell's regime raised taxes three times higher than they were under Charles, confiscated lands from defeated royalists, imprisoned dissidents without due process, and indemnified all crimes committed by soldiers during the war. Documented cases of theft, rape, and murder were erased with the wave of a hand and a splash of ink, but left a burning hatred of standing armies in the hearts of every citizen from the highlands of Scotland to the Isle of Wight. "Parliament was forced to break with all the cherished nostrums conjured up by their propaganda," writes the historian John Morrill. "They fought to protect a herd of sacred cows each of which was slaughtered to propitiate the god of war."

Cromwell died just seven years after the war ended and was succeeded by his son, Richard, who by most accounts was a "meek, temperate, and quiet man." Most of the actual power lay in the hands of Cromwell's generals, who were largely unqualified and uninterested in governing England. Despite being dismissed by Cromwell, Parliament reconvened to plot a fresh course for the nation. Most Englishmen despised this new "Rump" Parliament, as it was known, created when Cromwell's minions culled away royalists sympathizers from Parliament so none could speak up for the king when they voted for his execution.

Fearing the ire of the people, the Rump members set about securing their power by whatever means necessary. To this end, they instituted the first national gun registry in England. The Rump required landlords in London and Westminster to create "a true and perfect list of all Arms or Ammunition, as also all Horses" and give it to the local militia leader within one week. They gave the rest of the country twenty-five days to produce the same list. Anyone who didn't present this list by the due date was imprisoned until they paid a fine. If the governmental authorities felt someone on their list was a potential troublemaker or political opponent, they ordered the militia to disarm them. Parliament even rewarded citizens for informing officers if their neighbors owned unregistered arms or ammunition. That's how it was supposed to work, anyway.

Chapter 3

The new gun registry and disarmament policy was carried out in some areas, but it was wholly ignored in others. Englishmen were disgusted at being asked to spy on and disarm their friends. Magistrates, mayors, and justices of the peace looked the other way as people bought, sold, and practiced with weapons as they had for hundreds of years. As one writer commented, "thousands of arms are bought daily... but none are seized."

These measures, combined with the Rump's inability to agree on a new government, convinced many aristocrats and commoners the old ways were best. Supported by generals from both sides of the war, the aristocracy orchestrated a coup to have Charles I's exiled son, Charles II, made king. A handful of Parliamentarians urged caution and recommended they only let Charles wear the crown if he agreed to a list of restrictions on his powers as king, but the majority brushed these concerns aside in their haste to restore balance to the realm and avoid another war. They crowned Charles II king on his thirtieth birthday, May 29, 1660.

England had high hopes for Charles II, but he quickly turned into a busted flush. He dragged the English into two unsuccessful wars with the Dutch, racking up massive debts. Constant war coupled with Charles' extravagant lifestyle pushed the country into the red. While his grandfather had only spent £5,000 per year and his father £10,000, Charles II blew through over £100,000 per year, along with money collected from royal family members, friends, and wealthy followers.

Although the Catholic Charles II promised fair treatment to Protestants and Catholics alike, his words rang hollow. Less than a year after becoming king, he prevented Presbyterians from practicing their faith and elevated undeserving Catholics to positions of power. Even Anglicans, who Charles treated with more leniency, were concerned over his treatment of other Protestants. As one Anglican cleric wrote, "There were great murmurings of discontent... especially among the Presbyterians, who were unsatisfied for there was no toleration allowed them for the exercise of their religion although his Majestie... promised so much vpon [sic] the word of a King..." Catholics, in contrast, "... were permitted to have their Assembl[ies] and meetings without any contradiction or gainsaying."

Charles further enraged his subjects by marrying a Catholic princess, arranging a Catholic marriage for his younger brother James when his Protestant wife died, and quietly dismissing Protestants from government office. Although it wouldn't become public knowledge until after his death, Charles connived with the king of France to publicly announce his conversion to Catholicism in return for an annual pension and military support (although it's unclear if he ever truly planned to honor this pledge).

To be fair, Parliament wasn't any better when it came to religious freedom. They killed a bill that would have protected freedom of religion because they wanted to restrict the ability of Catholics to worship, and many of them had rolled over a few years before when Cromwell had persecuted Catholics. They were playing the same twisted game as Charles, and their principal objection was that he was winning.

Charles II was even more determined than his father to reinforce the ancient divide between commoner and crown at all costs. He had tried in vain to save his father before the Parliamentarians chopped off Charles' head, and he believed that unless he alone controlled the power of the sword in England, the same thing would happen to him. In a move echoed by tyrants throughout history, Charles began aggressive measures to disarm his enemies and take control of the army. Charles was clever, though, and began to consolidate power in the most subtle of ways.

Parliament was suspicious of Charles' intentions and attempted to limit his influence by disbanding the army that was raised during the civil war. Charles agreed, but three days before the bill was passed, he made the innocuous request to retain a small force of veterans, funded out of his own pocket. Eager to pass the new bill and knowing Charles could only afford to pay for a few thousand men, Parliament acquiesced. To placate the public—who looked askance at even a small standing army—Charles insisted his private army were "guards," not soldiers. No one bought it. As one member of Parliament put it, Charles' guards were "too many to make the people love him, and too few to protect him." By hook or by crook, Charles raised more and more money, and by the time he died, his guards numbered 9,000 men. This small force of warriors formed the nucleus of Charles' military might during his reign.

Parliament deluded themselves into thinking they could control Charles II by limiting his allowance, which led to the ill-fated decision to pass the Militia Act of 1662. This act gave Charles sole command over the militia, satisfying his request for more troops on paper, but only granted him £70,000 per year for three years to pay militiamen on active duty. Some Parliamentarians worried this risky gambit would backfire, but most were confident it would work. "I know of nothing that can hinder the King from raising what forces he pleases, if he pays for them himself," remarked Secretary Williamson. "My argument is," he continued, "you are the paymasters . . . how can any man think you will pay these men that are not employed to the interest you mean they should." Parliament members believed that if Charles directed the militia in a way they didn't like, they could rein him in by tightening their purse strings.

They were wrong.

Charles put his militia to work confiscating weapons from anyone suspected of being hostile to his policies. Under past kings, the law required three to five militia officers to agree that someone was a threat before disarming them, but Charles II lowered this number to one, giving his officers unfettered discretion to disarm anyone they pleased.

Just as this three-year limit was about to expire, Charles found another opportunity to enlarge the number of soldiers at his disposal: War. In 1665, he raised a large army to fight the Dutch, leading many people to believe that "the war was made rather for the army, than the army for the war." People came to so distrust their king that they called for the disbandment of the army even while the English were still fighting the Dutch—they feared their own soldiers more than foreign ones.

The war with the Dutch proved a disaster for the English, for they accomplished few of their objectives, took heavy casualties, and lost a good chunk of their navy. There was a silver lining for Charles, though, as the war gave him yet more military control. Throughout the war, the king and Parliament disarmed both Catholic and Protestant political enemies, and in 1666, Charles created the first "select militia" in England.

The regular militia usually mustered infrequently, in response to immediate threats like Dutch raids, after which they would return home. The select militia, however, remained on active duty for long periods of time, similar to modern full-time soldiers on tours of duty. Most importantly, the select militia were paid directly by Charles, making them little more than home-grown mercenaries. While the select militia were supposed to help fight the Dutch, Charles also hoped to use them as another piece of his personal army. The select militia started with 1,500 men, but quickly swelled to 15,000 as funds were siphoned away from other areas of government to pay for more soldiers. This infuriated many Parliamentarians and regular militiamen, who knew they would soon be overpowered by what was really a private army.

Parliament voted to disband the army after the war concluded in 1667, but Charles still had his royal guards and control of the regular and select militia. It was around this time that he began disarming Englishmen in earnest.

After several rumors circulated about a potential plot against Charles, the Privy Council—a group of advisers handpicked by Charles—issued an order to all gunsmiths to deliver up a list of all of the weapons they had produced in the past six months and the names of customers who had purchased them. Furthermore, they were required to produce this same list of guns made and sold every Saturday evening in the future. At the same time, Charles forbade arms or ammunition from being shipped outside of major cities where they would be more difficult to track and steal, and prohibited the importation of all guns and gun parts into England. In effect, this new order gave Charles complete control over the production and distribution of all firearms in England.

New reports of intrigues, plots, and potential coups came in daily. Whenever a whisper of dissent reached Charles' ears, he ordered a wave of Protestants, political opponents, and "unreasonable men" of "restless and perverse disposition" watched, arrested, and disarmed. Almost none of these conspiracies materialized, and it became clear that the king and Parliament were just using these imagined plots to pass acts, laws, and statutes to disarm citizens. Those arrested as "conspirators" were quietly released several months after the hullabaloo subsided, but the new laws against bearing arms remained and the confiscated weapons were rarely returned. As the 1st Earl of Clarendon put it, "There hath not been a Week since that Time, in which there hath not been Combinations and Conspiracies formed against his Person, and against the Peace of the Kingdom." It turns out that Clarendon was the source of many of these rumors. Several years later, he was exiled for fabricating plots to give Charles the excuse he needed to grow his personal army and steal weapons from law-abiding, loyal Englishmen.

Charles II also deprived over 60,000 Englishmen of their legal right to bear arms when he banished all veterans from London who had fought for Parliament during the civil war—including many soldiers who had helped restore him to power after Cromwell's death. As part of their banishment, Charles prohibited them from carrying guns, swords, or any other weapons. To further strip his subjects of the ability to fight back against his growing might, he had the town walls of former rebel strongholds demolished.

It's worth noting that Parliament—the official representative of aristocrats and commoners—was complicit in many of these measures. As a whole, they readily agreed to the Militia Act of 1662, the Conventicles Act of 1670, and other proclamations that disarmed innocent citizens, banished political opponents, and suppressed religious nonconformists. They rarely objected to Charles' encroachments on liberty, unless it affected them personally, believing they could keep the "Crown, Church, towns, Catholics, dissenters and vagrants all equally within their control." Instead of Parliament opposing the abuses of the king, one hand washed the other.

Step-by-step, Charles II worked with Parliament to snuff out the chances of armed insurrection. The selfish, amoral policymaking of England's leaders reached its zenith when Parliament passed the Game Act of 1671, the first major restriction on the right to bear arms of every Englishman. As the name implies, the law was ostensibly passed to protect the royal game of England.

Poaching was always a serious problem in England, especially during the civil war when enforcement slackened and people were desperate for food. To make matters worse, rebels took revenge on King Charles I by slaughtering the wildlife in royal game preserves to the point that some wondered if the deer population would ever recover.

Unlike today, there were no hunting seasons or licenses to restrict the killing of wild game. Instead, laws restricted hunting by requiring citizens to reach property or income requirements before they were allowed to hunt. Englishmen who didn't meet these requirements were considered poachers. Although this did prohibit many people from hunting, the requirements were within reach of most middle-class citizens who earned a decent wage or owned a modest estate. When a poacher was caught, offenders would typically have to give up whatever weapons they were using and pay a fine.

The Game Act of 1671, also known as "the Game Act," perverted these laws in a way that was almost certainly designed to disarm the populace. As William Blackstone observed, "prevention of popular insurrections and resistance to the government, by disarming the bulk of the people . . . is a reason oftener meant, than avowed, by the makers of the forest and game laws." There were four things that made the Game Act so heinous:

1. It drastically raised the income requirements to be eligible to hunt, making it so expensive that only the wealthiest citizens could afford the privilege.
2. It made the mere possession of weapons that could be used for poaching such as guns, bows, or spears illegal for anyone who didn't meet the new property requirements.
3. It only allowed landowners to hunt, whereas in the past wealthy people with no land could hunt so long as they met the minimum personal property qualification.
4. It gave game wardens and wealthy landowners unprecedented power to search and disarm anyone suspected of breaking the new law.

Before the Game Act, Englishmen had to make at least £40 from land per year, £80 from land leases per year, or have at least £400 of personal property to hunt, qualifications that most upper middle-class citizens could afford. The new law more than doubled these requirements, so that a citizen had to make £100 per year from land or £150 per year from land leases, and the personal property qualification was abolished. Overnight, this raised the income requirements so high that 99 percent of the English population no longer qualified to hunt. As William Blackstone pointed out, the property requirement for hunting was now fifty times the property requirement for voting.

The second and most serious problem with the Game Act was how it changed the legality of arms ownership. Under the new law, anyone who didn't meet the property qualifications for hunting was prohibited from owning *any* weapon that could conceivably be used for hunting, including guns, bows, and spears. Thus, the Game Act made it illegal for 99 percent of the population to "... have or keepe for themselves or any other person or persons any Guns, Bowes, Grey hounds, Setting-dogs, Ferrets, Cony-doggs, Lurchers, Hayes, Netts, Lowbells, Hare-pipes, Ginns, Snares or other Engines aforesaid." (Yes, it outlawed some dogs, too.) The law also caused food shortages in two ways: by depriving people of venison and by preventing them from killing deer, rabbits, birds, and other wildlife that consumed their crops.

To limit the number of people who were qualified to hunt (and thus own weapons) even further, the Game Act also removed the personal property qualification for hunting. Now, only deep-pocketed landowners—less than one percent of the population—were allowed to hunt or own weapons. As the historian Joyce Lee Malcom writes, "Wealthy merchants, prosperous lawyers, and others who had a goodly amount of personal wealth but insufficient income from land were instantly deprived of their right to hunt and grouped together with those defined in the law as 'idle and disorderly.'" This was a major annoyance to many middle-class citizens, but not enough of one to encourage them to rebellion.

Finally, the Game Act also made it much easier for game wardens to search people's homes for illegal weapons, which now included almost all kinds. In the past, game wardens were allowed to search the homes of suspected poachers so long as they had a warrant signed by two justices of the peace. The new game act allowed a single game warden or anyone else authorized by a royal official to search someone's home for weapons. If someone was caught with a weapon, they could be tried by a single royal official with the testimony of one witness, whereas in the past suspected poachers were tried before two officials with testimony of two witnesses. The new law also stated that officials didn't have to record the charges, evidence, or verdict from these trials, so the victim had no recourse to prove his innocence or to recover his weapons after they were taken.

Effectively, the Game Act of 1671 deprived almost all Englishmen of the right to bear arms—something they had been allowed and required to do for 900 years—and granted it only to wealthy landowners. The carefully worded law was a Trojan horse for gun control.

It's understandable why Charles II would support this law, but why was Parliament so eager to disarm their countrymen? There were already ample provisions to protect wild game when the Game Act was passed, and there's little evidence that poaching was a big enough problem to warrant disarming almost the entire populace. Guns were rarely used for poaching. They were too loud to conceal, too bulky for sneaking through forests, and too hard to hide in one's home. Most poachers preferred nets, snares, and other traps, which killed quietly and didn't require the hunter to wait in the woods. For example, of the thirty-four poaching cases that were appealed between 1658 and 1683 at the Hertfordshire Quarter Sessions, just three involved the use of a gun. A similar analysis of seventy-one poaching cases brought before the Warwickshire Quarter Sessions revealed only twenty-six, or around one-third, involved guns.

The most likely explanation for Parliament's support of the Game Act is that it was a political chess move intended to gain power over the king and commoners. For example, the law gave wealthy landowners—many of whom were members of Parliament—the right to pick game wardens, whereas in the past this had been a privilege of the king. Since game wardens now had broad powers to disarm most of the English population, and Parliament controlled many of the game wardens, this was a covert way for Parliament to decide who would and wouldn't be allowed to own guns.

If Parliament had truly wanted to protect wild game, they could have easily passed measures to beef up enforcement of existing laws and raised the fines for convicted poachers. Instead, they introduced a law that criminalized arms ownership and made disarmament the primary punishment. Aside from having their guns stolen, people violating the law were only fined ten shillings. This fine was even more lenient than in the past, again suggesting the intent was more to disarm citizens than to protect deer.

As with previous measures to disarm Englishmen, though, the Game Act was loosely enforced. Much like police officers in modern-day Second Amendment sanctuary cities, the Lords Lieutenant often turned a blind eye to those who flouted the Game Act, and there was little Parliament or the king could do to make them comply. For some, this was a practical precaution, as they didn't want to enrage the people in their jurisdiction; for others, a political and moral demonstration against unjust rule.

Dying in 1685 without a legitimate male heir, Charles II was succeeded by his brother James II, who only amplified the mistakes of Charles. Like Charles, James II harbored secret ambitions to convert England to Catholicism—by force if necessary. One of the first things he did was disarm all Protestants in Ireland. He ordered his commanders in Ireland to confiscate weapons from Protestant militia members, implemented a firearms registry for Protestants, and only permitted shipments of gunpowder to Irish Catholics. At the same time, he replaced Protestant officers with Catholic ones, and removed restrictions that made it difficult for Catholics to join the army. Within a few months of these policies being enacted, nearly two-thirds of the Irish Army was Catholic.

James knew it would be harder to implement these policies in England where the population was better armed and better positioned to strike back, so he went about molding the political landscape to his will. He started by removing as many opponents from Parliament as possible. James ordered elections held in the middle of the night, constantly changed voting locations, enacted last-minute decrees that forbade rivals from running for local office, and modified election rules to reduce the number of people who could be elected. When all of that failed, he would simply have armed men show up at elections to intimidate potential candidates and voters.

Charles had used many of the same tactics, but he was more subtle. James dispensed with the pretense of being a benevolent ruler and made it clear from the get-go that subjects would have to give up their guns, their freedom, and their position in government—or else. James was pleased with the fruit of his labors, claiming that out of 505 Parliamentarians, "There were not above forty members, but such as he himself wished for." This new hand-picked Parliament quickly granted James II what he really wanted: money and men.

They gave James almost £1 million per year, a vast sum that allowed him to quadruple the size of the standing army from 9,000 men in 1684, to 19,000 men in 1686, to 40,000 men in 1688, mostly staffed with Catholic officers. One of the reasons he was able to inflate his army to such a colossal size were two simultaneous failed uprisings that occurred early in his reign.

The first was a short-lived rebellion led by the Scottish Earl of Argyll, who returned from exile with several hundred men and was captured and executed in a little over a month. The second was led by the Duke of Monmouth, Charles II's bastard son. Promising to protect Protestant freedom of religion, he landed in southwestern England, an area whose inhabitants were known for housing many proud and restless Protestants.

Monmouth's decision to land there proved to be a double-edged sword. On the one hand, his small force of 1,500 men soon grew to an army of 7,000 as locals flocked to his banner. On the other hand, almost none of these people had guns.

Filled with ardent Protestants, this was one of the few areas in England that *had* been successfully disarmed by the Game Act. Monmouth landed in a veritable firearms desert, and it was clear his forces stood no chance against the English militia or the army. He sealed their fates by proving to be an abysmal leader who led his army in circles until it was annihilated at the Battle of Sedgemoor in 1685. He was then captured, tried, convicted, and beheaded (after multiple swings of the axe).

These two bootless rebellions gave James just the excuse he needed to strengthen the power of his standing army, which at this point numbered

20,000 men. Although this may not seem like a large force by modern standards, this meant that England had the same proportion of soldiers to civilians as the French did under Louis XIV, who was considered one of the most absolute monarchs of all time.

More important than the size of the army, however, was that James declared the soldiers no longer under Parliament's control, but the crown's. Any crimes or legal issues involving the army would be addressed in a weekly military court answerable to the king, and it was a known fact that most soldiers were treated with kid gloves. This led to large scale abuses where criminals seeking to escape justice "had only to be mustered into the army to avoid its clutches."

Although Charles II had mostly kept his troops confined to particular areas around London, James II stationed his army throughout England. The Petition of Right of 1628 and the Disbanding Act of 1679 made it illegal to force citizens to house soldiers against their will, but James disregarded these laws and illegally billeted his men among civilians across the country. These soldiers knew their privileged status as the King's men protected them from the law and so took advantage of the situation to terrorize their hosts. According to one contemporary, Edmund Bohun, the soldiers were allowed "to outrage and injure who they pleased almost without restraint." Also, because the king funded the army, not Parliament, almost all of the officers and most of the men were Catholics, many of whom had few qualms about disarming, intimidating, or arresting Protestants.

Now that James had a large standing army, he set his sights on sapping the military strength of Parliament. He knew they'd never agree to disband the militia, so he forbade it to muster, rendering it useless as a check against his vast legion of troops. To further defang the militia and suppress dissent, James decided to rigorously enforce archaic firearm laws that had become dead letters. In 1686, James informed the Lords Lieutenant that he had heard that "a great many persons not qualified by law under pretence of shooting matches keep muskets or other guns in their houses," and ordered them "to cause strict search to be made for such muskets or guns and to seize and safely keep them till further order."

In James' feverish desperation to disarm his subjects, he even tried to use the 1328 Statute of Northampton to arrest the political dissident Sir John Knight for carrying a gun in a church. This was the only time someone was charged with a firearms violation under this law, and it didn't work. John Knight walked free and kept his gun, as did many others.

The result of these policies—the perversion of the army and the subversion of the militia—was that most free Englishmen were barred from owning weapons, whereas criminals were given guns and allowed to run roughshod over their countrymen.

It seemed James II was doomed to repeat his brother's failures in every way, but like a snare, the more he constricted the rights of the English, the more fiercely they resisted. Despite James' efforts, Englishmen openly admitted to carrying guns, game cases involving firearms continued to appear in court, and Lords Lieutenant were being fired left and right for failing to disarm their fellow citizens. Nevertheless, James' aggressive expansion of the army and oppressive gun control laws worked well enough that "... it was no longer possible to start a great rebellion against the King," as historian J.R. Western put it.

It seemed that James and his followers had finished the work his brother had started, but in the end, his obsessive pursuit of absolute power proved his undoing. At this point, James had alienated almost every one of his allies, and most Englishmen were simply waiting for him to die. He was nearly sixty years old and had no male heir, but he did have a daughter, Mary, who was married to the Protestant Prince William of Orange. Should James die without a son, there was a sliver of hope that William might ascend the throne with the help of Mary.

Their hopes were dashed in 1677 when James' wife, Queen Mary, had a son, presaging another generation of oppression and strict gun control. This was the final straw for the English. After decades of political corruption, religious suppression, and violent persecution, the English were willing to do almost anything to restore harmony, prosperity, and peace to their country. What's more, they saw this as one of their last chances to save their rights as Englishmen before the country descended into out-and-out totalitarianism.

Chapter 3

James could see which way the wind was blowing and began frantically reinstating officials he had recently sacked. He implored his subjects to "lay aside all jealousies and animosities," but the public were sick of his empty promises. Recently fired politicians rebuffed James' offers, preferring instead to throw in their lot with whoever replaced him.

They didn't have to wait long.

In a bloodless coup that later became known as the Glorious Revolution of 1688, William and Mary invaded England and deposed James II. James had underestimated his subjects and overestimated the army's loyalty. Both Catholics and Protestants were enraged with the way he had disregarded the laws and disarmed law-abiding citizens. Instead of blindly accepting James' orders, the soldiers in his army endlessly debated government policies, religious freedoms, and which side they would take in a war "as if they were in the House of Commons." And when that pivotal moment arrived, they chose William. The militia either joined William's army or stood down, and as he approached London, James' 30,000-man army trickled away until only 4,000 remained. Hated by his subjects, abandoned by his allies, and facing hoards of determined English and Dutch soldiers, James fled to France, casting his royal seal into the river Thames, never to set foot in England again.

The Glorious Revolution was a watershed moment in the timeless battle between liberty and tyranny. In one of the first times in history, "A great king with strong armies, and mighty fleets, a vast treasure, and powerful allies, fell all at once," observed the Bishop of Salisbury, "and his whole strength, like a spider's web, was so irrevocably broken with a touch, that he was never able to retrieve what for want both of judgement and heart, he threw up in a day."

The victors couldn't rest on their laurels, though. England had no leader for the first time since the civil war, and some Parliamentarians wanted to accept William and Mary as king and queen unconditionally and immediately. They worried that if England remained leaderless, various political factions would plunge the country into chaos as they grappled for power. Better to trust William and Mary to do the right thing than risk another civil war, they thought. Others dug in their heels, determined not to repeat the mistake they'd made when they recklessly crowned Charles II king.

Protestants and Catholics, commoners and nobles, militiamen and soldiers, were all wounded from the political and religious whiplash of the previous five decades. They had endured the subtle abuses of Charles I, the slings and arrows of civil war, the hard-handed regimes of Cromwell, Charles II, and James II. Mismanagement, disarmament, and religious persecution had pulled the country apart at the seams.

Before agreeing to hand the reins of power to William and Mary, Parliament demanded that they acknowledge and swear to protect the rights the country had been denied for so long. The legislators wanted a bill of rights. As the nobleman and politician Anthony Cary put it, they meant to not just "change hands, but things." Speaking to his fellow members of Parliament, Cary enjoined them to "resolve, what Power you will give the King, and what not."

This strategy wasn't without risks. In a preview of the debates over the American Bill of Rights a century later, some Parliamentarians worried that it would be impossible or dangerous to list their rights. Others were concerned that if they created such a list, a future tyrant could wave the document in their face as they took away any right not written down. Others feared it would take years to come up with a list, and in the meantime, England would be vulnerable to rebellion and invasion without a king. Finally, still more worried that it would end up like Magna Carta—a slip of parchment that provided a veneer of protection from the king's tyrannous actions, but which was often ignored in practice.

These arguments were scorned by some Parliamentarians, such as Edward Seymour, who challenged his colleagues, "Will you do nothing, because you cannot do all?" Seymour's argument prevailed, and Parliament finally agreed that they needed to secure at least a small measure of protection for the most "true, ancient, and indubitable" liberties before they allowed William and Mary to settle into their thrones.

One of the first protections they demanded was their right to bear arms. The previous decades of civil war and strife had left the English with what historian Charles Firth referred to as "a rooted aversion to standing armies and an abiding dread of military rule." Since the first days of the war, the army had been used as a scythe to cut down political opponents, steal weapons, and compel obedience by force, and one of Parliament's primary motivations for extracting a bill of rights from their new monarchs was to protect themselves against being disarmed or bullied by a standing army.

Sir John Maynard complained that "... it was an abominable thing to disarm a nation, to set up a standing army." Hugh Boscawen highlighted how, at the king's orders, the militia had "... disarmed and imprisoned men without any cause." He had reason to complain, as he had been personally disarmed. A Mr. Finch declared that their rights would never be secure unless they also had a right to own weapons. "The constitution being limited, there is a good foundation for defensive arms—It has given us right to demand full and ample security."

They got what they wanted. The first draft of the English right to bear arms read, "That the Subjects, which are Protestants, may provide and keep Arms, for their common defense." This wording troubled some Parliamentarians, as the last phrase, "for their common defense," implied citizens only had the right to use arms in groups such as the militia. They struck out the word "common" to make it clear the right applied to individuals, so that the final version of the bill read:

> "That the Subjects which are Protestants may have Arms for their defense suitable to their Conditions, and as allowed by Law."

Parliament probably added these last two restrictions on the right to bear arms, that they be "suitable to their conditions" and "as allowed by law," to appease William's concerns of an uprising while simultaneously limiting his power. Parliament knew that if they overplayed their hand by asking William to guarantee that every subject be guaranteed the right to own guns (Catholic and Protestant, rich and poor, Parliamentarian and Royalist), they risked scuttling the entire project and earning the disfavor of their new king. At the same time, the "as allowed by law" clause ensured the king could never again arbitrarily disarm Englishmen without their consent, because only Parliament was allowed to decide the laws.

It's also telling what rights weren't included in the English Bill of Rights. Freedom of speech was only protected in Parliament, and freedom of the press, of assembly, and of religion weren't mentioned. But the right to bear arms—cherished, enforced, and exercised throughout English history—was law at last.

Of course, the wording of the new right was imperfect. It only specifically protected the right of Protestants to bear arms and only permitted people to own guns "suitable to their conditions and as allowed by law," loose terms that gave Parliament tremendous leeway in deciding who could and couldn't own guns. Although vague, rushed, and riddled with inconsistencies, the English Bill of Rights secured a legal foothold for the English right to bear arms.

Sadly, in time these mistakes and oversights would form the thin edge of the wedge as Parliament simply legalized new forms of tyranny. One hundred years later, the torch of liberty was once again dimming in England, but across the sea a new generation of philosophers, warriors, and statesmen would ensure it blazed brighter than ever before.

The Founders of the United States would remember the lessons of the English Civil War, and would transmogrify the English Bill of Rights into the broader, wiser, and more complete guarantee of individual liberty for Americans—the United States Bill of Rights.

4

America's Love Affair with Guns Is Older than America

"Both oligarch and tyrant mistrust the people, and therefore deprive them of their arms."
—Aristotle, Greek philosopher, polymath, author, and personal tutor of Alexander the Great, 4th century BC.

"I don't care if you want to hunt, I don't care if you think it's your right. I say 'Sorry' it's 1999. We have had enough as a nation. You are not allowed to own a gun, and if you do own a gun I think you should go to prison."
—Rosie O'Donnell, American talk show host, 1999.

For centuries, Englishmen had only known life under autocratic rule. Their lives were dedicated to serving kings, queens, barons, dukes, and other aristocrats.

Depending on where they lived or what monarch occupied the throne, they were compelled to worship one religion and persecuted for worshipping another. They were forced to fight wars they didn't understand, for causes they didn't believe in, and for monarchs they despised more than the enemy. And the moment their "betters" smelled the slightest whiff of disobedience, they were disarmed, imprisoned without trial, and if the offense was great enough, executed.

But what if there was no one around to tell them what to think, how to behave, and what religion to worship? What if they were left alone—not dependent upon or answerable to a king? What if they were free to govern themselves? This is exactly what happened when Englishmen sailed to the New World.

"America was opened," wrote Ralph Waldo Emerson, "after the feudal mischief was spent, and so the people made a good start. We began well. No inquisitions here, no kings, no nobles, no dominant church. Here heresy has lost its terrors." Separated from the stifling strictures of monarchy, American colonists began to dream of a country where the government was created, run, and controlled by the people, not the king. As their convictions crystallized into a new political philosophy, Americans set themselves on a collision course with England that would forever shatter the bonds of monarchy, lay the foundations of the United States of America, and lead directly to the creation of the Second Amendment.

The seeds of American independence began to take root shortly after English colonists created the first permanent settlement at Jamestown in 1607. Like a plant given fresh soil, civil liberties flourished in America. The colonists faced astonishing risks, but they were also exposed to freedoms and opportunities unheard of in most of Europe. There were no kings, barons, or lords, and, in the beginning, few slaves. Wealthy, well-born gentlemen toiled in the swamps alongside their manservants. Many of those who risked the perils of the New World hoped it would offer a chance to escape the crushing class and religious restrictions of Europe, and whether they liked it or not, they were soon united by suffering, starvation, and death. Eighty percent of the members of the first expedition succumbed to disease or were killed by Powhatan Indians, but together they held onto their small strip of land and were soon joined by thousands of others who shared their independent spirit and appetite for risk.

Just twelve years after the colonists arrived, Jamestown created the first representative government in North America. Each settlement elected two citizens who would vote on new laws, along with a council appointed by the Virginia Company. The new system was a tremendous success, and it encouraged more settlers to risk the voyage from Europe. English men and women who had come to the colonies with little more than threadbare clothing could earn a voice in government, a patch of land, and a respectable place in society through merit, industry, and creativity, and these stories of triumph fired the imaginations of their countrymen at home.

In England, only a fraction of the population owned land and were entitled to the political and economic rights of landowners. In the colonies, though, many people owned land, and they demanded the same rights as landowners in England, such as not being governed without their consent or in ways obviously against their interests. Right from the start, the stage was set for a more inclusive, meritocratic government ruled by the people.

England inadvertently fanned the flames of individual liberty by granting colonial charters to men of all faiths. Desperate for wealthy investors and effective leaders, and eager to gobble up as much of North America as possible before the French, Spanish, and Dutch claimed it, the king and Parliament allowed the Catholic Cecil Calvert to settle Maryland, the Baptist Roger Williams to settle Rhode Island, and the Quaker William Penn to settle Pennsylvania and Delaware.

While Protestants and Catholics butchered one another in England and across Europe, they peacefully coexisted in North America in the mid-seventeenth century. Unimpeded by a corrupt crown, Parliament, or aristocracy, Americans secured a degree of individual liberty, religious freedom, and representative government in a few decades that took the English hundreds of years to achieve.

The colonists also enshrined their hard-won liberties in a series of documents that were far more comprehensive and binding than the English Bill of Rights. The Massachusetts Body of Liberties of 1641 protected freedom of assembly and freedom of speech at public meetings, equal protection under the law for all citizens, and required citizens to be compensated if their property was taken for public use. It guaranteed them the right to bail, to employ a lawyer in one's defense, to trial by jury in civil cases, to challenge jurors, and to a speedy trial; the freedom to emigrate to other areas and limitations on imprisonment for unpaid debt; and it prohibited the charging of people for crimes of which they'd already been acquitted, as well as cruel or unusual punishments. It was also one of the first documents to specifically protect women, prohibiting physical abuse by husbands, guaranteeing widows a portion of a husband's estate even if they were written out of the will, and allowing daughters to inherit their parents' estate if their parents had no will or male heirs.

The Charter of Fundamental Laws of West New Jersey, adopted in 1677, specified "fundamental rights" such as representative government, religious freedom, and the right to a trial by one's peers, and prohibited the legislative authority from revoking them under any circumstances.

The colonization of North America also opened a new chapter in the history of the right to bear arms. While Englishmen had been allowed to own weapons, it was a necessity in North America. Alone on the edge of the world, surrounded by hostile tribes and foreign settlers, and menaced by starvation, a gun was an indispensable tool—like a hammer for building, a plow for farming, or a pot for cooking. Owning a gun was considered of such paramount importance that settlers were not just allowed to own any gun they liked, they were *obligated* to own a gun to protect the community.

From the beginning, English colonies required all adult males (and sometimes adult females if they were the head of the household) to own a gun and rally together in case the colony was attacked. A handful of hard-to-replace professionals, like doctors, were exempt from the requirement of joining in the defense of the town, but they were still required to own guns. These traditions and laws endured all the way up to the beginning of the American Revolution. Although there were almost no European countries that required people to own guns by the early 1700s, this was not the case in America. As late as 1770, there was a law in Georgia that required citizens to carry a rifle or pistol to church, and church officials were allowed to search every parishioner up to fourteen times per year to ensure they were armed.

Before, during, and after the American Revolution, most households either had a gun or were within a few paces of one that did. Although it's hard to quantify exactly how many guns existed in America in the 1700s due to shoddy record-keeping, some old tax records suggest an answer. In a study aptly titled *Counting Guns in Early America*, Northwestern University researchers James Lindgren and Justin Heather parsed through tax records ranging from the early 1600s to the early 1800s to estimate how many people owned guns in America. They found that throughout early colonial America, 50 to 73 percent of male-led households and 6 to 38 percent of female-led households owned guns. Based only on records from just before the revolution, guns were found in 54 percent of households on average. While that may not sound like many, consider that at the time, only...

- 30 percent of estates had any cash.
- 14 percent had any swords, daggers, or other edged weapons.
- 25 percent had Bibles.
- 62 percent had one or more books.
- 79 percent had clothes.

Lindgren and Heather also point out that these numbers "are likely to be substantial underestimates." This data was taken from probate records which were notoriously incomplete. Many property owners would remove prize items, family heirlooms, and other portable valuables from the home before the records were collected (hence why 70 percent of estates supposedly didn't have a single penny of cash). In other cases, the appraisers creating the list would get lazy and lump certain items together or overlook them entirely. For example, they might record a rifle, cleaning tools, and butchering knives as "hunting tackle," instead of recording each item individually, or simply overlook smaller items like pistols, cookware, and so forth to finish the job faster.

Based on these findings, it's fair to assume that significantly more than 60 percent of the population owned guns in early colonial America. Although there's much hand-wringing about the high rates of gun ownership in the US today, data collected from the Pew Research Center shows that only about 42 percent of American households currently have a gun, an 18 percent decrease from the time of our Founding Fathers.

The fact is that the founding generation was one of the most well-armed groups of people in the world at the time. Gun ownership started as a common sense necessity, was institutionalized as a duty, and finally became an inseparable aspect of American society. Ultimately, it was a combination of this long tradition of gun ownership and use, Americans' keen appreciation for personal liberty, and their inherited right to bear arms from England, that would lead to the creation of the Second Amendment.

Throughout this period, Americans were tied to England through blood, law, and loyalty, but their views on the rightful role of government had wholly diverged from their mother country by the time of the American Revolutionary War in 1775. Liberated by the wilderness of the New World, instructed by their spartan existence, and influenced by the work of enlightenment philosophers, the colonists came to believe that individual liberties were more important than blind obedience to a king and parliament 4,000 miles away.

To those who made the journey across the sea, England began to appear as a benighted backwater and America as the promised land, and they were soon forced to fight for it.

5

Everything You Know About the American Revolution Is Wrong

> "A man's rights rest in three boxes: the ballot box,
> the jury box, and the cartridge box."
> —Frederick Douglass, African-American orator, writer, and abolitionist, 1867.

> "Every Communist must grasp the truth, 'Political power
> grows out of the barrel of a gun.' Our principle is that the
> Party commands the gun, and the gun must never
> be allowed to command the Party."
> —Mao Zedong, Chinese communist leader believed to be responsible for the
> deaths of thirty to eighty million of his countrymen, 1938.

You've probably heard the traditional story of how the American Revolutionary War started.

It goes like this: The English imposed new laws, taxes, and tariffs on their American colonies to help pay off the debt from their wars with France. This enraged the colonists, who had no say over how the money was spent. "No taxation without representation" became their war cry as they threw crates of tea into Massachusetts Bay, flouting the new laws. The British occupied Boston in retaliation, then shot protestors at the Boston

Massacre. Taxes soared, tensions escalated, Americans started shooting back, and the American Revolutionary War was afoot.

That's true as far as it goes, but it's not the whole story. Yes, the war was partially about taxes, tea, and the monarchy, but this version of history gives short shrift to the colonists' deeper motivations, making it seem like they revolted simply because they had to pay more money to the government.

At bottom, the American Revolution was not an uprising against excessive taxes. It was an ideological crusade intended to uproot the last tentacles of monarchy from America and establish a new way of life for its inhabitants. Before the war, the American colonists were some of the most prosperous, free, and economically advantaged people on Earth. Their per capita income was higher than almost every European country. They were well-defended, had many political supporters in the British government, and had tremendous personal liberties compared to most countries. In short, they had everything to lose by fighting England, and yet they did so anyway.

Why?

Although the sun was shining on the colonies before the war, some Americans could see a storm was brewing. While many Americans contented themselves to live rich, peaceful, pleasant lives as vassals to King George, the Founders knew these halcyon days could never last so long as a monarch held the reins of their destiny. They had the foresight to see something better on the horizon, the courage to fight for it, and the wisdom to help their fellow Americans glimpse the same vision—a country built from the ground up on the principle that all men are created free, equal, and independent. A state designed solely to protect the liberties of its citizens. A government of the people, by the people, and for the people, as Abraham Lincoln put it a century later. And they were willing to fight a war to see their dream come true.

Plato once lamented that, "All wars are due to the desire to acquire wealth," but he might have changed his mind if he'd lived another 2,123 years to see the beginning of the American Revolutionary War.

At the outset of the war, the colonists were flush with cash. The average colonist's purchasing power was fifty percent higher than his fellow's in Britain, and income inequality was much lower in the colonies than in England, Wales, and the Netherlands. The colonists also had a higher quality of life, a longer life expectancy, and a lower infant mortality rate than their English counterparts.

What's more, the colonists paid almost nothing in taxes. In 1763, the average British citizen paid twenty-six shillings per year in taxes, whereas the average New England colonist paid *one shilling per year*. To further disprove the "taxes started the war" myth, we can look to research compiled in 1979 by economic historians Gary Walton and James Shepherd, who created a scale to measure the relative tax burden of England's various colonies in 1765. Here's what they found:

- Great Britain (England and Scotland): 100 (highest tax rate)
- Ireland: 26
- Massachusetts, Pennsylvania, and Maryland: 4
- New York: 3
- Connecticut: 2
- Virginia: 2

In other words, citizens of Great Britain paid about twenty-five to fifty times more in taxes than the colonists, despite making considerably less money and having a lower quality of life.

In a game of economic cat and mouse, the colonists thwarted almost every attempt the English made to raise taxes. The Sugar Act of 1764 and the Stamp Act of 1765 would have only paid for a small slice of England's cost of protecting the colonies, but the colonists quickly forced their repeals through lobbying and the boycotting of English goods. The Stamp Act caused such an uproar that Prime Minister George Greville, who supported the act, was forced to resign the year after it was passed. Next came the Townshend Acts of 1767, which would have cost the average colonist 1 percent of their income per year. Once again, the acts were repealed through boycotts, protests, and political lobbying.

The Americans had also developed a prosperous trade relationship with Britain that was heavily slanted in their favor. In return for protection against France, Spain, the Netherlands, and Native Americans, they adhered to a pocketful of loosely enforced trade restrictions, such as only exporting and importing certain goods from Britain, and not making hats, woolen clothes, and other cloth, so as not to compete with British manufacturers. All in all, these trade restrictions amounted to about 3 percent of the colonies's gross domestic product (GDP) and were "economically irrelevant" in the big scheme of things. For comparison's sake, social security taxes in America today make up about 6 percent of the nation's GDP.

Britain spent £100 million fighting the French in the Seven Years War, and much of the expense came from financing military operations in North America (known as the French and Indian War). This nearly crushed their economy, doubling Britain's national debt so that nearly half of all tax money collected went to paying off the interest from their many loans. Even after the war, Britain spent £350,000 pounds per year defending the colonies from Native American attacks and foreign incursion, funding other public services, like the post office, and protecting trade routes for the Americans up and down the Atlantic coast. Most of the taxes the British imposed on the colonists—the Townshend, Coercive, Tea, and Stamp Acts—would have only covered a fraction of the costs Britain incurred on the colonists' behalf.

America was a moneymaking machine, insulated from taxes, exempted from paying for their own military, and spared the squalid living conditions of many Englishmen at the time. The colonists also knew that war with England would be ruinous for their economy, and that the costs of the war would far outweigh any bumps in taxes. Thanks to the work of economic historians John McCusker and Russell Menard, we know that from 1774 to 1790 per capita income in the colonies plummeted 48 percent. By 1805—thirty years after the war began—per capita income was still 14 percent lower than it was before the war. And this figure doesn't include the direct costs of feeding, training, and equipping the army during the war or paying the nation's debt to France, who helped bankroll the conflict.

The bottom line is this: Plato was wrong about the Americans. They had the financial, political, and military support of one of the most powerful empires in the world, and they were just getting started. Yet they still went to war knowing it could cost them everything.

Our forefathers didn't go to war because they had to pay a few pennies to the crown. They went to war because they were willing to fight and die for the principles that would become the bedrock of all the freedoms we enjoy today. They were willing to sacrifice their pole position in the British Empire, their material comforts, and their lives, because they had collectively decided they would not tolerate even the slightest infringements on their rights.

The American Revolutionary War was an ideological war fought over the future of the American government. As the Pulitzer Prize-winning historian Rick Atkinson explained:

> "This would not be a war between regimes or dynasties, fought for territory or the usual commercial advantages. Instead, what became known as the American Revolution was an improvised struggle between two peoples of a common heritage, now sundered by divergent values and conflicting visions of a world to come."

To the founding generation, it was better to build a new nation from the wreckage of war than to live the rest of their lives beholden to a monarch who could snuff out their liberties, seize their arms, and spike any efforts to secure their lawful freedoms.

So, what did the British do that so incensed the colonists? What caused them to put down the pen and take up the sword? The colonists made it clear on numerous occasions they would pay higher taxes and peacefully remain part of Britain if they were allowed to participate in Parliament, but the British stubbornly refused.

Many people on both sides proposed various ways to settle their differences without bloodshed. The renowned economist Adam Smith pondered a solution to the problem in his magnum opus, *The Wealth of Nations*, which involved giving the colonists and inhabitants of Britain representation in

Parliament proportionate to how much they contributed to the British treasury. In other words, the citizens would be rewarded with greater say in the government based on how much they produced.

Thomas Pownall, a political theorist, member of Parliament, and governor of Massachusetts from 1757 to 1760, proposed a variety of conciliatory measures to cool tempers on both sides of the Atlantic. He advocated a form of joint government staffed by colonists and representatives from Britain that would administer the colonies, and many of his ideas were later put into practice as Britain grew to become the largest empire in the world in the 19th century. Other members of Parliament supported Pownall's proposals, but they were stymied by their peers.

Even the shrewd William Pitt, 1st Earl of Chatham and the Prime Minister who had masterminded the defeat of France during the Seven Years War, could see Britain was on the verge of making an irreparable mistake. "All attempts to impose servitude upon such men, to establish despotism over such a mighty continental nation must be in vain," Pitt admonished Parliament. "We shall be forced, ultimately, to retract. Let us retract while we can, not when we must." In a prediction that would become real all too soon, he further warned, "The very first drop of blood will make a wound that will not easily be skinned over." Twice he urged Parliament to reach an agreement with the Americans, and twice they shot him down in a landslide vote. He lamented to his wife of the experience that Parliament seemed "violent beyond expectation, almost to madness."

The key powerbrokers of Parliament at the time were the landed gentry—aristocrats who viewed any step toward representative government as a threat to their imperium over British politics. Many of them had also accepted generous royal appointments from King George in return for loyalty, and others owed their positions to the Prime Minister, Frederick North, a close friend of the King. All of this led the writer Horace Walpole to observe "This Parliament appeared to be even more corrupt and servile than the two last." They ignored the proposals from Smith, Pownall, and Pitt and scotched any motion to allow Americans to join Parliament.

While barring Americans from Parliament with one hand, they dunned them for taxes with the other and threatened to revoke their rights should they refuse. The relationship was starting to smack of serfdom, with the colonists toiling away to produce taxes for the British elite. As you now know, the absolute amount of money the British demanded was miniscule, but to the colonists it represented the camel's nose under the tent for future abuses.

Moreover, it was how these tax monies were demanded, collected, and used that ignited American fury. For one thing, some of the tax money was siphoned off to pay for a 10,000-man-strong standing army in the colonies. This was ostensibly for their own protection, but the colonists saw it as a prelude to more oppression by Parliament. For years, British soldiers had forced colonists to house and feed them in open violation of the Mutiny Act passed a few years before, and this was allowed to occur largely thanks to the cooperation of colonial governors and judges. It just so happened that much of the money raised from these new taxes was also paid to colonial governors and judges to keep them firmly under the thumb of the British government—officials who were supposed to be in the colonists' corner.

The colonists also had no representatives in Parliament to advocate for their interests or help decide how their money would be spent, which meant that Parliament could pass whatever legislation they wanted without their consent. Hence the phrase, "No taxation without representation." Although the Americans paid few taxes compared to the British, Englishmen at least had some say about them. This wasn't the case for the colonists, who were expected to pay taxes but were denied a voice in Parliament.

The colonists responded to all of these measures by boycotting the purchase and import of most British goods, drafting official complaints to the crown, and hoarding firearms. Many openly defied the new tax laws and tariffs, smuggling supplies and weapons throughout the colonies. These boycotts had ruinous ripple effects throughout the British economy. After the Stamp Act went into effect in 1765, which taxed paper in the colonies, Americans responded by terrorizing tax collectors and boycotting British goods so thoroughly that factories across Britain shuttered and thousands of laborers were put out of work. All in all, it's estimated that Britain squeezed less than £45 out of all of the colonies.

When the Townshend Acts went into effect two years later, American boycotts caused British exports to the colonies to drop by half, again idling many Englishmen and souring relations with the crown. These actions would later lead Adam Smith to conclude the colonies were "mere loss instead of profit."

Ironically, the infamous Tea Act of 1773 actually benefited the colonists and Britain. The act gave the East India Trading company a monopoly on tea sold in America, eliminating wholesalers and other middlemen who pushed up the price. This dropped the price of tea by nearly a third across the colonies, so that it was cheaper to buy it from the East India Company than from Dutch, Danish, and Portuguese smugglers. All import taxes on tea were lifted except for a paltry three pence per pound, which Parliament insisted upon to assert their authority in the colonies. It was carefully calculated to benefit both parties, but Britain got their math wrong.

The colonists flipped their lid.

Ignoring the financial benefits of the agreement, the colonists saw the Tea Act as another underhanded ploy to manipulate the American economy. They refused to allow the British to put a price on their independence. Americans realized the British would never allow them to establish the kind of free society they yearned for, and the British came to believe the Americans wouldn't concede to their demands unless threatened with violence.

At almost the same time the Tea Act was signed into law, the colonists' darkest suspicions about the British were confirmed. In late 1772, an anonymous informant gave Benjamin Franklin a letter written by a royal official serving in Massachusetts to a British undersecretary, urging harsher measures be used to force Americans to capitulate. One line even suggested "an abridgement of what are called English liberties." Franklin forwarded the letters to America, where they were widely circulated. This outraged the colonists, but it was just a snippet of what the British were saying about them behind closed doors.

The influential British writer, poet, and lexicographer Dr. Samuel Johnson referred to the Americans as "a race of convicts," who "ought to be thankful for anything we allow them short of hanging." King George's temper was rising as well, hissing to Parliament that he wished to quell the "dangerous spirit of resistance" among "my deluded subjects."

The nucleus of resistance was the trading center of Boston, and English authorities worried that this fever of rebellion would spread if not dealt with. Many prominent Patriot agitators, such as Paul Revere, John Hancock, Samuel Adams, John Adams, James Otis, and Dr. Joseph Warren, also lived in and around Boston. To bring the recalcitrant colonists to heel, Parliament ordered the British army to occupy the city in 1768, five years before the Tea Act was passed.

Two thousand troops were stationed in Boston—almost the same number as there were able-bodied American men—and a huge force considering the population was only 16,000 at the time. The colonists were well aware of the dangers of a standing army, and saw this as one more maneuver to strip away their liberties as protected under the English Bill of Rights. Naturally, the quartering of thousands of troops among a hostile populace didn't go well and clashes broke out. British soldiers rough-housed supposed "rebels," and Patriots vandalized Loyalists' stores and harassed the soldiers ("Loyalists" or "Tories" were those who wished to remain British subjects).

Christopher Seider, an eleven-year-old boy, was shot and killed by a British customs official in 1770 when he joined a crowd of violent protestors throwing rocks at the man's house. Eleven days after Seider's death, British soldiers fired into a crowd after being pelted with snowballs, rocks, and sticks, an event that later became known as the Boston Massacre. Five people died and six were wounded, and several of the British soldiers were charged with murder.

In an ironic twist of fate that's often forgotten in modern history, the soldiers were defended by the Patriots, John Adams and Josiah Quincy II, as well as by Loyalist Robert Auchmuty. Adams argued that the Patriots had been the aggressors, and it would be hypocritical to say British soldiers didn't have a right to defend themselves when the colonists did. Quoting the great Roman orator and litigator Cicero, Adams won the case after appealing to the primacy of the universal law of self-preservation, "The man who had employed a weapon in self-defence was not held to have carried that weapon with a view to homicide."

The British continued to pass new taxes and tariffs and attempted to enforce the old ones, and the colonists responded as they had before: They smuggled, complained, protested, and fought back. When the British customs boat *Gaspee* ran aground on a sandbar in Rhode Island, Patriot smugglers attacked and torched the ship. The next winter, members of the Patriot organization The Sons of Liberty disguised themselves as Mohawk Indians, boarded three British trading vessels, and dumped 342 crates of tea into Boston Harbor—worth about $2 million in today's money.

After this open act of defiance, the British decided to bear down on the colonists. In a series of diktats later called the Intolerable Acts, the British blockaded Boston Harbor, replaced the democratically elected town officials with their own, revoked the Massachusetts royal charter, declared the colony to be in open rebellion, and appointed General Thomas Gage as military governor of the colony.

Gage was in his mid-fifties, with fleshy jowls, thin gray hair, and a stern gaze. He was also a seasoned combat veteran, having fought toe-to-toe against the French from Belgium to Pennsylvania, and helped subdue the Scots in the decisive and vicious battle of Culloden. In 1755, he was at the vanguard of a column of British soldiers that were nearly annihilated in the wilderness of western Pennsylvania by the French and their Native American allies. His commander and five hundred of his fellow soldiers were killed, bullets grazed his stomach and eyebrow and, thanks largely to the clear-eyed actions of a young Lieutenant-Colonel named George Washington, he narrowly escaped with his life.

The British also passed a law allowing the newly appointed governor to hold trials of Massachusetts officials in other colonies with jurors and judges who were more sympathetic to the king than the colonists. Finally, they passed the Quartering Acts, which required colonists to feed and house British soldiers in peacetime. In effect, this brought Massachusetts under direct control of the British Parliament and King George—precisely what the colonists had been protesting. Whispers of rebellion spread across North America as all eyes turned on Massachusetts.

The British were extremely uneasy about the prospect of fighting the Americans—and for good reason. "There are, in the different provinces, about a million of people," cautioned William Gerald Hamilton, a member of Parliament who opposed taxing the colonies, "which we may suppose at least 200,000 men able to bear arms; and nor only able to bear arms, bur [sic] having arms in their possession, unrestrained by any iniquitous Game Act. In the Massachusetts government particularly, there is an express law, by which every man is obliged to have a musket, a pound of powder, and a pound of bullets by him . . ."

He underestimated the Americans. In reality, modern estimates show that the colonists could muster some 500,000 fighting men if push came to shove, a force nearly twice as big as the largest European land army at the time, the Russian Empire. The Americans' reputation as exquisite marksmen and fierce fighters also gave the British pause. "The Yeomanry of America," wrote British Lieutenant-Colonel Charles Lee, "are accustomed from their infancy to fire arms; they are expert in the use of them:— Whereas the lower and middle people of England are, by the tyranny of certain laws almost as ignorant in the use of a musket, as they are of the ancient Catepulta."

As armed conflict loomed large in the minds of both sides, the colonial militia began to prepare for war. Nearly every free adult man in Massachusetts from sixteen to sixty was required to serve in the militia, with most using their own guns. Instead of drilling once every three months as they were required, some units drilled three times per week. This was not an armed rabble, but a citizen army.

The colonial militia also began husbanding away as much weaponry, powder, and ammunition as possible. In a mirror image of what happened in the English Civil War, both sides started wrestling for control of the colonies' arsenals. The British army had stockpiles of gunpowder in "powder houses" across the colonies, to be used in emergencies or for training exercises. As tensions rose between the Patriots and Loyalists, the British began quietly sending soldiers to retrieve the powder and bring it back within the walls of Boston. Although this powder was military property, the colonists saw this as a clear sign the British were readying themselves to suppress them by force. Some colonial militias and private citizens also stored their powder in these powder houses, and they feared losing those supplies as well.

In September 1774, 260 British soldiers sailed under the cover of night up the Mystic River and seized hundreds of barrels of gunpowder from the Charlestown powder house outside of Boston. Rumors spread that this was the opening salvo of the war, and within hours, there were 20,000 militiamen marching toward Boston. The force later dispersed when word spread that the powder was British army property, but British authorities were dismayed by the speed and ferocity of the militia's response.

Lord Dartmouth, the Royal Secretary of State for America, was particularly peeved at the militia's actions and dashed off several letters urging General Gage to "arrest and imprison the principal actors and abettors" and subtly suggested "disarming the Inhabitants of the Massachusetts Bay, Connecticut and Rhode Island . . ." In a line that would come back to haunt him several months later, Dartmouth also added that "I think that a small force now, if put to the test, would be able to conquer . . ." the American militia.

Gage, a generally loyal, honest, and even-handed man, agreed with the idea in principle, but pointed out that it would take military force and probably martial law to disarm the Americans. "Your Lordship's Idea of disarming certain Provinces would doubtless be consistent with Prudence and Safety," Gage acknowledged, "but it neither is nor has been practicable without having Recourse to Force, and being Masters of the Country." However, although Gage's response suggests that the British were reluctant to openly disarm Americans, they began doing so anyway using indirect means.

Two days after Lord Dartmouth suggested disarming the colonists, King George III blocked the import of all guns and ammunition to America. On the surface, the new statute simply required merchants to obtain a permit to export weapons from Britain to America, but in reality, no permits were given until the end of the war in 1783. Luckily, it didn't much affect the Americans. American gunsmiths were already some of the best in the world, and wily old Benjamin Franklin was already outflanking the law by smuggling weapons into America from the Netherlands, France, and Spain.

Back in America, Gage refused to allow merchants who had stored gunpowder in the local powder houses to sell to colonists and forced firearms retailers to sell the British their excess inventory so Americans couldn't buy more guns. Although Gage hadn't given orders to disarm Americans, some soldiers seem to have taken matters into their own hands. "They keep a constant search for every thing which will be serviceable in battle;" complained Dr. Joseph Warren in a letter to Samuel Adams on September 29, 1774, "and whenever they espy any instruments which may serve or disserve them,—whether they are the property of individuals or the public is immaterial,—they are seized, and carried into the camp or on board the ships of war."

Patriots quickly caught wind of what was happening and began raiding powder houses all across New Hampshire, Rhode Island, and Connecticut. Others began hiding powder, cannon, muskets, ammunition, salted food, and any other military supplies they could get their hands on in secret caches across the colonies. Around the same time, Patriots like George Mason organized independent militia companies after they were prevented from mustering the Virginia state militia.

By 1775, both sides were already loaded for bear when Loyalist spies informed Gage that the Patriots had stockpiled weapons at Concord, Massachusetts. In the early morning hours of April 19th, 800 British soldiers marched from Boston to confiscate the weapons, but the Patriots were well ahead of them. Thanks to an intricate intelligence network largely masterminded by Paul Revere and Joseph Warren, the Patriots knew where the British were headed before they even left Boston.

In his famous "Midnight Ride," Revere rode through the night to warn every Patriot he could find that "The Regulars are coming out!" Revere had other messengers fan out across the countryside, so that by the time the British began marching, the land was swarming with thousands of armed Patriots ready to confront the Redcoats.

The British realized the game was up shortly thereafter when they heard alarm bells and gunshots—signals the colonists used to alert the militia—along their marching route, which probably led to the ill-fated decision to enter Lexington, Massachusetts, a small farming village just outside of Boston, the kind of town that would have slumbered through history except that it lay along the route to Concord. Colonel Francis Smith, the commander of the British expedition, made the wise choice to send for reinforcements from Boston, but they would arrive too late.

The British could have marched right past Lexington, but Marine Lieutenant Jesse Adair—who would later lead a British charge at Bunker Hill—decided he should secure the flanks of their advance by making a slight detour into the town before the main column continued to Concord.

Just as the first glint of sunlight began to rise above the low hills surrounding Lexington, the British vanguard marched into town where they came face to face with seventy-seven armed militiamen arrayed in the town square, commanded by Captain John Parker.

Parker was a veteran of the British Army and fought as a sergeant in Louisbourg and Quebec in the French and Indian War. Unlike most British officers, who bought their rank, Parker was elected by the men he led and was close friends with many of them. A quarter of them were related to him through one side of the family or the other, and most had been born and raised in and around Lexington. Although his once robust body was racked by tuberculosis, he stayed up with his men through much of the night to ensure they were ready to face the British.

Parker had consulted with his men before the British arrived and decided that unless the soldiers harassed, searched, attacked, or arrested anyone, they were to be left alone. He knew that the guns the British were after in Concord had been moved to a new hiding place, so there was little point in provoking them—better to let them search the town and slink back to Boston, tired, hungry, and empty handed, than start a war with the most powerful army in North America. But as fate would have it, a war did start that day.

Parker had intentionally arranged his men in the open so the British would know this wasn't an ambush, careful not to block the road to

Concord. He wanted to show the British that the colonists were ready and willing to defend the town if provoked, but had no intention of actually fighting. "Stand your ground; don't fire unless fired upon," he told his men. "But if they mean to have a war, let it begin here."

The commander of the British vanguard, Major John Pitcairn, had given his men similar orders not to fire, but he seems to have harbored more militant views. Just a month before, he'd bragged to the Admiralty of the Americans' that "One active campaign, a smart action, and burning two or three of their towns, will set everything to rights. Nothing now, I am convinced, but this will ever convince these foolish bad people that England is in earnest."

Despite their orders, fear triumphed over forethought, and the British began fanning out around Parker's men, intending to surround them. Pitcairn rode forward waving a sword and demanded Parker's men lay down their weapons and disperse. Expecting this, Parker told his men to go home, but at this critical moment, his voice failed him. Though he didn't know it at the time, he only had five months to live before tuberculosis took his life, and his voice wasn't strong enough to rise above the shouts and stomps of nervous soldiers. The few men who heard him began to trickle away, but before they got far, a shot rang out. Both sides gaped at each other in confusion, trying to see who had fired, when the British soldiers let loose a hail of balls that ripped into Parker's men.

At first, they didn't believe they were really being shot at, thinking the British had only loaded their guns with powder and were trying to scare them off. As more balls tore into flesh and men toppled over, they quickly realized they were under attack. A handful of militiamen managed to fire off a ragged volley at the British just as a wall of red shapes came racing at them through a haze of gun smoke. Without orders, the British troops had charged into the fleeing militiamen, stabbing and slashing with their bayonets. Parker watched as his cousin James was gutted by a British blade. Another man, Jonathan Harrington, was shot in the torso, and crawled through the chaos to bleed to death on his own doorstep.

The militia fled into the hills, and shortly thereafter Colonel Smith arrived and brought the British Marines under control. Eight colonists were dead and ten were wounded, whereas the only British casualty was a man who'd taken a musket ball in the leg. The British fired off a volley of shots to mark their victory and continued their march to Concord. Little did they know that Parker wasn't finished with them yet.

As the British approached Concord, they quickly secured the surrounding area and began searching for weapons. Although the most important equipment and supplies had been moved, they found three massive twenty-four-pounder cannons, 550 pounds of musketballs, and over 100 barrels of salted food and flour, which they threw into a stream. They also burned several carriages and accidentally lit a house on fire, and as the smoke rose above the sky, the militia began to move in.

The commander of the Concord militia was James Barrett, sixty-five years old at the time, and the owner of the farm where most of the weapons had been hidden. He had pulled his men back to a hill overlooking the town when the British arrived, knowing he didn't yet have the numbers to confront them. While the British searched the town, militiamen poured in from the surrounding countryside, so that by the time Barrett saw the smoke over Concord, they numbered close to 400 men.

Still not knowing exactly what had happened at Lexington, Barrett ordered his men to advance to the North Bridge—a small wood-planked walkway across the Concord River that led into town and was guarded by about one hundred British regulars. Seeing they were outnumbered, the British commander ordered his men to retreat across the bridge. The militia advanced and were within fifty paces of the British on the opposite side of the river when a shot cracked from the British lines. Two more British soldiers fired, and soon the whole line was firing indiscriminately into the militia. Two Patriots were killed instantly by British balls and four were wounded. The militiamen returned fire, killing four British soldiers and wounding nine, forcing them to retreat toward the town and begin their march back to Boston.

The British tramped quickly through the countryside, but now they were being dogged by close to a thousand armed militiamen. When the

British were forced into a narrow column to cross a bridge, militia marksmen began sniping at the soldiers, killing two men and wounding six others. The British were in trouble, and General Gage's worst fears were coming true. Far from being overawed by the might of the British Empire—a force that had recently bested soldiers from France, Spain, Sweden, Scotland, and Bavaria—this ragtag force of citizen soldiers unleashed their fury into the fleeing regulars.

As the British column approached Boston, they entered a gauntlet of near constant sniper attacks and coordinated ambushes. At one point, they charged a hill packed with five hundred militiamen, hoping to drive them off. The militia stood their ground and stopped the attack cold with a shower of well-placed shots before moving to set another ambush in front of the British advance. Halfway to Lexington, the British met a sharp curve in the road where they were suddenly pelted with musketballs from both their sides and rear, and by the time they made it through the thicket, another thirty men were dead or wounded.

The British column was exhausted, burdened with dead and wounded comrades and running out of ammunition as they jogged toward Lexington, where John Parker was waiting for them. In an encounter that would become known as "Parker's Revenge," the Lexington militia cut down more British troops from a hilltop just outside of their hometown. One ball struck the British commander, Colonel Francis Smith, in the leg, knocking him from his horse.

The British endured the onslaught and stumbled into Lexington, where they were joined by a relief force of one thousand British soldiers, including two cannons, under the command of Brigadier General Hugh Percy. While the British rested, Massachusetts Brigadier General William Heath assumed command of the colonial militia and prepared his men to inflict more punishment.

As the British resumed their march to Boston, the militia performed a series of moving ambushes: They spread out in small groups along the flanks of the British advance, waiting behind trees, hills, and walls, and took shots at long range to chip away at the British force. Whenever the

British counterattacked, the militia would vanish into the woods or mount their horses to ride off ahead of the column, only to reform, reload, and renew the attack.

As the British approached the small town of Menotomy (present day Arlington), they were met with more musket fire from the houses and hills surrounding the town. Furious at these tactics and their humiliating losses, British soldiers began killing anyone they suspected of aiding the Patriot attack. They killed two drunks in a tavern, ransacked houses and the local church, and stole valuables and liquor from local residents. According to one Patriot account, British troops "pillaged almost every house they passed by, breaking and destroying floors, windows, glasses . . . and carrying off clothing and other valuable effects. Not content with shooting down the unarmed, aged, and infirm, they disregarded the cries of the wounded, killing them without mercy . . ."

Although wartime atrocities are often embellished for propaganda purposes, even the British admitted they stooped low that day. "Our Soldiers . . . were so wild and irregular," admitted British Lieutenant John Barker in his diary, "that there was no keeping 'em in any order; by their eagerness and inattention they kill'd many of our own People; and the plundering was shameful; many hardly thought of anything else; what was worse they were encouraged by some Officers."

It was just outside Menotomy that Samuel Whittemore saw the British column while walking in his fields. Whittemore was seventy-eight, old enough to be alive when William of Orange was on the throne of England, and had spent most of his life fighting for the British Empire, rising to the rank of captain. He fought in King George's War, where he helped capture the fortress of Louisbourg. He also fought in the French and Indian War, and some sources say he took part in the British expedition against Chief Pontiac. Now he was just a farmer, grandfather, and community organizer, but when he heard the storm of gunfire and saw the British approaching, he grabbed his old weapons and hurried to join the fight.

Whittemore found a low stone wall close to the road and waited until the British were just a few paces away, then stood and fired point-blank into a soldier, killing him instantly. He then drew a pair of dueling pistols with which he killed another soldier and wounded a third. With no time to reload, he drew a sword and charged as the British rushed him. Before he could reach them, a British musket ball tore through his face, and he was beaten to the ground with rifle butts and skewered with bayonets.

The soldiers left him to die in a pool of his own blood as they retreated toward Boston, but militiamen found him shortly thereafter, trying to reload his musket. They took him to a doctor (who happened to be John Adams' cousin), who did his best to patch up his wounds, but he didn't expect him to live. Against all odds, Whittemore not only recovered but lived another eighteen years before dying at age ninety-six—long enough to see the British defeated, the ratification of the U.S. Constitution, and George Washington elected as the first President of the United States. He was buried not far from where he helped win the War for Independence.

The British column eventually reached the safety of Boston, but not before they had lost three hundred men—killed, wounded, or missing—while the Patriots lost only ninety-three men. It was a minor skirmish by any standard, but a skirmish that split the colonies like an earthquake. As John Adams commented, "The Die was cast, the Rubicon crossed." There was no turning back now. When George Washington heard what had happened at Lexington and Concord, he wrote to a friend: "The once-happy and peaceful plains of America are either to be drenched in blood or inhabited by slaves ... Can a virtuous man hesitate in his choice?"

Pushed to the wall, the virtuous men of America did not hesitate. With guns in hand, militiamen came from every corner of New England to lay siege to Boston. By the morning of April 20, 1775, fifteen thousand armed Patriots under the command of William Heath surrounded the city.

Horrified at his predicament, Gage finally began disarming all of the inhabitants of Boston. He ordered soldiers to search homes without warrants and refused to allow any citizens to leave unless they surrendered their weapons. Many people either smuggled their weapons out of the city or decided it was better to live in Boston with their weapons than leave without, but on April 27, the townsfolk surrendered 1,778 muskets,

634 pistols, 973 bayonets, and 38 blunderbusses (a kind of short-barreled musket)—a massive stockpile of weapons. Despite complying with his demands, Gage refused to let many of the people leave. The few he let go were forced to abandon most of their possessions in Boston. At this point, all of these citizens were still British subjects entitled to the rights of free Englishmen, including the right to bear arms. This disarmament and deceit by Gage would be a key motivation for the *Declaration of the Causes and Necessity of Taking Up Arms*, published on July 6, 1775, by Thomas Jefferson and John Dickinson, which explained why the colonies felt it necessary to use violence against the British to protect their rights.

The British would attempt to break the siege of Boston in June, in what would become known as the Battle of Bunker Hill (although most of the fighting occurred on nearby Breed's Hill). Americans caught wind of a British plan to occupy the hills north of Boston, which would give them control of the entire harbor. Twelve hundred militiamen promptly wrong-footed the British by digging trenches and erecting walls across the hills under cover of darkness. The next morning, the British charged up the hills into a murderous storm of musketballs and cannon fire, repulsed twice with heavy casualties. The Americans were running out of ammunition, though, and a third and final British charge broke their lines.

Although it was a British victory on paper, these losses, and those at Lexington and Concord, convinced many British commanders that they had severely underestimated the "deluded Americans," as King George had referred to them. The British suffered over one thousand casualties and twenty slain officers, whereas the colonists lost just 450 men. General Henry Clinton, the newly appointed commander-in-chief of the British forces in North America, paraphrased Pyrrhus of Epirus in his diary, writing, "A few more such victories would have shortly put an end to British dominion in America."

The comparison was perhaps more accurate than he realized. Pyrrhus of Epirus was a Greek king who invaded Italy and won two battles against the Romans at Heraclea and Asculum in the third century BC. The army of the Roman Republic—made up of citizen soldiers much like the colonists—rallied and eventually forced Pyrrhus to flee back to Greece, where he was allegedly killed when an old woman hurled a tile at his head from her roof as Pyrrhus fought her son in the streets.

Major John Pitcairn, the marine commander who'd waived his sword at Captain John Parker across the Lexington commons, and once boasted that, "If I draw my sword but half out of my scabbard, the whole banditti of Massachusetts will run away," was shot six times before receiving his coup de grâce just after reaching the American trenches.

A year later, the British garrison in Boston was forced to retreat to Nova Scotia, and the skirmishes fought by a band of armed citizens at Lexington, Concord, and Bunker Hill ignited a war that blazed across the colonies.

The Patriots fought for a simple idea: That all men are created equal, free, and independant and are entitled to inherent natural rights that no one—not even a king—can take away. They had tried to negotiate for these rights with pen and paper, but when words failed, they were forced to reach for musket and ball.

They held fast to this philosophy like a lifeline through the bloody, chaotic, and desperate war that followed. It was this conviction that propelled the Americans to early victories against the British at Ticonderoga, Saratoga, and Trenton, and bolstered their resolve after crippling defeats at Quebec, Long Island, and Charleston. It stayed their nerves as they shivered through the bitter winter at Valley Forge, slogged through the septic swamps of South Carolina, and tramped through the peaks and valleys of Appalachian mountains. It gave them hope as their bodies were ravaged by smallpox, malaria, and typhus.

Nearly a quarter million Americans served in the American Revolutionary War—almost a tenth of the entire population—and one in ten of those who served would never live to see the country they helped create. It took eight years, thirty thousand American deaths, billions of dollars (in today's money), and the efforts of countless men like Paul Revere, John Parker, and Samuel Whittemore, but in the end, the Americans won their freedom.

Once the war with Britain was over, however, the colonists faced a new challenge—building a government that would protect the rights of every generation yet to come.

They learned many lessons fighting the British, one of which was that men with guns could shatter an empire if they had good reason to do so. Not only did the Founders understand this, they drafted the Constitution to ensure that Americans could do this to their own government should the need arise.

In the next chapter, you'll learn why and how they did so.

6
Why Does the United States Have a Bill of Rights?

"A sword is never a killer, it is a tool in the killer's hands."
—Lucius Annaeus Seneca, Roman Stoic philosopher,
statesman, and writer, 1st century AD.

"We cannot have assault weapons in our society . . .
They need to be banned . . . military-grade assault weapons,
those just don't belong in the hands of everyday people."
—Bill de Blasio, Democratic mayor of New York City, September 5, 2019.

After the war, the Founders held the destiny of the new nation in the hollow of their hand. They had escaped England's thrall, and now set themselves to the task of crafting a government that would secure the liberties they fought for in the revolution.

Luckily, the Founders were something of an intellectual dream team, well equipped to rise to the challenge, and the citizens of the new nation were cut from a similar cloth. Long before the first shots were fired in Lexington, Americans had embraced the philosophy that all men were created free, equal, and independent, and possessed inherent *natural rights* that transcended government, man, and king. As John Dickinson declared in 1766, "They are born with us; exist with us; and cannot be taken from us by any human power without taking our lives."

What's more, they believed these rights were as old as mankind—a fact of nature just as real as the earth, sea, and sky—and by taking up arms against the British, they weren't trying to create new rights, but to reclaim and protect those rights which had been so long denied to so many. The purpose of the government, they believed, was to protect these natural rights—nothing more, nothing less. To ensure the government fulfilled its obligations admirably, they also believed the only legitimate form of government was one that existed with the consent of the people, was created by the people, and that the people had the right to modify or destroy their government if it failed to protect their rights or actively infringed upon them. As Jefferson put it so eloquently in *The Declaration of Independence*:

> "We hold these truths to be self-evident, that all men are created equal, that they are endowed by their Creator with certain unalienable Rights, that among these are Life, Liberty and the pursuit of Happiness.
>
> —That to secure these rights, Governments are instituted among Men, deriving their just powers from the consent of the governed,
>
> —That whenever any Form of Government becomes destructive of these ends, it is the Right of the People to alter or to abolish it, and to institute new Government, laying its foundation on such principles and organizing its powers in such form, as to them shall seem most likely to effect their Safety and Happiness."

Brilliant as the Founders were, though, they didn't come up with these ideas. They borrowed them from Enlightenment thinkers like John Locke, Thomas Hobbes, and Jean-Jacques Rousseau, whose concepts colored much of the Founders' decisions about the new government.

One idea in particular was a linchpin of their beliefs: The *social contract theory*. The theory states that, in a hypothetical "state of nature," where humans are unbound by any social, political, or legal limitations, we have every freedom imaginable—both good and bad. Of course, if humans were to act on all of these freedoms, we would be little more than beasts. "The life of man," warned Hobbes, would be "solitary, poor, nasty, brutish, and short."

To prevent this chaotic existence and protect their most fundamental rights of life, liberty, and the pursuit of happiness, the theory goes, humans must enter into a *social contract* with one another. Essentially, this libertarian theory states that while man is born completely free, some of these freedoms need to be restrained for the benefit of all. However, these restraints need not infringe on the most important, fundamental rights of man. Here's how Leonard Levy, one of the foremost historians on constitutional law and winner of the Pulitzer Prize for History, describes their thinking:

> "Born without the restraint of human laws, he [man] had a right to possess liberty and to work for his own property. Born naked and stationless, he had a right to equality. Born with certain instincts and needs, he had a right to satisfy them—a right to the pursuit of happiness."

What's more, a central assumption of social contract theory is that all humans have a right to life, and thus have a right to defend their lives. "I should have a right to destroy that which threatens me with destruction," wrote John Locke in 1690, "for, by the fundamental law of nature, man being to be preserved as much as possible, when all cannot be preserved, the safety of the innocent is to be preferred: and one may destroy a man who makes war upon him." In other words, if a criminal uses violence against you and violates your sacred right to self preservation, you have every right to inflict violence upon them to prevent it from being done to you.

As a corollary, you also have the right to possess the same *means* to defend yourself as the criminal has to harm you. You can't effectively preserve your right to life if your enemies are significantly better armed than you, and thus you have a right to possess weapons on par with those who could harm you. These ideas would be embodied in the Second Amendment which, as you'll learn in this chapter, is first and foremost a guarantee of the right to self-preservation.

When the social contract theory was first proposed, it was meant more as a thought exercise to help explain how humans formed societies, but the Founders took this concept to its logical conclusion and created a government founded on a literal contract—the Constitution. This was a radical departure from the British system, where laws, privileges, and punishments would change with the whims of whatever monarch sat on the throne. Although Magna Carta, the Petition of Right, and the English Bill of Rights had secured a modicum of liberty for Englishmen, these documents were vague, incomplete, and riddled with loopholes that were frequently exploited by autocratic kings and corrupt parliaments. This was particularly true when it came to the right to bear arms. Both the king and Parliament disregarded Britain's liberty documents when they needed to disarm political opponents, but the Americans weren't going to let the same thing happen to them.

Part of the reason it was so easy for the ruling class of Britain to oppress their countrymen, was that Britain never had a single, clear, universal constitution that explained what the government could and could not do (in fact, they still don't). Instead, they had a loose collection of liberty documents that only limited the power of the crown, but not Parliament. Thus, members of Parliament were free to strip away the rights of anyone they pleased, impose fines, taxes, and punishments, disarm innocent citizens, and enrich themselves at the expense of the common British citizen, which they did with gleeful abandon.

The Founders sought to turn this system on its head and developed a wholly different concept of a constitution: Cardinal law that served as the keystone of effective government. To them, a *constitution* should codify the natural rights of man, specify how the government was to protect these rights, and clarify the regular, fair procedures of law that would preserve these liberties for every citizen. It "signified to them a supreme law creating government, limiting it, unalterable by it, and paramount to it," explains Levy.

Chapter 6

The fundamental difference between the American and British systems of government was this: The British system of government started with the assumption that power resided in the monarch, who could dispense certain freedoms to the people as he would throw crumbs to a beggar. To them, the question was, "What liberties will we grant to the people?"

The system of government envisioned by the Americans was the polar opposite. It started with the assumption that *all* power resided in the people, who carefully granted certain privileges and powers to the government that would benefit everyone. To them, the question was, "What liberties will we grant to the government?"

War with Great Britain was just the opportunity the Founders needed to bring these ideas to life, and the colonists began scribbling the first state constitutions soon after the first shots were fired at Lexington and Concord. Even before the Declaration of Independence was signed on July 4, 1776, visionaries such as George Mason and Thomas Jefferson had already drafted and adopted the Virginia Constitution of 1776—the first permanent state constitution. Pennsylvania, Delaware, Maryland, Vermont, Connecticut, Rhode Island, New Jersey, Georgia, New York, South Carolina, and Massachusetts followed suit, so that by the end of the war, almost every American was guaranteed more freedoms than their British counterparts.

These state constitutions were a tremendous leap forward for individual liberties, especially considering the documents were drafted in wartime by men who would likely be hanged for treason if caught. Their courage was laudable, but their eagerness and haste also meant that the new state constitutions were poorly worded, omitting important rights, and inconsistent with one another. In effect, each state had a slightly different "rule book" for how the government was supposed to work, which many believed weakened the country from within. Many failed to protect freedom of speech, assembly, and petition, and the right to habeas corpus (which prevents people from being jailed without proof of guilt). Others excluded freedom from double jeopardy (being tried for a crime after acquittal), bills of attainder (legal writs that allowed authorities to imprison and execute people without trial), and ex post facto laws (which retroactively declared certain activities criminal, increased the penalty for a crime, or changed the rules of evidence to obtain a conviction despite a past acquittal.) Many of these constitutions were also contradictory and vague when it came to securing the right to bear arms, with some emphasizing the right of states to maintain a militia and others the right of individuals to own and use guns.

Thus, the founders met to draft a new federal constitution that all of the states would agree to and that would supersede the state constitutions. In essence, this would be a "master" rule book for how the country would be run, and while states could still have unique constitutions and laws depending on their circumstances and citizens' wishes, they all had to conform to the overarching rules of the federal Constitution. They finished the first draft on August 6, 1787, after just four months of work, but it would be five years before all of the states agreed on the purpose, scope, and wording of this new pact.

Why did the process take so long? Well, although the Founders are often depicted as a kind of enlightened political fraternity—united by principle and patriotism, untarnished by petty politics, and all working harmoniously for the good of the common man—this is looking at history through rose-colored glasses. There's no doubt the Founders had good intentions for their countrymen and were a cut above most modern politicians, but they were also possessed of great passion, pride, and pugnacity, and they fought each other in debate with as much fervor as they did the British on the battlefield. And they disagreed fiercely over the new Constitution.

Specifically, they fought over whether or not the new federal constitution should have a bill of rights. This argument split the founders into two parties:

The *Federalists*, led by men like Alexander Hamilton, James Madison, and John Jay, who believed that a federal bill of rights was unnecessary, foolish, and even dangerous.

The *Anti-Federalists*, led by men like Patrick Henry, George Mason, and Samuel Adams, who believed a federal bill of rights was a vital component of the new US government.

Chapter 6

Now, over 200 years later, it's easy to look back in hindsight and say the Anti-Federalists were right and the Federalists were wrong. After all, who could argue against things like freedom of speech, the right to a speedy trial, and protection against unreasonable search and seizure? The Federalists have earned a particularly bad rap among gun owners for their opposition to the Bill of Rights because, if they'd gotten their way, we'd have no Second Amendment. Is this really fair, though? Did the Federalists really want to deny these inalienable rights to their countrymen?

No.

In fact, the Federalists and Anti-Federalists agreed on almost every right that would eventually be added to the Bill of Rights on principle, but they disagreed on the best way to protect these rights from government infringement. As George Washington (a Federalist) confided to the Marquis de Lafayette about the debates over the Constitution, "There was not a member of the Convention, I believe, who had the least objection to what is contended for by the advocates of a Bill of Rights."

Ironically, when the Constitution was first being drafted, neither Anti-Federalists nor Federalists raised more than a finger to push for a bill of rights, and it nearly died on the vine. George Mason meekly suggested that he "wished the plan had been prefaced by a Bill of Rights," and Elbridge Gerry of Massachusetts supported him, but their proposal was quickly voted down 10 to 0. A few days later, Gerry and Charles Pinckney proposed inserting a clause that said "the liberty of the Press should be inviolably observed." Roger Sherman flatly harpooned this proposal, saying "It is unnecessary. The power of Congress does not extend to the Press." The motion was voted down again, 7 to 0. Reporting on the lack of debate over a bill of rights to his fellow Pennsylvanians, James Wilson wrote "So little account was the idea that it passed off in a short conversation, without introducing a formal debate or assuming the shape of a motion."

Things changed when it became clear that the Federalists wished to grant the new government supreme dominion over the states. Although most state constitutions already had bills of rights, the powers granted to the federal government allowed them to be overridden, which posed a clear threat to individual liberties throughout America. For example, Congress could now use its powers to tax as a mace to smash religious freedom. Catholics could be forced to pay three times as much as Protestants or vice versa. It could limit freedom of the press in the same way, taxing dissident newspapers or printers into extinction. Or, the government could place an exceptionally high tax on guns, making them too expensive for most people to possess (which occurred for certain kinds of guns in 1934 under the National Firearms Act, or NFA).

The most dangerous aspect of the new Constitution was the "necessary and proper clause," which allowed Congress to pass new laws to exercise its powers under the Constitution. According to the Anti-Federalists, this loophole gave the new federal government limitless power to infringe on individual liberties. Although there were checks and balances in place, if the wrong people were to climb the rungs of power and corrupt these positions, America would have no legal recourse to defend themselves against the government's actions.

For instance, although New Hampshire's Bill of Rights stated that citizens could never be disarmed by the government, what if the new federal government declared New Hampshire to be in rebellion for not paying taxes? Then, they could deem it "necessary and proper" to send in the army to quell the "rebellion" and disarm the inhabitants, just as the British had done fifteen years before. Or, the government could pass new laws that directly violated individual liberty, such as a law that criminalized criticizing the government. Then, since there was no ban on ex post facto laws, the government could declare anyone who had spoken out against the government in the past a criminal. These people could be forced to stand trial without counsel or the right to produce evidence on their own behalf, imprisoned or even tortured, and then subjected to the same treatment all over again *for the same crime*, because there was no law against double jeopardy. The new government could do all this while thumbing their nose at state bills of rights, because they were only limited by the rules of the Constitution, which didn't explicitly prohibit any of these offenses.

The Federalists countered that none of this was actually possible for one simple reason. The cornerstone of the new Constitution was the fact that it only granted the government the powers explicitly listed, and any right, power, or privilege not listed was automatically and unequivocally granted to the states or the people. In other words, they had carefully crafted the new federal constitution so that it precisely conformed to the principles you learned about in the beginning of this chapter. According to the Federalists, the federal government was granted a handful of responsibilities for the benefit of everyone, but all other freedoms were retained by the people. In essence, the Constitution gave the government a narrow to-do list, and anything not on the list was none of their business.

Thus, the Federalists believed that because the federal government was granted no power to violate individual rights, it tacitly guaranteed individual rights. As Alexander Hamilton claimed in *The Federalist No. 84*, "the Constitution is itself, in every rational sense, and to every useful purpose, a Bill of Rights." Adding a bill of rights, he believed, would be unnecessary.

Hamilton and his Federalist allies even went so far as to claim a bill of rights would be "dangerous," because it "would contain various exceptions to powers not granted; and, on this very account, would afford a colorable pretext to claim more than were granted." If the Constitution attempted to define even one or two individual rights, the Federalists claimed, that would imply the federal government *did* have the authority to decide individual rights on the whole. They could then use this precedent to rapidly expand their powers beyond the bounds of the Constitution into the personal lives of every American. "For why declare that things shall not be done which there is no power to do?" asked Hamilton. "Why, for instance, should it be said that the liberty of the press shall not be restrained, when no power is given by which restrictions may be imposed?" From the Federalist perspective, telling the government they weren't allowed to infringe on personal liberties would be like telling your dog it doesn't have the right to drive your car.

Finally, the Federalists also argued that when push came to shove, a corrupt government would simply ignore "parchment barriers" like a bill of rights and impose their will by force, and here they had a point. After all, the first battle of the American Revolutionary War was fought when the

British attempted to infringe on the colonists' right to bear arms, which was already protected under the English Bill of Rights, a "parchment barrier" if there ever was one.

In the Federalist's minds, the Constitution was an elegant solution to the many pitfalls of previous governments. Instead of granting a monarch, oligarchy, or corrupt Parliament the unfettered ability to decide how the country was run, the Constitution laid out exactly what the new federal government was allowed to do, and specifically barred them from having a hand in any other matter. It was a noble idea, but like Pygmalion and his statue, many Federalists were so infatuated with their proposed form of government, they willfully ignored its flaws.

For one thing, the Constitution did give the federal government power to control a few individual rights. The Constitution already guaranteed trial by jury in civil cases, bans on religious tests for public office, and the right to habeas corpus. Throwing the Federalist's argument back in their faces, Robert Whitehall posed the obvious question, "Have the people no other rights worth their attention, or is it to be inferred... that every other right is abandoned?" Patrick Henry picked up the argument and pointed out that since the Constitution protected the writ of habeas corpus but allowed it to be suspended when necessary for public safety, "It results clearly that, if it had not said so, they could suspend it in all cases whatsoever. It reverses the position of the friends of this Constitution [the Federalists], that every thing is retained which is not given up; for, instead of this, everything is given up which is not expressly reserved."

In other words, the Federalists' main argument against a bill of rights was that future tyrants or corrupt governments could revoke any rights not expressly included on the list. As the Anti-Federalists pointed out, though, the version of the Constitution the Federalists were trying to have signed into law *already* listed several individual rights. If the Constitution was going to list individual rights, as it clearly did, why not make it a proper list of the most important rights?

Richard Henry Lee, a prominent Anti-Federalist, pointed out another contradiction: The Constitution prohibited Congress from granting titles of nobility, but according to the Federalists' logic, this clause should be unnecessary because no other part of the Constitution implied they had any right to grant such titles. "Why then by a negative clause, restrain congress from doing what it had power to do? This clause, then, must have no meaning, or imply, that were it omitted, congress would have the power in question ... on the principle that congress possess the powers not expressly reserved."

Remember, one of Hamilton's chief arguments against a bill of rights was that this would imply the government had some control over individual rights. In essence, a bill of rights was simply a list of things the government wasn't allowed to do. Creating such a "not to do" list, though, would imply the government did have some say over individual liberties, or so the Federalists contended. As Lee pointed out, though, the Constitution already listed certain things the government wasn't supposed to do, like granting titles of nobility, refuting Hamilton's own argument.

Perhaps the strongest argument for a bill of rights was also the simplest: what harm could it do?

After all, the founders all agreed on the rights that were to be included. They all believed in the importance of freedom of speech, religion, and association. They all abhorred unreasonable search and seizure, ex post facto laws, and double jeopardy. And virtually all of them believed in an individual's right to bear arms and the importance of an armed militia.

James Winthrop, an Anti-Federalist who'd been librarian of Harvard College before the war and had been wounded in the Battle of Bunker Hill, rightly observed that most governments—whether democracies or autocracies—have a "disposition to use power wantonly. A bill of rights," he continued, "is therefore as necessary to defend an individual against the majority in a republick as against a king in a monarchy."

One Federalist whose feet stayed firmly on the ground throughout this debate was James Madison, who worked harder than any other man in America to pass the Bill of Rights into law. Madison had been ambivalent about a bill of rights in the beginning but, influenced by the Anti-Federalist arguments and personal correspondence with his friend, Thomas Jefferson, he came to believe it would do little harm and might do much good. As he explained in a letter to Jefferson, "I have favored it because I supposed it might be of use, and if properly executed could not be of disservice." He agreed with Jefferson's point that although a bill of rights may be just a "parchment barrier," at the very least it would educate the people about their most important rights, so they would know when the government was infringing on them.

In Britain, "rights" were a hazy concept, largely left up to subjective interpretation by Parliament, the king, and custom. Madison believed the United States should aim higher and clearly spell out exactly what rights its citizens were entitled to, even if the list might be incomplete or imperfect.

Madison realized that the argument over a bill of rights had devolved into an internecine quarrel that threatened to sabotage the entire Constitution and took it upon himself to unite both parties in compromise. He defected from the hardline position of Hamilton and his cronies, and single-handedly fought tooth and nail to pass the Bill of Rights into law. Standing alone before an apathetic House of Representatives on June 8, 1789, Madison threw down the gauntlet to both parties in a rousing speech before Congress, where he proposed they set aside their differences to protect "the great rights of mankind." Through clear reasoning and stirring rhetoric, Madison dismantled all of the major arguments against a bill of rights, addressing Anti-Federalist worries over a despotic government and reassuring Federalists that any new amendments would not hamper the effectiveness of the new federal government.

And his words fell on deaf ears.

Every speaker that followed Madison either opposed a bill of rights or believed they had far better things to debate. Six weeks later, he went hat in hand to the House and "begged" for them to reconsider his amendments. Instead, they grudgingly granted him a place on a committee to draft the amendments, giving him one week to report his progress.

After carefully drafting his list of amendments and delivering it to the House, they promptly pigeonholed it for future consideration. After more prodding and pleading, the House finally considered his amendments on

August 13. The bill bounced back and forth between the House and the Senate, and Madison's proposed nineteen amendments were whittled down to twelve, and over the next two years, ten of these amendments were ratified and signed into law, including the Second Amendment.

Despite facing overwhelming odds, enduring many disappointments, and being ostracized by many fellow politicians, Madison pushed the Bill of Rights through to completion. "There is no question that it was Madison's personal prestige and his dogged persistence that saw the amendments through the Congress," writes historian Gordon S. Wood. "There might have been a federal Constitution without Madison but certainly no Bill of Rights."

As you'll learn in the next chapter, this is particularly true when it comes to the Second Amendment, which might have looked entirely different if it hadn't been for Madison's steady hand and superior intellect.

7

What the Second Amendment Was *Really* Meant to Protect

> "The whole aim of practical politics is to keep the populace alarmed—and hence clamorous to be led to safety— by menacing it with an endless series of hobgoblins, all of them imaginary."
> —H.L. Mencken, journalist, essayist, and historian, 1918.

> "Yes, people pull the trigger—but guns are the instrument of death. Gun control is necessary, and delay means more death and horror."
> —Eliot Spitzer, Democratic governor of New York, August 7, 2012.

The Founders spent half a decade ironing out the nuances of the Constitution, but ironically, there was little debate about the Second Amendment at the time. They probably never imagined that these twenty-seven words would become the most disputed sentence in the entire document.

The final draft of the Second Amendment of the US Constitution, as written by James Madison, reads:

"A well regulated Militia, being necessary to the security of a free State, the right of the people to keep and bear Arms, shall not be infringed."

At first glance, this might seem like a strange way to describe such a simple concept. If the Second Amendment is about protecting the right of citizens to own guns, why not just say so? Why doesn't it read "The people have a right to keep and bear arms that the government shall never infringe." Why the strange preamble about the militia? Why the explanation about it being necessary to protect "a free State?"

The short answer is that Madison was trying to shoehorn multiple meanings into this single sentence and, as a result, the wording became tangled.

The long (and more interesting) answer is that the Founders wished for the Second Amendment to serve several important roles for the people of America. Although most of these roles have been forgotten or rendered impotent by subsequent legislation, the primary purpose—to protect the right of the people to keep and bear arms—remains as important now as it was then.

Fundamentally, the Second Amendment is about securing the right of self-preservation for Americans, both as individuals and as a group. To this end, it protects Americans' *individual* right to bear arms in defense of themselves, their families, and their communities, and it protects their *collective* right to form militia groups to defend their state and country from invaders or tyrannical governments. In other words, the reason the Second Amendment starts by talking about the militia's role in protecting the state and finishes by talking about the right to keep and bear arms is because it was meant to protect *both* of these privileges.

The Founders fought each other over many things, but they agreed on this: An armed citizenry was an indispensable part of the new American republican government. And first and foremost, the Second Amendment was written to protect a citizen's right to own guns.

As you recall, the Founders drew most of their ideas from Enlightenment philosophy, which starts with the assumption, as Thomas

Hobbes put it, that people have every right imaginable in a "state of nature." Of course, human nature being what it is, this kind of absolute freedom would be little more than anarchy, something like a medley of *Fight Club*, *A Clockwork Orange*, and *Joker*—constantly infringing on the rights of others. This chaotic way of life, most importantly, would infringe on man's inalienable right to self-preservation—the right to defend one's life against violence from others. Thus, although individuals have to sacrifice some rights to form a peaceful society, they must never sacrifice their rights to life, liberty, and the pursuit of happiness.

If further steps weren't taken to protect these sacred liberties, though, some of the Founders feared they would become "dead letters." It's all well and good to say that citizens have "inalienable" rights, but if careful measures aren't taken to protect them, they'll wither and blow away like leaves in an autumn wind. Thus, a free society must guarantee "auxiliary rights," which are rights that are necessary to protect the three fundamental rights of life, liberty, and the pursuit of happiness.

For example, the right to a jury trial isn't a sacred, inalienable right, but history has proven that you can't have liberty unless you have fair, regular, speedy trials by your peers. Thus, you have a right to a jury trial. Likewise, being able to own a car isn't an inalienable right, but being able to earn a living is essential to protecting your life and pursuing happiness, and thus all free societies ensure that individuals have the right to own property like cars. And finally, being able to own a gun isn't an inalienable right the same way the rights to life, liberty, and the pursuit of happiness are, but it is necessary for shielding those rights from tyranny, oppression, and violence by others. Thus, you have a right to own guns.

In other words, if someone wishes to take away your right to life, liberty, property, or the pursuit of happiness, you have the right to defend yourself. As any person wishing to take away your rights could (and probably would) use a gun if they intended to use force, you also have the right to own a gun so you have a chance of successfully defending your rights. This was the single most important reason the Founders believed in gun ownership: It was an absolute expression of the Enlightenment belief that all men are created free, equal, and independant, possess the right to self-preservation, and have every right to defend themselves from violence. Although some rights must be sacrificed for the sake of civilization, the right to keep and bear arms must never be surrendered under any circumstances in free society.

So, that's the first reason the Founders created the Second Amendment—to give you the right to defend yourself. The second reason the Founders created the Second Amendment is more controversial—to protect the citizens' right to overthrow a tyrannical government by organizing into militia units that could resist a professional army.

If the government threatens the security of a free state, Americans have the right to band together and abolish the government by force, just as the Founders did in the American Revolution. This idea may seem strange, even absurd. Attacking the government is and has always been considered an act of treason—a crime punished by death for most of history—but theoretically, Americans have the right to overthrow their government to correct intolerable and systemic abuses when all other options have been exhausted.

This "right to revolution" was another concept that arose from Enlightenment thinking, and it was a core tenet of the Founding Fathers' vision for the United States. They made this explicit in the Declaration of Independence, which states that "when a long train of abuses and usurpations... evinces... to reduce them [Americans] under absolute Despotism, it is their right, it is their *duty*, to throw off such Government." While this was written to the British monarchy, the same principle applies to any government that repeatedly violates the rights of its citizens.

The Enlightenment philosopher, John Locke, explained this idea in detail in his *Two Treatises on Government*, writing that "... whenever the Legislators endeavor to take away, and destroy the Property of the People, or to reduce them to Slavery under Arbitrary Power, they put themselves into a state of War with the People." In other words, when those in power prove they're unworthy to lead by abusing their position, "they forfeit the Power... and it devolves to the People, who have a Right to resume their original Liberty."

Chapter 7

In a way, this is just an extension of the concept of self-preservation from the individual to the citizenry as a whole. Instead of just defending their *own* lives or property, the citizens of America also have the right to join forces to defend their *collective* rights against the most powerful potential enemy of all: their own government.

As you learned in chapter four, this was also the purpose of the English Bill of Rights. Embittered at the Catholic Stuart Monarchy, Parliament secured the right of Protestants to bear arms, with the proviso that they be "suitable to their condition and as allowed by law." This slippery caveat enabled Parliament, who decided the laws, to disarm more or less anyone they pleased—in this case, the Catholics.

The Founding Fathers didn't believe in any such caveats. They didn't have to compromise with a monarch, kowtow to Parliament, or make any concessions when it came to the right of Americans to defend life, liberty, and the pursuit of happiness. In a land ruled by the people—not an autocratic monarchy or corrupt oligarchy—*all* of the citizens would have the right to bear arms. Period. This wasn't just a moral issue, but also a practical one. The more armed citizens, the better they would be able to resist a tyrannical government.

To the Founders, this was the essence of the republican system of government—a nation of moral, learned, armed men who had the wisdom to take an active part in politics, the perception to see when the government slid toward tyranny, and the skill with a gun to prevent it from infringing on their rights.

In a way, the Founders were simply taking what they saw as the most effective elements of the English Bill of Rights and removing needless or counterproductive portions. One of the Founder's primary sources on British law was the jurist, writer, and legal scholar William Blackstone, who pops up repeatedly in colonial debates, newspaper articles, and writings. Blackstone's *Commentaries on the Laws of England*, first published in 1770, served as the definitive source on British law in the colonies, and it heavily influenced the Founders' views on arms ownership.

Blackstone wrote pages about the importance of keeping arms under

British law, declaring that arms ownership enabled citizens to protect "the natural right of resistance and self-preservation, when the sanctions of society and laws are found insufficient to restrain the violence of oppression." He continued, writing that the right to have arms was indispensable "to protect and maintain inviolate the three great and primary rights of personal security, personal liberty, and private property." (Originally, most people referred to "private property" as the third right of man after life and liberty, but Thomas Jefferson modified this to "pursuit of happiness" to give it a broader, less materialistic meaning).

When England finally absorbed Scotland into the Kingdom of Great Britain in 1707, the Scottish politician, writer, and scholar Andrew Fletcher proposed placing limitations on England's control over Scotland, including one which read, "That all fencible (fighting) men of the nation, between sixty and sixteen, be with all diligence possible armed with bayonets, and firelocks all of a calibre, and continue always provided in such arms with ammunition suitable." In other words, he wanted every able-bodied man of Scotland armed to the teeth to keep England honest and Scotland free.

The Founders also drew inspiration from James Burgh, a British politician and writer who was one of the first to defend the universal right to free speech in his book, *Political Disquisitions*, published in 1774. In the same book, he dedicated more than one hundred pages to extolling the values of an armed citizenry over a standing army. "A militia-man," he wrote, "is a free citizen; a soldier, a slave for life."

Most of the Founders, including Thomas Jefferson, George Washington, James Madison, and John Adams, also received a classical education in the works of great ancient historians such as Cicero, Livy, Thucydides, Tacitus, and Plutarch, and these lessons heavily influenced their decisions when forming the new American government. John Adams wrote that whenever he read Thucydides and Tacitus, "I Seem to be only reading the History of my own Times and my own Life."

The Founders often quoted these ancient sources and used their works to justify their own political positions, as George Mason did when decrying the possibility of a corrupt President using the military to impose tyranny.

Chapter 7

"When he [the President] is arraigned for treason," warned Mason, "he has the command of the army and navy, and may surround the Senate with thirty thousand troops. It brings to recollection the remarkable trial of Milo at Rome."

He was referring to one of the most famous legal cases of antiquity, which occurred 1,844 years before the ratification of the Bill of Rights. In the twilight of the Roman Republic, Cicero recorded one of the best defenses of the right to bear arms. A politician named Milo had long been at odds with another politician named Clodius. The two had met along the Appian Way, a quarrel ensued, and Clodius was killed. The exact circumstances of the death were and still are a mystery, but Milo was put on trial and his friend, Cicero, agreed to defend him. Before Cicero could deliver his final statement, however, a mob of Clodius' followers drowned out his words and intimidated him into submission. The court pronounced Milo guilty, and he was forced into exile, but Cicero sent him a copy of the prepared statement. It reads as if it were written by one of the Founding Fathers themselves:

"There exists a law, not written down anywhere, but inborn in our hearts; a law which comes to us not by training or custom or reading but by derivation and absorption and adoption from nature itself; a law which has come to us not from theory but from practice, not by instruction but by natural intuition.

"I refer to the law which lays it down that, **if our lives are endangered by plots or violence or armed robbers or enemies, any and every method of protecting ourselves is morally right.** When weapons reduce them to silence, the laws no longer expect one to wait their pronouncements. For people who decide to wait for these will have to wait for justice, too—and meanwhile they must suffer injustice first.

"Indeed, even the wisdom of a law itself, by sort of tacit implication, permits self-defense, because it is not actually forbidden to kill; what it does, instead, is to forbid the bearing of a weapon with the intention to kill.

"When, therefore, inquiry passes on the mere question of the weapon and starts to consider the motive, **a man who has used arms in self-defense is not regarded as having carried with a homicidal aim.**"

In other words, Cicero had already articulated the concept of the right to self-preservation two millennia before the Founding Fathers and pointed out the obvious fact that there's nothing wrong with simply possessing a weapon—it's how you use it that counts. In a fitting end to this little story, Cicero, Milo, and even the man presiding over the trial, Pompey, all became martyrs to what happens when a government turns tyrannical, for they all perished resisting the rise of Julius Caesar.

At this point you might be wondering, how exactly does the Second Amendment protect against a tyrannical government? Are armed men and women to grab guns and start shooting politicians simply because they do or say something they don't like? Wouldn't this just lead to anarchy?

No, no, and yes.

Let's address the "you can't just start shooting people" strawman first. Often, when people hear that the Second Amendment was created to allow Americans to overthrow a tyrannical government, their first response is something along the lines of, "What, you're just going to grab your AR-15 and shoot the President?" This is a caricature of the "right to revolution." In reality, the Founders took careful measures to prevent anarchy and laid out several important preconditions that had to be met before the citizens had a right to use violence against the government.

First of all, the government had to repeatedly violate individual rights on a large scale. For example, taxing citizens without allowing them to participate in government, forcing citizens to billet soldiers, and seizing private property (including guns) were considered "a long train of abuses and usurpations" by the Founders. Saying something silly on television or

Twitter doesn't count. Passing a new, inconvenient law that gets your goat isn't justification for violence.

Second, the government had to deny citizens any recourse for justice against abuses. For example, just because the government issues an unfair speeding ticket doesn't mean Americans have the right to start shooting traffic cops. So long as there are fair legal procedures by which you can get justice—arguing your case in court, for instance—Americans *do not* have the right to attack the government. This is what Blackstone meant when he wrote that people have the right to revolution when "the sanctions of society and laws are found insufficient to restrain the violence of oppression."

Finally, although the Founders didn't state this explicitly, it was also understood that the oppression had to be so widespread that it affected the body of the people and rippled into nearly every aspect of society. The Founders, for example, attempted to resolve their differences with King George for years before finally taking up arms, and they only did so when they felt they had no alternative. "Private individuals were forbidden to take force against their rulers either for malice or because of private injuries," notes historian Pauline Maier. "And not just a few individuals, but the 'Body of the People' had to feel concerned... a broad consensus involving all ranks of society," before revolution was justified.

The Founders viewed revolution as a last resort, and cautioned Americans that "Governments long established should not be changed for light and transient causes; and accordingly all experience hath shewn, that mankind are more disposed to suffer, while evils are sufferable, than to right themselves by abolishing the forms to which they are accustomed."

Ultimately, Americans do have a right to revolution, but this doesn't mean they have the right to take up arms and attack the government at the slightest provocation. The government needs to oppress individual rights of citizens on a large scale, deny them any recourse for justice, and reject peaceable options before citizens have the right to overthrow it.

But... what if the government does all of these things?

What if they do repeatedly infringe on individual rights and deny the citizens peaceable means to resolve their disputes?

If you lived in any society before 1792, the answer was usually the same one the Romans received after their city was sacked for the first time. "Woe to the vanquished." In other words, if you don't like the terms, you shouldn't have lost.

This is more or less how "negotiations" have always taken place between despots at the head of an army and disarmed citizens. Throughout history, tyrants and corrupt politicians of all stripes have always derived their power from the soldiers under their command. After the fall of the Roman Republic, it became commonplace for the Imperial Legions to decide who became emperor (often after assassinating the previous one), and by the third century, the Senate was rendered irrelevant. This practice became so common that these soldiers-turned-emperors were dubbed "barracks emperors." Famously, the Praetorian Guard once auctioned off the position of "Emperor" to the highest bidder after murdering the previous one. Then they killed him too.

During the Middle Ages, kings often muscled their way to the top of the hierarchy, not by the consent of their subjects, aristocrats, or church, but by the strength of their housecarls and men-at-arms. Americans remembered well that Charles I and II, Cromwell, and James had only been able to suppress their countrymen because they commanded hoards of obedient soldiers. Americans had come to loathe standing armies before and during the war, and one of their chief complaints against the British was that they used their Redcoats to carry out their political aims. Jefferson admonished King George in the Declaration of Independence for keeping "among us in time of peace, standing armies without the consent of our legislatures." When it came to the subject of standing armies, though, the Founders were caught on the horns of a dilemma, based on the difference between a standing army and a militia.

A *standing army* is a permanent army of paid soldiers. Typically, people sign up for a specific length of time and focus on nothing else but serving in the military while enrolled. A *militia* is a military force raised from the civilian population, and people who serve in the militia are sometimes referred to as "citizen soldiers." These are people who spend most of their time working normal jobs—farmers, doctors, craftsmen, and so forth—who also own and train with weapons. When their community or country is threatened, they join together, fight the enemy, and return to their lives when the threat is gone.

Aside from a handful of exceptions, most armies throughout history have been made up of militias or volunteer citizens. The main reason for this was because most societies simply couldn't afford to maintain a large army and were forced to recruit soldiers from the citizenry. Why drain the national treasury to feed, equip, and train a large army year-round, when you could simply require citizens to contribute military service as needed? These citizen soldiers could also police the populace during peacetime. They could (and were expected to) take care of themselves and their country, not wait for their country to take care of them.

Over time, leaders in more enlightened nations of the world, such as Rome, Greece, Venice, and England, realized that a militia system had other advantages. As stated previously, Machiavelli taught us that a militia is far less likely to be co-opted by the intrigues of a tyrant or to turn against their fellow citizens. After all, they'd be looting, raping, and killing their own kin, whereas mercenary or standing armies often had no such qualms. The Founders witnessed this firsthand, when hired German mercenaries—the Hessians—plundered homes, killed civilians, and gang-raped women as young as ten years old when occupying New Jersey.

In fact, there was little distinction between the military and the citizenry throughout much of history. It was simply expected that, if physically able, men would fight if called upon. Even the indefatigable army of the Roman Republic was more akin to a militia than a modern full-time military. Starting at age seventeen, male citizens were expected to put their names forward for military service, and it was considered not just a duty but a privilege and rite of passage to protect the nation. Those who didn't submit their names for selection were sold into slavery as punishment. Soldiers would serve a few weeks to a few months—just one campaign season—before returning to civilian life and would often volunteer for multiple terms.

Many historians have pointed to the decline of the Roman militia system as one of the causes of their eventual downfall. After proudly serving as citizen soldiers for almost a thousand years, Romans increasingly foisted the responsibility of defense to hirelings, mercenaries, and foreign legions, soldiers who often cared more about enriching themselves than defending Roman liberty.

Edward Gibbon, author of the tour de force *The History of the Decline and Fall of the Roman Empire*, was one of the first people to popularize this idea. "In the purer ages of the [Roman] commonwealth," remarked Gibbon, "the use of arms was reserved for those ranks of citizens who had a country to love, a property to defend, and some share in enacting those laws which it was their interest, as well as duty to maintain." In other words, the citizens of Rome had skin in the game. They weren't fighting for gold and slaves, but for life and liberty.

This all changed when they "... trusted for their defense to a mercenary army," Gibbon explained. Roman citizens grew complacent. They trusted their government officials to raise mercenary armies and conduct wars on their behalf, unwilling or unable to realize that their government would one day turn these armies against them. Roman citizens sealed their own fate when they laid down their arms. As Gibbon concluded, a people "... possessed of arms, tenacious of property, and collected into constitutional assemblies, form the only balance capable of preserving a free constitution against the enterprises of an aspiring prince."

Ironically, Gibbon was also a member of Parliament during much of the American Revolutionary War and was a strident supporter of the British monarchy, claiming in January 1775 "... we have both the right and the power on our side ..." Proving his worth as a historian, though, he later admitted the war had been a mistake.

James Burgh, a contemporary of Gibbon, lamented the passive, pleasure-seeking nature of the average Englishman, and lauded the dynamic, militaristic condition of the Scots, "Bred up in hardy, active, and abstemious courses of life, they were always prepared to march." He continued, "The common people of England, on the other hand, having been long used to pay an army for fighting for them, had at this time forgot all the military virtues of their ancestors."

In many ways, the colonial militias of early America resembled the armies of Republican Rome. The British didn't form a standing army until 1660, and didn't station an army in North America until almost a century later. The early settlers of North America had to depend almost entirely on their own weapons and training to defend themselves, and they became quite effective. Almost every settlement required citizens to own arms, and over time, these groups of people organized themselves into militia units. By the time of the American Revolution, nearly every colony had its own militia, and some, like Virginia, had multiple.

Although the militia distinguished itself admirably in the beginning of the American Revolutionary War at the battles of Lexington and Concord, it stumbled as the war dragged on.

For one thing, it could be difficult to control. Men would often leave at the worst possible times to attend to their farms and families. Others would simply refuse to follow orders. While they were highly effective at skirmishing and waging guerilla warfare, they frequently proved ineffective in large pitched battles against the British regulars. At Bunker Hill, for example, many militiamen came and went as they pleased during the battle. At one point, twenty men escorted a single wounded man away from the fight under the pretense of making sure he was taken care of. "Others were retreating seemingly without any excuse," wrote John Chester, the commander of a company of Connecticut militia.

In the two months between the battles of Lexington and Concord and the Battle of Bunker Hill, the militia force withered from 30,000 men to less than 16,000, with most troops simply wandering home when they got hungry or grew impatient. With no clear chain of command, the militia was also constantly dogged by supply problems, and it was probably this lack of discipline, leadership, and logistics that was responsible for their defeat at Bunker Hill and many subsequent battles.

One of the greatest critics of the militia system was George Washington, who had to deal with its deficiencies firsthand. As he bemoaned in a letter written to John Hancock just after his army was squeezed out of New York by the British, "To place any dependance upon Militia, is, assuredly, resting upon a broken staff." Hamilton expressed the same sentiment in softer words, praising the militia for their service but reminding them that "the liberty of their country could not have been established by their efforts alone, however great and valuable they were." Washington conceded the militia was "more than competent to all the purposes of defensive war," but he, Hamilton and others were right that the militia was inadequate for protracted campaigns against massive foreign armies.

Ironically, although the Americans had railed against standing armies on many occasions, most grudgingly acknowledged they had major advantages. If America was to protect her borders and possibly expand west, they would need troops to man the forts and keep an eagle eye on the wilderness of North America. It also made practical sense. With a standing army, tacit knowledge of military life, tactics, and training could be handed down from the older veterans to the new recruits. Men could focus entirely on perfecting the art of war for years or even decades without distraction. And a standing army with a well-oiled military structure would be more efficient than a ragtag conglomeration of freewheeling militia units. Thus, the Founders decided it made sense to establish and maintain a small standing army, with a few major caveats.

First, the army would be under strict civil control. That is, people who were not generals or military officials would be in charge (reducing the chances of a general "pulling a Caesar" and turning the military against the state). The army was only to be 3,000 men strong, just barely enough to have a military presence on the frontier and to deter insurrections. The army could be enlarged during wartime, but only with approval from Congress, and the army was to be reduced to its normal size when the conflict was over. And of course, none of the troops were to be housed among American civilians.

The greatest check and balance against the new standing army, though, was to be the American militia. "Before a standing army can rule, the people must be disarmed, as they are in almost every country in Europe," wrote Noah Webster. "The supreme power in America cannot enforce unjust laws by the sword; because the whole body of the people are armed, and constitute a force superior to any band of regular troops."

In the Virginia ratifying convention, Patrick Henry proclaimed that the people's "last and best defense" against an army controlled by Congress was the militia. "The great object," he roared, "is that every man be armed ... Every one who is able may have a gun." At this same ratifying convention, George Mason reminded those attending that the British standing army had previously sought to disarm the colonials, and that a militia was their best defense against an American army doing the same. "Who are the militia?" he asked. "They consist now of the whole people."

Alexander Hamilton, writing in the *Federalist Papers*, called a well-regulated militia "the most natural defense of a free country." His Anti-Federalist critics agreed with the need for a militia, writing that "a well regulated militia, composed of the Yeomanry of the country, have ever been considered as the bulwark of a free people."

The Founders all agreed that a standing army was an existential threat to democracy, even if it was necessary, and that a militia was the best way to keep it in check. Thus, they treated the standing army as if it were an attack dog. It could be useful if kept on a short leash and trained to only assault intruders or enemies, but if it turned on its masters—the citizens of America—it was to be quickly put down by the much stronger militia.

James Madison had this in mind when drafting the Second Amendment, even doing the math to show how a militia would square up against a standing army. "According to the best computation," he reasoned, a standing army in the United States couldn't be more than about "one twenty-fifth part of the number able to bear arms. This proportion would not yield, in the United States, an army of more than twenty-five or thirty thousand men. *To these would be opposed a militia amounting to near half a million of citizens with arms in their hands*, officered by men chosen from among themselves, fighting for their common liberties, and united and conducted by governments possessing their affections and confidence. It may well be doubted, whether a militia thus circumstanced could ever be conquered by such a proportion of regular troops." [emphasis added] In other words, the largest possible standing army in the US could still be crushed by the militia, which was the only reason the Founders felt comfortable allowing a standing army to exist.

Many Founders were completely opposed to a standing army, especially considering it would be under the direct control of the new federal government, which they already eyed with suspicion. They feared the standing army would swell to an unstoppable Goliath, as had happened in most European nations, and be used to squash state governments. Patrick Henry was one of the most outspoken critics, and many Americans shared his sentiments.

In the final analysis, it's clear the Founders knew they were playing with fire by creating a standing army, and that the militia was intended to be a bucket of water close at hand. The reason the Second Amendment declares that "A well regulated Militia" is "necessary to the security of a free State" is because it was meant to check the standing army, should it break free from its leash and bite the hand that fed it.

Although the Second Amendment is only twenty-seven words long, it's the result of thousands of years of careful study of the rights of Man and the proper role of government in free society. In its broadest sense, the Second Amendment was meant to protect the right of self-preservation—the right to protect one's life, liberty, and pursuit of happiness from violence, and it does so in two ways:

1. By guaranteeing citizens the right to own guns, so they can effectively resist violence from others.
2. By guaranteeing citizens the right to form militia units, so they can resist a tyrannical government and, specifically, the standing army that gives that government its power.

It was never intended to give individual Americans the right to assault politicians for petty grievances, but it was meant to prevent the government from using an army to suppress the populace. The Founders knew that there would always be aspirant autocrats hiding in the darkest corners of democracy, itching for their chance to seize power, and they would only be able to do so with the support of the military. By maintaining a robust, well-armed militia, they sought to deter the dreams of these would-be tyrants.

That's what the Founders intended, at least, but times have changed. The modern US military is far larger, more powerful, and better equipped than any militia force in the United States today, making any chance of armed insurrection slim at best. The "militia," as most courts recognize it today, has been transformed into the National Guard, which can be "activated" by the President and placed under the command of the federal government at a moment's notice.

All of this has led some politicians, lawyers, and activists to claim that the Second Amendment *only* guarantees your right to own guns if you serve in the militia. Some even claim this was the Founders' original intention. The Second Amendment was never about giving individuals the right to own guns, they say, but to ensure the militia was prepared to fight off foreign enemies and put down riots and rebellions.

Are they right? We'll answer this question next.

8

Are Guns Only for People in the Military? Here's What the Founders Wanted . . .

> "Necessity is the plea for every infringement of human freedom: it is the argument of tyrants; it is the creed of slaves."
> —William Pitt (the Younger), Member of Parliament, November 18, 1783.

> "The fact of the matter is that there is no legitimate use for these [assault] weapons."
> —Chuck Schumer, Democratic New York senator, 2003.

Based on what you now know about the Second Amendment, you may be wondering—why do so many states have laws that prevent people from owning certain guns?

After all, if the Second Amendment affirms "the right of the people to keep and bear arms," why do so many states seek to suppress that right? If owning guns is a protected right in the United States, then why don't we look at gun control with the same scorn we would at controls on free speech and our right to a speedy trial?

The answer may seem absurd, but over the past century or so, most

US courts have developed a very different understanding of the Second Amendment than that of the Founders. Specifically, most courts have ruled that the Second Amendment doesn't guarantee Americans the right to defend themselves or own guns, but only to join the militia. Where did this idea come from?

As you know, the Second Amendment has two clauses: one that was meant to protect the right of Americans to own guns and one that was intended to protect their right to form militia units.

Some US courts, lawyers, historians, and gun-control groups, though, focus exclusively on the militia clause and claim that the Second Amendment was really *only* meant to protect the right of citizens to join the militia. Some of these people go even further and claim the Second Amendment was only meant to protect the state's right to form militias, and that it has absolutely nothing to do with individual rights.

This idea is known as the *collective right* interpretation of the Second Amendment, because it's based on the idea that the Second Amendment only guarantees your right to use guns *collectively*—that is, in a group with other militia soldiers. For simplicity's sake, I'll refer to people who support this idea as *collectivists*. In opposition to this idea, there's the *individual* interpretation of the Second Amendment, which states that the amendment was created not just to protect the right to form militia groups, but also to guarantee Americans the right to own guns as private citizens.

Let's talk about the collectivist interpretation first, as it's less well-known than the individual interpretation of the Second Amendment. The first thing to know about the collectivist right interpretation is that the name is a bit of a misnomer, because when you look at what this theory entails, it really means that you only have the right to own or use a gun when serving in the US military. Thus, it would be more accurate to call the "collective" interpretation of the Second Amendment the "military-only" interpretation of the Second Amendment.

To understand why, you first have to understand how the modern US "militia" differs from the militias that helped win the American Revolutionary War. Before, during, and shortly after the Second

Amendment was signed into law, the US militia included more or less all able-bodied free men who could shoot a gun. The Militia Act of 1792, passed the same year the Bill of Rights was ratified, narrowed the definition slightly to "each and every free able-bodied white male citizen... who is or shall be of age of eighteen years, and under the age of forty-five years..." Nothing about this law implied people outside the militia were not allowed to own guns, either.

Over time, though, the US militia has mutated into more or less another branch of the US armed forces—the National Guard—which is nothing like the militia the Founders envisioned. While the militia of the Founder's era supplied their own weapons, only operated within the borders of the United States, and was funded by and under the control of the states, the National Guard is the opposite: all weapons are provided by and kept by the state, members are regularly sent overseas to fight foreign wars, and funding and military control is largely provided by the federal government.

The Founders wished for the US militia to serve as a civil defense force against insurrection, foreign invasion, and a standing army led by internal tyrants, but General Joseph L. Lengyel, the Chief of the National Guard Bureau, openly admits that "... fighting America's wars is the primary mission of the National Guard." Thanks to the 2007 National Defense Authorization Act, the President can even take control of a state's National Guard without the consent of the governor—treating it as just another pool of troops to fill the ranks of the U.S. military.

At best, the Founders would call the modern-day National Guard a *select militia*, which is simply a group of civilians who receive weapons and training from the government and who carry out its bidding. As you'll recall, one of the reasons the English Bill of Rights protects the right to bear arms is because King Charles II created a select militia to control his people. The Founders were vehemently opposed to the creation of a select militia. Both at the Constitutional Convention and the Third Congress, the Founders rejected proposals to create a select militia for the federal government. During debates over the Constitution, Anti-Federalists repeatedly accused the Federalists of attempting to create a select militia, something they fiercely denied and denounced.

"Today's National Guard is thus a far cry from what the Founders' understood a militia to be," writes historian David Yassky. "Indeed, the Founders' did have a concept that approximates today's National Guard—but it was a concept they disapproved. This is the 'select militia' - a specially trained part of the citizenry. To the Founders, a select militia was little better than an army." In much the same way the statesman and general Gaius Marius transformed the Roman Republican Army into a full-time, mercenary military, the US militia has evolved into a cog in the US war machine. Technically, thanks to the Militia Act of 1903, there is also an "unorganized militia" in the US, which includes all able-bodied men aged 17 to 45. Few courts take this concept seriously, though—if you try to claim that you have the right to own a gun because you belong to the unorganized militia, you're probably going to lose in court.

In the final analysis, the collectivist position that the Second Amendment guarantees your right to own guns if you join the militia is the same as saying you have the right to own guns if you join the military. Hence the "militia-only" theory of the Second Amendment should be called the "military-only" theory.

The reason lawyers, historians, and gun-control advocates have been trying to topple the individual interpretation of the Second Amendment since the 1960s is that it's the single greatest legal impediment to new gun laws. They know that if they can rewrite the meaning of the Second Amendment, it gives lawmakers across the US carte blanche to enact whatever gun-control laws they want. "Unless a state's constitution protects individual firearm ownership or has been interpreted as protecting such," writes Patrick Charles, a legal historian and proponent of the military-only theory, "that state may impose any firearm legislation it deems proper."

The military-only interpretation of the Second Amendment opens the door for implementing more or less unlimited, absolute, European-style gun control in the United States. The hot topics parroted on the news—"red flag" laws, increased background checks, a national gun registry, and high-capacity magazine, assault weapon, and handgun bans—are trivial matters compared to the fundamental meaning of the Second Amendment. If the collectivists get their way, any argument about gun "rights" is rendered null and void, because according to their interpretation, you don't have a "right" to own guns. Gun ownership is a privilege, like driving a car, and like any other privilege, it can be regulated or revoked by the state. Any state in the US could pass laws for confiscating your guns, banning you from owning any guns in the future, and shuttering any gun store that sells to civilians... if these people win.

At this point you're probably wondering, why haven't I heard of this before?

The answer is that although the military-only interpretation has steadily gained ground in the courts and the ivory towers of academia, it's been losing ground in the court of public opinion. As lawyer, legal scholar, and researcher Don Kates wrote in 1983, "The individual right view is endorsed by only a minority of legal scholars, but accepted by a majority of the general populace who, though supporting the idea of controlling guns, increasingly oppose their prohibition, believing that law-abiding citizens may properly have them for self-defense. Though the individual right view reigns among nonlegal scholars, the exclusively state's right [collectivist] position is dominant among lawyers and law professors and enjoys the support of the American Bar Association."

Despite the collectivists' best efforts to brand gun owners as a militant fringe of society—a deluded minority that cares more about playing with guns than protecting their fellow citizens—research shows Americans are becoming more pro gun, not less.

For example, between 2007 and 2016, the number of concealed handgun permits issued to Americans soared from 4.6 million to 13 million. Polls from the Pew Research Center and Roper have also noted a significant uptick in support for gun rights and waning support for gun control. In the early 1990s, when they first started measuring Americans' attitudes on guns, Pew and Roper both found that about 60 percent of Americans supported stricter gun control and 30 percent opposed it. By 2010, the gap had narrowed—only about 50 percent of Americans supported more gun control and about 50 percent opposed it. So from about 1990 to 2010, there was a 10 percent decrease in support for more gun control, and a 20 percent increase in support for gun rights.

The latest Pew polling data from 2019 shows Americans' views are still more or less evenly divided, with half supporting more gun control and half supporting less.

A 2015 Rasmussen poll also found that 68 percent of Americans feel safer living in neighborhoods that allow guns, putting the lie to the notion that most people object to private gun ownership. Polling data collected by Gallup shows that in 1959, about 60 percent of Americans said they'd be okay with a law banning handguns except for the police and military, and only 40 percent opposed it. By 2019, the tables had turned: 70 percent of Americans said they'd oppose such a law, and only about 30 percent said they'd support it. Finally, more guns were sold in 2020 than in any previous year in recorded history, with many stores seeing sales double, triple, or quadruple over 2019.

While it's nice to know how Americans feel about guns, what matters is what's *true*.

So, who's right? Does the Second Amendment really protect the right of Americans to own guns? Or, does it only guarantee your right to use guns in the military? Should states be allowed to pass any gun laws they want?

To answer these questions, you first have to understand where the military-only interpretation of the Second Amendment comes from. Their argument hinges on three key points:

1. The Second Amendment begins with the phrase "A well regulated militia," and so the rest of the sentence should be interpreted as *only* applying to people serving in the militia.
2. At the time the Second Amendment was written, the term "to bear arms" was only used to refer to soldiers carrying guns, thus only applying to a government-controlled militia. In other words, "to bear arms" really meant "use weapons in the military."

3. US courts have consistently interpreted the Second Amendment as only protecting the right of people to serve in state militias, making this the only correct interpretation.

These people believe a modern translation of the Second Amendment might read something like this:

"Because a well-regulated military is necessary for the security of a free state, the people's right to keep and bear arms in the service of this military won't be interfered with."

There are several major problems with this idea, though.

Are Guns Only for the Militia?

As you learned in the last chapter, the Founders clearly believed in the importance of armed citizens. Just because the Second Amendment begins with the phrase "A well regulated militia" doesn't mean the right to bear arms *only* applies to the militia.

One of the first pieces of evidence that the Second Amendment was intended to protect an individual right comes straight from the man who wrote it: James Madison. Originally, Madison proposed inserting the amendments that make up the Bill of Rights, including the Second Amendment, throughout the Constitution instead of attaching them as a separate list. His idea was rejected (the Founders wanted to make it clear what had changed from the original Constitution when they added the Bill of Rights), but his preference for where the Second Amendment would have been inserted gives us a powerful clue as to its intended purpose.

At the time the Second Amendment was drafted, the Constitution already gave the federal government authority for "organizing, arming, and disciplining, the militia," in Article 1, Section 8. Thus, if Madison only intended for the Second Amendment to preserve the right of states to form militias, it would have made the most sense to insert it here—in the section dealing with the militia. Instead, Madison proposed inserting it in Article

1, Section 9, which included clauses protecting individual rights such as habeas corpus, bans on bills of attainder and ex post facto laws, and rules against unfair taxation. Clearly, Madison wanted the Second Amendment grouped with other guarantees of individual rights already contained in the Constitution, not with the section dealing with the militia.

After the Bill of Rights was drafted, Madison's friend Tench Coxe published a series of newspaper articles explaining the meaning of the amendments that were widely circulated in Boston, Philadelphia, and New York. When describing the purpose of the Second Amendment, Coxe never even mentions the militia:

> "As civil rulers, not having their duty to the people duly before them, may attempt to tyrannize, and as the military forces which must be occasionally raised to defend our country, might pervert their power to the injury of their fellow-citizens, the people are confirmed by the next article in their right to keep and bear their private arms."

Coxe sent a copy of his article to Madison, who praised his interpretation and noted that it was already published in New York newspapers, where the First Congress was meeting. Thus, it's fair to assume that Madison—the very author of the Second Amendment—felt it was largely designed to protect Americans' *individual* right to own guns.

Then, there's also the fact that the vast majority of people serving in American militias before, during, and after the American Revolutionary War used their own weapons. Militias were only possible *because* Americans owned tens of thousands of guns and knew how to use them, and were brave, selfless, and talented enough to contribute their skills to the militia. As George Mason pointed out, the militia were "the whole people"—the entire male populace of the colonies, and all of the colonies allowed (and some encouraged) women to own and use guns, too, especially if they were the heads of household.

Even after the American Revolutionary War, Americans were still required to use their own guns when serving in the militia. In 1792, when

Chapter 8

Congress enacted the Uniform Militia Act, it also stipulated that every person enrolled in the militia was to "provide himself with a good musket or firelock, a sufficient bayonet and belt, two spare flints, and a knapsack, a pouch, with a box therein to contain not less than twenty four cartridges... each cartridge to contain a proper quantity of powder and ball." In other words, every member of the militia was to buy, keep, and maintain their own guns, ammunition, and other kit.

This was still how most legal authorities understood the Second Amendment a century later. Thomas Cooley, a law professor and Michigan Supreme Court justice who was considered "the greatest authority on constitutional law in the world" at the time, wrote in 1891 that:

> "It may be supposed... that the right to keep and bear arms was only guaranteed to the militia; but this would be an interpretation not warranted by the intent... the people, from whom the militia must be taken, shall have the right to keep and bear arms, and they need no permission or regulation of law for the purpose."

According to Cooley, the Second Amendment wasn't about guaranteeing your right to join the militia, but was instead a guarantee of your right to own guns, which *enabled* the state to form militias. "To bear arms implies something more than the mere keeping," he continued. "It implies the learning to handle and use them in a way that makes those who keep them ready for their efficient use." In other words, the right to keep and bear arms means you have the right to buy, own, and train with guns, whether you're in the militia or not. Any law that restricts those rights is unconstitutional.

In the 1840s, the individual right interpretation found new champions among abolitionists of slavery. In his book *The Unconstitutionality of Slavery*, the firebrand abolitionist Lysander Spooner wrote that both free men and slaves have the right to bear arms "in defense of life, liberty, chastity..." The anti-slavery lawyer Joel Tiffany argued that the right to bear arms was "accorded to every subject for the purpose of protecting and defending himself, if need be, in the enjoyment of his absolute rights to life, liberty and property," and that this guarantee was to be "without any exception." He went on, writing "the right to keep and bear arms, also implies the right to use them if necessary in self defence; without this right to use the guaranty [sic] would hardly have been worth the paper it consumed." Neither of them, nor any other abolitionists, claimed the Second Amendment was about joining the militia.

The bottom line is that colonial militias were only possible because *individual* Americans owned guns, and the Second Amendment was designed to protect both the right to own guns and to serve in the militia. That's how it was understood at the time, and how Americans understood it for decades later. Despite these interpretations, however, the courts began to favor the military-only interpretation.

What Does "Bear Arms" Really Mean?

The collectivists' second main claim is that the term "to bear arms" was a kind of military jargon—only used to refer to soldiers carrying weapons in the military. While they have a point that the term "to bear arms" was primarily used in this context, it wasn't *only* used this way.

Before we look at the historical evidence, let's flip to page 213 of Samuel Johnson's *A Dictionary of the English Language*, published in 1755, by far the most widely used dictionary during the time the Second Amendment was written. It is reasonable to assume that whatever definitions Johnson gives for the words "bear" and "arms" are the ones the Founding Fathers would have had in mind when drafting the Second Amendment.

Johnson writes that the definition of the word "bear" is:

To carry as a burden
To convey or carry
To carry as a mark of distinction
To carry as a mark of authority

In other words, it means "to carry." And if we look at the latest *Oxford English Dictionary*, the definition of "bear" is:

(of a person) to carry.

The definition of the term "bear" nowadays is exactly the same as it was when the Second Amendment was written.

And what about the word "arms?" Johnson defines them as "weapons of offence, or armour of defence." And if we look at Timothy Cunningham's *A New and Complete Law-Dictionary*, published in 1771, another common reference at the time among lawyers and politicians, the definition is listed as "any thing that a man wears for his defence, or takes into his hands, or useth in wrath to cast at or strike another."

Thus, if we look at the literal definition of the phrase "bear arms," it clearly means "to carry weapons or armor." Nothing about either word implies arms were only meant for soldiers.

What's more, you can find many examples of the term "bear" being used in reference to weapons owned by individuals before the Second Amendment was written. For example, in the epic Anglo-Saxon poem *Beowulf*, written between the 8th and 11th centuries, the eponymous hero mentions that he will decline "To bear a blade or a broad-fashioned target" when fighting the monster Grendel, and instead opts to best the beast with his bare hands. The poem also mentions "bearers of war-shields." The poem wasn't referring to an official military or even a militia, which didn't exist in England at the time, but to men *bearing* weapons to defend themselves.

You can also find examples of the word "bear" used in reference to private arms in several English laws. For instance, one of Henry VIII's failed firearms laws made it illegal for any resident of Wales to "bring or bear ... any Bill [a kind of pike], Long-bow, Cross-bow, Hand-gun, Sword, Staff, Dagger, Halberd, Morespike, Spear, or any other manner of Weapon ..." (Most of Henry VIII's attempts to regulate weapons were ignored or repealed after his death, including this one).

Several centuries later, and shortly before the American Revolutionary

War, the English passed several laws prohibiting Scottish civilians—not soldiers or militiamen—from "bearing" arms. A 1715 statute passed shortly after Scotland was officially absorbed into Great Britain complained that "... the Custom that has too long prevailed amon[g]st the Highlanders of Scotland, of having Arms in their Custody, and using and bearing them in traveling abroad in the Fields..." Another statute prohibited Scottish citizens "To have in his, her or their custody, use or bear, broad sword," and other "warlike weapons" such as pistols and daggers, and went on to describe the punishment for Scots who chose to "bear arms" in violation of the statute.

Even the entire phrase "keep and bear arms" was used by the British before the Second Amendment was drafted. In a debate in Parliament on June 19, 1780, after a series of riots in London, Lord Richmond objected to British soldiers disarming civilians who used arms to protect themselves from violent rioters, as this was "a violation of the constitutional right of Protestant subjects to keep and bear arms for their own defence." He mentioned nothing about these people having to serve in the militia.

And finally, the Pennsylvania state constitution of 1776 declared that the people have a "right to bear arms for the defence of themselves and the state," despite the fact that Pennsylvania didn't even have an official state militia. Less than a year later, Vermont borrowed more or less the same wording for their state constitution. Thus, at the time the Founders were alive, the term "bear arms" wasn't tied to military service (nor has it ever been).

The bottom line is that the term "bear arms" means exactly what it sounds like: to carry weapons or armor. Nothing about this phrase indicates that it was only meant for soldiers enlisted in the US military or people serving in the militia.

What Does the Supreme Court Think About the Second Amendment?

Finally, the collectivists' strongest argument, and the one that's been used the most to support gun-control laws, is that US courts have repeatedly agreed with the collectivists' interpretation of the Second Amendment.

That is, most courts have interpreted the Second Amendment as *not* protecting an individual's right to own guns, but only protects the right of Americans to use guns in the militia. Some collectivists go a step further and claim that the idea that the Second Amendment protects your right to own guns is a modern machination designed to line the pockets of gun companies.

There's a kernel of truth here, but it's more wrong than right. Here's the reality: From the time the Second Amendment was written to around 1900, more or less every court in the US agreed with the individual right interpretation of the Second Amendment. Then, starting in the early 1900s, a handful of courts subtly twisted the meaning of the amendment, probably for political reasons. These rulings were criticized and largely ignored for several decades until the 1960s, when gun-control activists began looking for ways to undermine the right of Americans to bear arms. Realizing their utility, these groups latched onto these old, controversial court cases and began touting them as justification for more gun-control laws. Although the military-only interpretation of the Second Amendment is relatively new in the big scheme of things, it has now existed long enough to give the anti-gun movement significant legal momentum. Let's start at the beginning.

Before around 1900, most US courts believed in the interpretation of the Second Amendment you learned in the last chapter: That it was designed to protect an individual's right to own guns and join militia units. For example, in 1803, the lawyer, law professor, and friend of James Madison, St. George Tucker, published the first American edition of Blackstone's *Commentaries*. When comparing the American Bill of Rights to the English one, he wrote, "The right of the people to keep and bear arms shall not be infringed . . . and this without any qualification to their condition or degree, as is the case in the British government." The Second Amendment didn't have any caveats about owning guns "suitable to their Conditions and as allowed by Law," like the English right to bear arms did. Americans could own what they wanted.

This wasn't just legal theory, either. Most courts held the same opinion through the 1800s, such as *Nunn v. State* in 1846, which removed a Georgia law which prohibited the possession of most kinds of pistols. Even though the Georgia State Constitution had no "right-to-bear-arms" clause, the state Supreme Court ruled that the law violated the Second Amendment. The court concluded that, "The right of the whole people, old and young, men, women and boys, and not militia only, to keep and bear arms of every description, and not such merely as are used by the militia, shall not be infringed…"

Then things changed in the early 1900s. One of the first instances of a military-only interpretation of the Second Amendment comes from the Supreme Court of Kansas in 1905. In the case of *City of Salina v. Blaksley*, James Blaksley was charged with carrying and allegedly firing a .32-caliber pocket pistol inside the city while drunk, violating the city ordinances. Blaksley appealed his conviction to the Supreme Court of Kansas, insisting his "right to bear arms" was absolute under all conditions—even when drunk and shooting within a crowded city. As you can imagine, the Supreme Court was unmoved and upheld his conviction. That isn't surprising (firing guns in residential areas while drunk is generally frowned upon), but what is surprising is *why* the Supreme Court ruled the way they did, as their argument set an important legal precedent for the collectivists to latch onto.

First, the court ruled that the Second Amendment only protected the use of military-type guns, which they believed didn't include the .32-caliber revolver used by Blaksley. Second, the court claimed the Second Amendment only protected the right of people to use these kinds of guns if they were enrolled in the militia. "The right of the people to keep and bear arms for their security is preserved, and the manner of bearing them for such purpose is clearly indicated to be," the court claimed, "as a member of a well-regulated militia, or some other military organization provided for by law."

Wait, what?

This was the first time a US court had ever taken this view, and they supported their position with two weak pieces of evidence. They quoted the 1883 legal textbook *Commentaries on the Law of Statutory Crimes* by Joel Prentiss Brown, which states: "In reason the keeping and bearing of arms has reference only to war and possibly also to insurrections wherein the forms of war are, as far as practicable observed." Basically, what Brown was saying in the overly verbose style of his time, was that the primary purpose of the "keeping and bearing of arms," was so that citizens could defend the country from invasion (war) or a tyrannical government (insurrection). Brown never said that the Second Amendment only applied to people in the militia, but the Supreme Court of Kansas interpreted his writing this way.

Next, they referenced another court case called *Commonwealth v. Murphy*, which upheld a ban on militia organizations drilling and parading with firearms in Boston. In this case, the Massachusetts court said that ". . . it is within the police power of the legislature to regulate the bearing of arms, so as to forbid such unauthorized drills and parades." Once again, the court never claimed guns were only for people in the militia—they simply didn't want large groups of armed men running through the streets of Boston. (Ironically, the guns the men used in this case had been modified so they couldn't be fired, but the city of Boston still didn't want them scaring the residents.)

City of Salina v. Blaksley occurred over 100 years after the Second Amendment was ratified, and it was the first instance in which a court interpreted it as only guaranteeing the right of Americans to use guns in the militia. They built this new interpretation on two very weak pillars—a vague quote from a legal textbook, and a case about a relatively minor local firearms regulation in Boston, neither of which supported their position. Most courts brushed the results of *City of Salina v. Blaksley* aside, instead sticking with the traditional and well-supported individual interpretation of the Second Amendment. Courts consistently struck down various gun-control laws in cases like *People v. Zerillo* (1922), *Glasscock v. City of Chattanooga* (1928), and *People v. Nakamura* (1936), among others, on the grounds that they violated the Second Amendment. Then something happened in the 1930s that changed the legal battleground over the Second Amendment: the National Firearms Act of 1934 (NFA).

The NFA levied a $200 tax on several kinds of firearms and firearms accessories, including machine guns, silencers, and shotguns and rifles with a barrel less than 18 inches long—now known as "NFA Firearms" or "Class

III firearms." To enforce the tax, the government created a strict registration process for all of these items, and Americans were (and still are) required to complete a lengthy process of submitting paperwork, undergoing a background check, and waiting months before being granted permission to own these items. The law also imposed byzantine regulations and a $500 to $1,000 fee on any business that wanted to sell NFA firearms. The reason the tax was $200—in 1934, the equivalent of $3,827 today—was because this was roughly the price of a Thompson Submachine Gun. The goal of the tax was to make these guns so expensive that most people couldn't afford them, which did nothing to keep them out of the hands of gangsters who were brimful with cash and usually stole the weapons they used to commit crimes.

While we don't need to dive into a full history of the NFA, suffice it to say it was passed for a variety of reasons: The government was desperate to prove to the American public that they were doing *something* to curtail the bloodshed caused by armed gangsters, especially after the Saint Valentine's Day Massacre in 1929. Giuseppe Zangara had almost succeeded in shooting Franklin D. Roosevelt the year before. There's also strong evidence that Roosevelt and his Attorney General, Homer Cummings, were hellbent on regulating guns as part of a broader effort to impose federal authority on the states. Ironically, Cummings felt the NFA didn't go far enough. If he'd gotten his way, all pistols, shotguns, and rifles would have been regulated as NFA items, and he openly stated his goal was to enact firearms laws like those in England (which were much more restrictive than those in the US, and still are).

Many Americans felt the NFA infringed on the Second Amendment, especially considering how ineffective it was at preventing violent crime. Instead of repealing the law, though, the government doubled down and started looking for ways to make sure the NFA stayed on the books. It was a political win for the Roosevelt Administration, even if it didn't fulfill its intended purpose, and they weren't going to let it die without a fight. All of this leads us to the case of *United States v. Miller* in 1939.

Jackson "Jack" Miller and Frank Layton were a pair of bank robbers who were arrested on charges of violating the NFA. Specifically, they were caught trying to transport a "sawed-off" shotgun from Oklahoma to Arkansas. Miller was a career criminal who'd developed a habit of snitching on his accomplices. In 1935, he'd ratted out his entire gang, the Ozark Mountain Boys, in return for immunity from prosecution and protection from members of the gang who were still on the run. After the breakup of the gang, Miller laid low to avoid getting killed, and eventually fell in with Frank Layton, a small-time bank robber from Oklahoma. The police believed they were on their way to commit a bank robbery when they pulled them over and discovered the sawed-off shotgun.

Here's where things get weird.

At first, Miller and Layton pleaded guilty, but Judge Heartsill Ragon refused to accept their plea and insisted they be defended by a state-appointed lawyer. With the help of their lawyer, Miller and Layton claimed the indictment against them was unlawful because it violated their Second Amendment rights. Judge Ragon immediately dashed off a memo agreeing with Miller and Layton that the law was unconstitutional, and closed the case. The prosecution tried to indict Miller and Layton again, but Judge Ragon issued the same decision—not guilty.

Then things get downright bizarre.

Judge Ragon was a full-throated supporter of gun control and believed the Second Amendment was an annoying encumbrance, not a cherished American right. Before becoming a judge, he'd served as a Democrat in the US House of Representatives where he'd introduced, endorsed, and fought for a variety of new gun-control laws. At one point, he explained on the House floor, "I am unequivocally opposed to pistols in any connection whatever." In 1927, he was instrumental in pushing through a bill that banned the mailing of pistols.

So, why did Judge Ragon let Miller and Layton off the hook so easily? No one knows for sure, but it wasn't because he had a sudden change of heart about gun rights. According to extensive research published in the *New York University Journal of Law and Liberty*, Brian L. Frye concluded that Judge Ragon almost certainly connived to use this case to bolster the NFA.

When this case fell into his lap, Judge Ragon realized he had two choices. On the one hand, if he found Miller and Layton guilty, it would do little to burnish his personal bona fides or support his larger political aims. All he would have accomplished was locking up a pair of bank robbers who clearly had it coming. On the other hand, if he allowed Miller and Layton to go free, he'd kill two birds with one stone:

- By pretending to support Miller and Layton's Second Amendment rights, he transformed the case from a clear-cut decision about a pair of bank robbers breaking the law into a referendum on the meaning of the Second Amendment.
- By refusing to let Miller and Layton plead guilty in his district court, he gave the prosecution the opportunity to appeal the case to the US Supreme Court, which would almost certainly find them guilty.

Thus, by declaring Miller and Layton not guilty, he allowed the prosecution to bypass the state courts and go straight to the Supreme Court, where his political allies could make the most of the guilty verdict (and reward him accordingly). Judge Ragon realized this minor case about two bank robbers could be spun into the perfect "test case" for the government to argue that the new National Firearms Act did *not* violate the Second Amendment.

After all, the hapless duo were about as unsympathetic a pair of defendants as you could find: Lifelong violent criminals, one of whom squealed on his fellow crooks. Furthermore, Judge Ragon intentionally issued what's known as a *memorandum opinion*, basically a terse statement giving his verdict, with no discussion of how he came to his conclusion. With no arguments from Judge Ragon to muddy the waters, the Supreme Court could make up their own decision about the case without having to explain away Ragon's reasons for letting the robbers go free. The Supreme Court's job was made even easier due to the fact that the defense attorney for Miller and Layton, Paul Gutensohn, didn't even appear in court. Instead, he sent the court a telegram saying that Miller and Layton hadn't paid him, and that he would offer no argument in their defense. Judge Ragon was also close with the agency responsible for enforcing the NFA—the Treasury's Alcohol Tax Unit, describing its District Supervisor, John Burckett, as "a lifelong, close, personal friend of mine." Judge Ragon even requested Burckett be promoted due to "the smooth running of the Alcohol Tax Unit under his supervision." (The Alcohol Tax Unit was the precursor to the ATF).

In other words, Judge Ragon was a political insider who stage managed *US v. Miller* to be a win for the US Supreme Court, and thus an airtight defense of the NFA that would stand for decades.

The Supreme Court declared both parties guilty, just as Ragon and his cronies wanted. Their argument was simple: The Second Amendment only guarantees Americans the right to own guns when serving in the militia. As a corollary, they only have the right to own the kinds of guns that would be used in the militia, which, they believed, didn't include short-barreled shotguns. As Justice James Clark McReynolds put it, "We construe the amendment as having relation to military service and we are unable to say that a sawed-off shotgun has any relation to the militia."

Even at the time, though, this was incorrect. As is often the case, the people making the laws about guns had little to no technical knowledge about guns or how they were used. For example, the US government ordered thirty-to-forty-thousand short-barreled, aka "sawed-off," shotguns during World War I, which were issued to troops guarding German prisoners. The same thing was true in World War II, which broke out two years after *US v. Miller*. "As a G.I. in World War II, I can recall having to qualify on a variety of weapons, including short-barreled shotguns," writes the historian Leonard Levy. "The Court was not well informed on government-issued weapons." Just three years after the ruling in Miller, another court wrote "the rule of the Miller case ... would seem to be already outdated ... because of the well known fact that in the so called 'Commando Units' some sort of military use seems to have been found for almost any modern lethal weapon," including short-barreled shotguns and rifles, machine guns, and even silencers.

Ironically, if modern courts were to agree with Justice McReynolds' point that the Second Amendment only protects the right of citizens to own weapons used by the military, this would include all NFA weapons. For example, the standard issue rifle for the US Army, the M4 Carbine, is both a machine gun and a short-barreled rifle, as it can fire on full automatic and has a 14.5-inch barrel, and silencers are used by every branch of the US armed forces. Taken to the extreme, one could use Justice McReynolds' opinion to argue that personal explosives like hand grenades, rocket launchers, and mortars are fair game for civilians, too, as these are also used by every military in the world.

At bottom, the ruling in *US v. Miller* is a convoluted mess that created more questions than answers about what the Second Amendment really means. On the one hand, the Court claimed that the Second Amendment *does* protect the right of individuals to own guns "for lawful purposes," provided they're in the militia. The Court also concluded that the "militia," meant "all males physically capable of acting in concert for the common defense." Basically, they concluded that all men have the right to own military weaponry. The court also ruled that the federal government has the right to tax guns, but not to prohibit them. On the other hand, the government got what they wanted: a Supreme Court case ruling that the National Firearms Act was legal, and an opaque judicial opinion that the Second Amendment only protects the right of Americans to own guns in the militia.

Despite the vague conclusion of the Court, not to mention Judge Ragon's likely collusive behavior, gun-control advocates have tried to spin *US v. Miller* as an open-and-shut case proving that the Second Amendment doesn't protect an individual's right to bear arms. Their stance is "It says right there—'militia.' Case closed." But as you know, there's a lot more to the story.

And what of Miller and Layton? Layton was sentenced to five years probation and seems to have turned his life around after the case, dying in 1967. Miller didn't live long enough to hear the guilty verdict. On the night of April 3, 1939, Miller was picked up by a group of men at his home. At noon the next day, a farm worker discovered his bullet-ridden corpse in a dry creek bed. Although several men were charged with his murder, they were released, and his killers were never caught.

Over time, several other courts agreed with the ruling of *US v. Miller*, and this led to a snowball of legal precedents that gun-control advocates have wielded ever since. The nitty gritty details of these cases are beyond the scope of this book, but a few notable examples include *US v. Rybar (1996)*, *US v. Toner (1984)*, *US v. Warin (1976)*, *Cases v. US (1943)*, and others.

Over time, enough courts agreed with the ruling of *US v. Miller* that this idea became the accepted norm among lawyers, judges, and other legal professionals: The Second Amendment is about protecting the right of people to own guns in the militia, but not to own them individually. Circling back to the question posed at the beginning of this chapter, this is why many states have fairly strict gun laws, while claiming they don't violate the Second Amendment. Most courts simply don't see the Second Amendment as protecting the right of people to own guns.

This isn't to say that *all* courts have taken this limited view of the Second Amendment. Although collectivists like to cherry-pick the cases where courts have agreed with their opinion, they carefully overlook the many cases that contradict it. For example, in 1990, the US Supreme Court ruled that "'the people' protected by the Second Amendment are the same 'people'—individual human beings—protected by other portions of the Bill of Rights," concluding that the Second Amendment guaranteed individual Americans, not just militia members, the right to own guns. In most of these cases, though, the Second Amendment was never the central topic of debate. Instead, it was only discussed in passing when it was relevant to the main issue of the case (for example, whether or not the bank robbers Miller and Layton violated the NFA). It wasn't until 2008, in the landmark case of *D.C. v. Heller*, that the Supreme Court finally decided what the Second Amendment really means.

In 1976, Washington D.C. banned all pistols and semi-automatic rifles. The only people allowed to own such guns were police officers, security guards, and people who'd registered their guns before 1976. The law also required the few residents who did own guns to keep them "unloaded, disassembled, or bound by a trigger lock or similar device," so that they were completely inoperable, and banned all NFA guns and magazines that could hold more than ten rounds. This would be like only allowing people to own a few kinds of cars, and requiring that the gas tank be empty, the wheels removed, and the steering wheel locked at all times when the car wasn't being driven.

As a private, licensed security guard working in Washington D.C., Dick Heller was one of the few people in the city permitted to have a pistol, which he carried while protecting government employees. He was only allowed to have the gun at work, though, and surrendered it each day before going home. Heller lived in a dangerous neighborhood, and so applied for a permit to keep his pistol at home for self protection. His application was rejected out of hand, so he sued Washington D.C. for violating what he believed was his constitutional right to protect himself with a gun.

This set in motion what would become the single most important Supreme Court decision about gun rights in history. What made this case so impactful was that the meaning of the Second Amendment was *the* central question, not a sideshow. The court was forced to make a clear decision on whether or not the Second Amendment protects the right of Americans to own guns as individuals, or only protects the right of Americans to own guns in the militia or military.

Specifically, the court framed the question like this:

"Whether the following provisions [the handgun ban in Washington D.C.] violate the Second Amendment rights of individuals who are not affiliated with any state-regulated militia, but who wish to keep handguns and other firearms for private use in their homes."

After an exhaustive study of the Founders' writing, textual analysis of the Second Amendment, and previous court cases, Justice Antonin Scalia, speaking for the majority of the Supreme Court of the United States, concluded...

"The Second Amendment protects an individual right to possess a firearm unconnected with service in a militia, and to use that arm for traditionally lawful purposes, such as self-defense within the home."

He continued, eviscerating the core tenets of the military-only theory of the Second Amendment in crystal clear terms that could no longer be misinterpreted, modified, or muddled by legal legerdemain. The court ruled that the beginning of the Second Amendment—*A well regulated Militia, being necessary to the security of a free State*—"announces a purpose, but does not limit or expand the scope of the second part, the operative clause." That is, just because the Second Amendment begins with "a well regulated Militia," doesn't mean the right to keep and bear arms only applies to people *in* the militia. The Second Amendment was created in part out of fear the government "would disarm the people . . . enabling a politicized standing army or a select militia to rule," which is exactly what happened during and after the English Civil War and before the American Revolutionary War. One of the main goals of the Second Amendment was to "deny Congress power to abridge the ancient right of individuals to keep and bear arms . . ."

The Founders' writings from before, during, and after the time the Second Amendment was drafted, as well as those of various state constitutions, all point to the Second Amendment guaranteeing an *individual's* right to own guns, not just those who serve in the militia. Although some previous Supreme Court cases cast doubt on the individual interpretation of the Second Amendment, none of them truly refuted it. "There is nothing in the legislative history of the Constitution, state constitutions, writings, or even English history," concluded Scalia, "showing that the Founding Fathers intended to limit gun ownership solely for militia purposes."

At long last, the Supreme Court cut through the miasma of confusing, conflicting, and politically charged opinions about the meaning of the Second Amendment that had metastasized over the past century. Instead of clinging to the relatively recent and erroneous idea that the right to bear arms was only limited to the militia, the Supreme Court returned to the original interpretation of the Second Amendment—that it was intended to protect an individual's right to bear arms *and* to form militias.

However, Supreme Court opinions can always be overruled, and it's possible that one day a new court will overturn the verdict from *D.C. v. Heller*, but that would be a long row to hoe. For one thing, the court's verdict was quickly bolstered by a similar ruling in the case of *McDonald v. City of Chicago*, which determined that the ruling from *D.C. v. Heller* also applies to the rest of the United States. (Washington D.C. is not a state, so this needed to be clarified). This is also why you should be wary of any politician who advocates "packing" the Supreme Court—adding new justices in addition to the traditional nine—as the primary reason for this maneuver would be to gain a majority and push through unconstitutional laws, such as reinterpreting or repealing the Second Amendment.

So, based on all of this, why are there so many states with strict gun-control laws? The Supreme Court also ruled that while prohibiting gun ownership is unconstitutional, regulating it is not. To a certain point, the government is permitted to decide what kind of guns Americans are allowed to own, but not to completely prohibit them. Of course, this still leaves plenty of room for interpretation, which is why the debate over gun ownership in the United States will continue for years to come. The general position of the Supreme Court, though, is that the Second Amendment unequivocally protects the right of Americans to own guns for self defense, militia service, and for recreation.

This is exactly what the Founders wanted. That said, there are still many people who disagree with the court's ruling and who wish to abolish the Second Amendment or legislate it into a dead letter. So what is the next biggest threat to the Second Amendment? You'll learn the answer to that question in the next chapter.

9

"You Only Have the Right to Own a Musket" and Other Second Amendment Myths, Debunked

> "Experience hath shown, that even under the best forms of government those entrusted with power have, in time, and by slow operations, perverted it into tyranny."
>
> —Thomas Jefferson, author of the Declaration of Independence, Founding Father, and third President of the United States, 1778.

> "Repeal the Second Amendment. Concern that a national standing army might pose a threat ... that concern is a relic of the 18th century."
>
> —John Paul Stevens, Associate Justice of the US Supreme Court, 2018.

Many people have suggested that the Second Amendment is not just past its expiration date—it's stinking up the whole store.

Instead of looking at it as an essential feature of the American government, they look at it as a vestigial remnant of a bygone era, like a septic appendix that needs to be cut out.

Sure, they concede, it made sense for plainsmen, trappers, and traders in the wilds of the frontier to have a rifle to protect themselves from grizzly bears, marauding Native Americans, and hostile settlers. It made sense for Americans to own guns when we were a loose confederation of states and territories after the American Revolutionary War, with a battalion of superpowers salivating at the prospect of biting off a chunk of North America. It made sense for Americans to be armed as they trudged westward on the Oregon and California trails to settle distant coasts.

Many of these people even acknowledge that guns were invaluable tools in the early 1900s, when large swathes of America were anarchic backwaters and Poncho Villa and Geronimo were running roughshod through the Southwest.

But now?

Do Americans really *need* guns now?

Isn't the Second Amendment a bit passé?

The police protect us from criminals, and the military protects us from invasion and insurrection. Not only are US police ubiquitous, they're better trained, equipped, and organized than most country's militaries. And if you still cling to some anachronistic notion of civic militarism—the idea that citizens should defend their country—you can join the National Guard.

What's more, violence has plummeted around the world in recent decades. From 1990 to 2015, global homicide rates dropped twenty percent on average. In North America and Western Europe, homicide decreased by forty-six percent. At this point, there's no question we live in one of the most peaceful, prosperous, and promising ages of mankind, perhaps the apogee of human existence.

This worldview is what leads people like Deborah Prothrow-Stith, the former Dean of the Harvard School of Public Health, to say things like "I hate guns and I cannot imagine why anyone would want to own one." To people like her, guns look like all cons and no pros.

According to Prothrow-Stith and others like her, American civilians don't need to make war against other countries (the military handles that). They don't need to defend state borders (the National Guard does that). And they don't even need to protect themselves (the police do that).

In other words, the Second Amendment is obsolete, and it's time we struck it from the Constitution. There's just one little problem with this idea...

Technology Changes. Humans Don't.

Looking down at the relics of history from a rarified perch, it's easy to convince ourselves that we could never again descend into the chaos, violence, and oppression of the past.

Never again will a king rule over us, or shackled humans be sold as chattel, or religious pogroms decimate "heretics" or "infidels," or proscription lists condemn people to death for having the wrong political beliefs. That's what we tell ourselves, anyway.

Not only is it hard for most people to put themselves in the shoes of our ancient ancestors, it's hard for most Americans to imagine a return to the 1960s and 1970s, when civilians were conscripted to fight a war they didn't believe in, when African Americans were denied entry into schools, and when terrorists committed over 500 attacks against American citizens.

We're beyond all of that, we assure ourselves. We've transcended our savage nature and sectarian beliefs, and we will forever march to new heights of peace, freedom, and prosperity for all. We've achieved a spiritual enlightenment, of sorts.

And if our ancestors could see us now, they'd split their sides laughing.

Between fits of mirth, they'd probably say something to the effect of: "You've done well for yourselves, but remember: 'Pride goeth before destruction, and an haughty spirit before a fall.'"

In other words, don't think you're so different from me.

Imagine, for a moment, all of the historical figures you've learned about in this book seated in front of you. Try to picture their weathered faces and finery—the pressed tunic of Polybius, the puffy mutton sleeves of Machiavelli, the powdered wig of George Washington. Debating politics, morals, and theology in Latin, Italian, and English. Thousands of years of collective wisdom crammed into a single room.

If there's one thing they'd all agree on, it would probably be this:

Cultures change, societies evolve, technologies advance, and our lives become more sophisticated, enjoyable, and safe, but no amount of time, modern trappings, or trinkets can disguise our innate values, virtues, and vices, which all remain unchanged.

"Human nature is the one constant through human history," wrote Thucydides, the Athenian general and historian. "It is always there."

We're the same trousered apes we've been for millennia. Anyone who tells you something different is either a naive optimist or ignorant of human history. If this sounds harsh, let history bear witness:

Nine thriving, highly-advanced Mediterranean civilizations of the late Bronze Age were ripped asunder by a mysterious and violent band of marauding "sea peoples." "Within a period of forty to fifty years at the end of the thirteenth and the beginning of the twelfth century," writes the historian, Robert Drews, "almost every significant city in the eastern Mediterranean world was destroyed, many of them never to be occupied again."

The Assyrians felt they had reached the highpoint of civilization before their empire was wiped from the face of the earth with the fall of Nineveh in 612 BC—you can still glimpse the ruins next to Mosul in Iraq.

The Persians believed their empire to be the most powerful and enduring that would ever be, until Alexander and forty thousand Greek soldiers shattered it in a decade.

The Romans held nearly all of Europe in their grasp, until Goths, Vandals, and Germans pulled it apart and devoured it in the fifth century AD, sacking "The Eternal City" in the process.

Chinese emperors had ruled over eastern Asia with impunity for 1,500 years before being subjugated by Mongol tribesmen in three generations.

The Holy Roman Empire lasted a thousand years before being trampled in the mud and blood of the First World War.

After the Great War, the French, English, and Poles believed they'd clipped the wings of Germany until 1939, when Panzers, Stukas, and storm troopers swarmed over Europe.

From 1992 to 1995, Bosnians, Serbs, Croats, and other peaceful Balkan citizens were subject to acts of barbarism that could have been found etched into an Assyrian tablet: mass rape, ethnic cleansing, plundered cities, and butchery of surrendering soldiers and unarmed civilians on a biblical scale.

More recently, Venezuelans watched as their country transformed from a thriving democracy and the richest country in South America into a stunted, impoverished dictatorship in the blink of an eye. Now, Nicholas Maduro imprisons political enemies, cancels elections that threaten his rule, guns down protestors, and attempts to rewrite the constitution. He also banned civilians from owning guns in 2009.

Even now, it is estimated that forty million people are still held as slaves across Asia, Africa, India, and the Middle East.

The lesson?

Humans have not changed, yet we pretend that we have. Are we really so naive as to think that our current version of life will endure forever? That our predictable, peaceful existence will persist until the end of time? That we've seen the end of tyranny?

A glance at the pages of human history proves this a mirage. Throughout the world, there are still people who are willing to climb a mountain of corpses in their lust for power. There are still those who'd stab their fellow man in the back to steal his property. And there are some who, through despair or mental illness, simply wish to sow chaos—to break the things they wish they could build.

Evil exists and always will. And as long as it exists, it can infiltrate and corrupt even the best forms of government.

The Greeks put their finger on this problem over two thousand years ago and came up with a name for the process by which governments sour from good to bad: *anacyclosis*. Developed by the Greek sages Plato, Aristotle, and Polybius, the theory of anacyclosis states that governments continually transform in a series of predictable stages. According to Polybius' interpretation, the three forms of "benign" government—monarchy, aristocracy, and democracy, eventually and inexorably devolve into "malignant" forms of government—tyranny, oligarchy, and ochloarchy (mob rule). These ideas influenced many political thinkers from Cicero to Machiavelli to

John Adams. According to the ancients, whether a government becomes corrupt is not a matter of *if*, but *when*.

As society has advanced, we've hemmed in the dark side of human nature with new carrots and sticks, but no system can eliminate it altogether. While our modern government tends to reward the honest and productive, and penalize the devious and indolent, it doesn't always work.

The Founders devoted their lives to building a system of meritocratic government that was based on the idea that most people are inherently good and *can* work together for the betterment of all. That said, they also understood that many people have bad inclinations that must be restrained, especially as they gain power. As Madison reminds us in *The Federalist Papers*, "It may be a reflection on human nature, that such devices [the Constitution] should be necessary to control the abuses of government. But what is government itself, but the greatest of all reflections on human nature? If men were angels, no government would be necessary."

This is why political philosophers from Aristotle to Montesquieu to Madison advocated for a separation of powers in government—to prevent any one person or group from collecting too much influence and oppressing others. This is why all free societies have, to one degree or another, protected free speech—so that citizens could voice their concerns in public and hold their leaders accountable. This is why nearly every aspect of the American government was designed to check our bad side—to keep Dr. Jekyll, and not Mr. Hyde, in the driver's seat. At the end of the day, though, the Founders also understood that these institutions and "parchment barriers" would not be enough to contain the ambition of a Caesar, the greed of a Gengis Khan, the sadism of a Stalin, or the tendency for power to corrupt even the best of us.

Most importantly, they also understood that even "democratic" institutions can become oppressive and tyrannical.

"The fundamental article of my political creed," wrote John Adams to Jefferson, "is that despotism, or limited sovereignty, or absolute power is the same [whether] in a majority of a popular assembly; an aristocratic council; or oligarchical junto and a single emperor—equally arbitrary, cruel, bloody and in every respect diabolical." "The right of a nation to kill a tyrant, in cases of necessity," Adams continued, "can no more be doubted, than to hang a robber, or kill a flea."

All of this is why Americans have the Second Amendment—to retain the means to defend themselves against tyrannical statesmen, depraved plutocrats, corrupt councils, petty criminals, and any other person or group who threatens their liberty. Those who wish to use violence against others can only be held in check with the threat—or use—of violence.

This is why the Second Amendment is not and will never become obsolete. Until human nature fundamentally changes, which history proves is unlikely if not impossible, violence will always be necessary to defend freedom. "Guard with jealous attention the public liberty," warned Patrick Henry. "Suspect everyone who approaches that jewel. Unfortunately, nothing will preserve it but downright force. Whenever you give up that force, you are inevitably ruined."

This is why Americans must never bargain away their right to bear arms.

Some people agree with this idea in theory, but point out that American civilians have a snail's chance in saltwater of defeating a tyrannical US government. It has the largest, most advanced military in the world. It has numerous overseas allies it could recruit to oppress its own people. It has nearly inexhaustible resources. As the court pointed out in the case of *D.C. v. Heller*, "It may well be true today that a militia, to be as effective as militias in the 18th century, would require sophisticated arms that are highly unusual in society at large. Indeed, it may be true that no amount of small arms could be useful against modern-day bombers and tanks." All of this is true—if the US military were to be turned against the American people, the chances of success would be miniscule.

There are two problems with this line of thinking, though.

First, the Second Amendment isn't necessarily about ensuring American civilians are just as well armed as the US military or can beat it in pitched battle. Instead, the Second Amendment is meant to be a deterrent. It's about giving citizens enough firepower to convince a corrupt government that oppressing the American people—even if successful initially—would be more trouble than it's worth. "You can build a throne out of bayonets," quipped Boris Yeltsin, "but you can't sit on them long." In other words, a despotic ruler or oligarchy could seize power, but it wouldn't be easy, pretty, or safe for those imposters for long.

Second, for all of the US military's strengths, it's not invincible. In Vietnam, Iraq, Afghanistan, and Syria, US soldiers were repeatedly stymied by relatively unsophisticated, atomized guerrilla forces using outdated weapons. There are a variety of reasons for this—unclear goals, massive financial costs, stifling rules of engagement, media misrepresentation, and misguided public opinion—but there's no reason to think American civilians would be any less ferocious when pushed to the wall.

History has also proven that success on the battlefield doesn't always win wars. Hannibal annihilated every Roman army sent against him for almost two decades, killed almost all of Rome's military leadership, and came within a few days' march of taking Rome itself, but failed to break Rome's resolve and eventually lost the Second Punic War. The 685,000-man Grande Armée under Napoleon conquered Moscow and much of western Russia, but destroyed itself in the process, limping away with only 120,000 men. Despite the Tet Offensive being a resounding military victory for Americans on paper—more North Vietnamese died in 1968 than Americans in the entire war—the campaign convinced many Americans at home that the war was not worth the cost.

History is filled with many such examples of "hopeless" causes turning into remarkable upsets. When Persia, with an army three times larger, invaded Greece in 480 BC, the Greeks could have been forgiven for laying down their arms and submitting to the Persian yoke. Instead, they closed ranks and fought tooth and nail to expel the invaders from their homeland. To any outside observer, the American cause in 1776 looked hopeless. The British had taken New York and New Jersey, and would soon take the capital of Philadelphia. Instead of bending the knee, the Americans held fast, dragged themselves back from the brink of destruction, and triumphed. In the Winter War of 1939, the full force of the Russian military descended on isolated, outnumbered, and outgunned Finland. Instead of agreeing to become a communist puppet state, the Finns repelled the Red Army through a combination of superior tactics, leadership, and sheer force of will.

As military historian Victor Davis Hanson puts it, "War is a laboratory, a barometer, a thermometer, it's a measuring device. That's all it is. It's a very bitter one. So, two sides have differences, and nobody knows who's stronger and who's weaker, because there's material consideration, tanks, planes, and there's willpower . . . War then tells you in a very very difficult way, who was stronger after all. But it doesn't need to occur if you can convey that message before the war breaks out."

Hanson was referring specifically to Hitler, Mussolini, and Tojo at the outbreak of World War II, but the same principles apply in the case of a civil war.

Hanson explains that the proper role of military force is ". . . to create deterrence. That's all its valuable for—to create a deterrent effect so that history's great monsters, and they're always there, don't try to do something stupid. Most wars are started by weaker powers who have convinced themselves that the stronger are either too complacent or don't want to take the trouble to police the area, and they're going to try something stupid."

There's no question that the US military is *materially* stronger than the US populace, but are they *morally* stronger? Do they have the fortitude to face off against millions of armed, highly-motivated, and desperate civilians, fighting on their own turf? Are millions of conscripted soldiers willing to risk their lives to find out who's stronger, on the orders of politicians who will be insulated from the carnage?

That's a tall order.

Wars aren't just won with guns, bombs, and tanks. They're also won with grit, persistence, and will. Tyrants and military rulers suddenly die. Oligarchs undermine one another. Resources dry up. Patience wears thin. Public support wanes. And whoever's left standing, wins.

There's also the possibility that other nations would come to the aid of a beleaguered, oppressed American populace fighting a tyrannical military—if not out of altruism, at least to gain a leg up on the US government. This is precisely why the French crown supported the

Americans against the British in the American Revolutionary War; why the Chinese supported the Vietnamese against the Americans in the Vietnam War; why the Russians supported the Syrian government against the Americans when we backed the rebels in Syria; and ironically, why the US funded the mujahideen (the precursors to the Taliban) against the Russians during their invasion of Afghanistan, who eventually turned on the Americans.

And finally, even if a situation truly is hopeless, Americans still have the right to resist a tyrannical government no matter what the odds. As Thomas Jefferson and John Dickinson explain in *The Declaration of the Causes and Necessity of Taking Up Arms,* "... the arms we have been compelled by our enemies to assume, we will, in defiance of every hazard, with unabating firmness and perseverance, employ for the preservation of our liberties; being with one mind resolved to *die freemen rather than to live slaves.*" (emphasis added) It doesn't matter if victory seems unlikely or death certain—Americans have the right to resist an oppressive, corrupt government, under any circumstances, full stop. Of course, the chances of an armed conflict between Americans and their own government is slim. But even if Americans never use guns against their own government, they still serve as an important hindrance against authoritarians.

The number one reason to own guns is not to hunt deer, to practice target shooting, to enjoy looking at them on your wall, or even to scare off a criminal. The number one reason Americans have the right to own guns is to deter the formation of and to defend themselves against a tyrannical state—an immortal, timeless, shape-shifting demon that has dogged free society since the beginning of civilization and can never be killed, only contained.

Now, the prospect of civil war can seem so remote that it's hard for most people to imagine, and many gun-control advocates dismiss it out of hand. According to these types, governments are good and won't turn against their own people, and anyone who says otherwise is a conspiracy theorist. (Never mind the last 3,000 years of recorded history or all of the contemporary counterexamples!)

Chapter 9

So, if the idea of a second American Civil War seems far-fetched or fantastical, let's turn our attention to more immediate, pressing questions, such as...

Do You Need a Gun to Defend Yourself?

US police are better trained, equipped, and armed than ever before.

So many people think, why would anyone need a gun? Why not call the police? Well, for several reasons, both practical and moral.

First, the practical problem: There's much truth to the saying that when seconds count, the police are minutes away. According to data collected by the Bureau of Justice Statistics, police arrive within five minutes after receiving a call about a violent crime only twenty to thirty percent of the time. This means that if you call the police because you're being robbed or attacked, there's a seventy to eighty percent chance you'll be waiting more than five minutes—sometimes much more.

If you look at data on 911 calls—the ones most likely related to life-threatening situations—the data isn't much better. Police in most major cities have an average response time of five to ten minutes, with some neighborhoods having to wait much longer.

This isn't a dig at police or first responders, but it illustrates how Herculean their job is. They're expected to arrive at the scene of the crime in minutes, make sense of the situation, and then quickly and safely stop the crime, which could include wounding or killing an attacker without hurting innocent bystanders. This is, of course, impossible to pull off all of the time.

Police can't be everywhere at once, and even when they get a call for help, it's almost always when a crime is in progress or has already occurred. Thus, it's not surprising that research shows most police support the right of Americans to defend themselves. They know better than anyone that they *aren't* omnipotent and won't always arrive in time to save the day.

For example, in one of the largest and most comprehensive surveys of its kind ever conducted, Police1.com asked fifteen thousand police officers from around the United States thirty questions about gun control. Here are some of the key takeaways from the report:

- Ninety-five percent said that a ban on the manufacture and sale of magazines that hold more than ten rounds would not reduce violent crime.
- Seventy-one percent said that a ban on the manufacture and sale of some semiautomatic guns would have no effect on reducing violent crime, 28 percent said it would increase violent crime, and only 7 percent said it would decrease it.
- Eighty-five percent said the proposed Assault Weapons Ban of 2013, which included banning AR-15s and high-capacity magazines, would have a zero or negative effect on public safety, and only 10 percent said it would have a moderate or significantly positive effect (the bill was defeated by a vote of forty to sixty in the Senate).
- Seventy percent said they had a favorable opinion of other police officers' public statements that they would not enforce more restrictive gun laws in their jurisdictions (i.e., most police supported their colleagues who established so-called Second Amendment sanctuaries).
- Sixty-one percent said they would not enforce more restrictive gun laws in their jurisdictions if they were police chief or sheriff.
- Twenty-eight percent said that more permissive concealed carry laws for civilians would help more than anything else in stopping large scale public shootings, followed by more aggressive institutionalization for the mentally ill (19 percent) and more armed guards/paid security personnel (15 percent). Only 2.4 percent favored tighter gun laws as a solution.
- Ninety percent said that fewer people would be injured if armed citizens were present at the onset of a shooting.
- Eighty percent said that they support arming school teachers and administrators who willingly volunteer to train with firearms and carry one in the course of their job.

- Eighty-one percent said that gun-buyback programs are ineffective in reducing gun violent crime.

The reason so many police support gun rights is probably because they know their own limitations better than anyone else. They know they can't arrive in time to stop every violent crime, much less catch the perpetrator or provide life-saving aid for a wounded victim. They also appreciate the terror that comes from feeling that your life is in imminent danger. Police are human; they won't always arrive in time to save a victim's life; and they're confronted with most people's "worst case scenarios" on a daily basis. Every day, people are attacked or threatened in situations where calling the police is impractical, and they have to defend themselves by whatever means available.

More specifically, a scientific study conducted by University of Chicago economist Jens Ludwig shows that there are probably about 400,000 to 1.3 million instances of "defensive gun use" per year in the United States. (Pinning down an exact number is almost impossible due to the way these kinds of surveys are conducted). This means that people use guns to defend themselves around 1,100 to 3,600 times *per day* on average across America.

Although the media likes to downplay these statistics, it's undeniable that every day, hundreds, if not thousands, of Americans use guns to protect themselves from violence. And it's the most physically vulnerable members of society who have the most to gain from using guns in self defense. A Glock 19 pistol allows a 50-year old, 5'2, 100-pound mother to fend off a 25-year old, 6'5, 350-pound former NFL lineman.

There are also many examples of private citizens stopping violent criminals from killing other people. For example...

On March 22, 2015, a man pulled out a gun and began shooting at another patron of a barbershop in Philadelphia. There was a crowd inside, including several children. Before he could kill anyone, another man pulled out his own gun and shot the attacker in the chest multiple times, killing him. "The person who responded was a legal gun permit carrier," said Philadelphia Police Captain Frank Llewellyn. "... I guess he saved a lot of people in there... it could have been a lot worse."

In April 2015, Everado Custodio was arguing with a group of people on the street in Chicago, when he pulled a gun and began shooting at them. John Hendricks, an Uber driver, US Army veteran, and one of the few concealed carry holders in Chicago at the time, was taking a break from work when he saw Custodio start shooting. He pulled his pistol and shot Custodio three times, stopping him from hurting anyone in the crowd.

On December 29, 2019, a man snuck into the West Freeway Church of Christ in White Settlement, Texas. He pulled out a shotgun and began shooting at the 242 people in the congregation, killing two within seconds. Before he could continue his rampage, seventy-one-year old concealed carry holder Jack Wilson drew his pistol, aimed, and shot the attacker in the head, killing him instantly.

Just two years earlier, a gunman managed to kill twenty-six people and injure twenty others at the First Baptist Church in Sutherland Springs, Texas, where no one in the congregation was armed. The gunman was still roaming the aisles and shooting at anyone he could see when he was confronted by Stephen Willeford, a former NRA firearms instructor who lived nearby. Willeford shot the attacker multiple times with his AR-15 and then pursued him for several minutes, before the attacker killed himself.

Although stories like this rarely get much media attention outside of the local news, there are myriad other examples of private gun owners stopping violent criminals faster than police would have been able to and saving lives in the process.

Then, there's the fact that even when police arrive in time to stop a crime, they don't always handle the situation well. One of the most salient and tragic examples of police mishandling a shooter is the infamous Marjory Stoneman Douglas High School shooting in Parkland, Florida.

At about 2 p.m. on February 14, 2018, a mentally ill former student snuck into the school and began shooting teenagers and teachers with an AR-15, killing seventeen people in six minutes. Although many gun control advocates held up this massacre as evidence that more gun laws are needed to prevent mass shootings, it's a better illustration of why you *can't* rely on police to protect you from violent criminals in all situations. In this case, police and other public servants failed to protect the students and teachers at the school in every way.

First, Scot Peterson, an armed, uniformed school resource officer (a police officer who is stationed inside a school to protect the students) was at the school during the entire shooting. When he heard gunshots, he lingered outside the building and then moved farther away, hiding for forty-eight minutes and never confronting the shooter, only emerging long after the last shots were fired and other police officers had begun securing the building. As of this writing, Peterson is still facing multiple charges for neglect of a child, negligence, and perjury.

Second, the first police officer to arrive (other than Peterson, who was already present) blocked off a nearby traffic intersection instead of confronting the shooter. When seven more police officers arrived, they remained next to their squad cars outside the school, even as they could hear gunshots from inside. The first police officers didn't enter the building until five minutes after the shooting was over, and the shooter had already escaped. When Captain Jan Jordan arrived and assumed control of the situation, she ordered her deputies to form a perimeter around the school instead of attempting to confront the shooter, contrary to police training. She resigned nine months after the shooting.

Broward County Police Chief Scott Israel, a Democrat, later admitted that he had changed the policy in his district so that officers "may" confront active shooters instead of "shall" confront active shooters. He was fired, and the Florida State Senate later voted to permanently bar him from ever becoming police chief in Broward County again. As Florida Governor Ron de Santis said, "These incidents demonstrate Sheriff Israel's repeated incompetence and neglect of duty."

Finally, the ultimate cause of the shooting was the complete and utter failure of the school and police to properly address the shooter's mental health and remove him from society. Although Sheriff Israel claimed his department "only" received twenty-three calls about the shooter and his family over the previous decade, a public records request proved that from 2008 to 2017, there were *forty-five* such calls to police. In the two years before the shooting, two separate callers told police the shooter had threatened to shoot up a school and might be a "school shooter in the making." When a fellow student warned the school resource officer that the shooter had tried to kill himself and planned to buy a gun, the school said they would do a "threat assessment." An investigator for the Florida Department of Children and Families claimed that the shooter was mentally stable, despite the presence of self-inflicted "fresh cuts" on his arms. A month before the shooting, the FBI received a tip on its public access line, and just two days before the shooting, released a statement saying, "The caller provided information about [the shooter's] gun ownership, desire to kill people, erratic behavior, and disturbing social media posts, as well as the potential of him conducting a school shooting."

In other words, multiple police agencies failed to prevent the shooting despite many warnings, and then failed to protect the students inside the school after the shooting began.

Of course, it's not fair to blame the events at Parkland entirely on the police. Multiple school safety officers saw the shooter enter the school with a rifle bag and did nothing to stop him, and one of them even recalled him as "Crazy Boy"—the student most of the staff thought most likely to shoot up the school. A student saw the shooter loading his gun before he began shooting his classmates, ran from the school, and informed another school safety monitor, who neglected to alert school officials or the police. Another school monitor hid in a closet after the shooting began and never used his radio to alert teachers or the school resource officer. The school had locked all of the bathrooms to prevent students from vaping, which made it impossible for them to be used as shelters. Two months before the shooting, retired Secret Service officer Steve Wexler conducted a thorough review of the school's security measures, and found numerous "blatantly obvious" mistakes, such as unlocked gates (one of which the shooter would stroll through) and classrooms that were organized in such a way that would make it easy for a shooter to hit almost anyone inside the room from the doorway. The school ignored his advice.

There are many other examples of police malfeasance, too.

Chapter 9

On May 31, 2020, police failed to prevent rioters from ransacking most of Santa Monica, California. After reviewing footage of the looters pillaging stores for hours, a former top police official remarked, "It kind of speaks for itself. The officers looked the other way. Squad cars drove by the looters and didn't stop. They were within twenty-five yards of people committing crimes." As a result of the police's supine response, sixty-five thousand people signed a petition to have Police Chief Cynthia Renaud removed.

On June 8, 2020, violent protestors attacked the East Precinct building of the Seattle Police Department. Police not only abandoned the building, but also six city blocks and a park inside the Capitol Hill neighborhood of Seattle. The police only retook the area from rioters three weeks later, after multiple people were killed and injured, including a 16-year old boy. During this time, people living in the area were at the mercy of armed thugs.

Ironically, when citizens in Denver, Colorado organized a peaceful, pro-police rally on July 19, 2020, members of "Antifa" arrived and attacked them ("Antifa," which stands for "anti-fascist," is a violent protest movement whose members claim to fight against people who hold "right-wing" beliefs). Police leaders ordered their subordinates to stand down for fear of media reprisals, allowing Antifa free reign to terrorize the very people advocating for the police—including old men and women. Luckily, one police lieutenant disobeyed orders and helped prevent the altercation from turning into a brawl. As he told reporters later, "These people are going to get killed if we don't stay."

None of this is to say that police are incompetent, but they are imperfect. They're forced to deal with potentially life and death situations every day; they're under immense media scrutiny; and they're often shackled by bureaucratic restrictions that make their jobs even more difficult. When you call the cops, you're placing your safety in the hands of another flawed human being with a gun.

And, like any profession, there are also bad apples. Some cops don't care as much as they should; others are indecisive or overly aggressive; and others are simply inept. This doesn't mean you *shouldn't* call the cops, but it's worth remembering that doing so isn't a panacea.

Many people have the misguided belief that if they just dial 911 and wait for police to arrive, everything will be okay. The problem is that life isn't a Marvel movie. Police don't swoop in out of the sky, subdue the bad guy in seconds, and save everyone. Instead, they often arrive too late, make mistakes, or even add to the carnage. And in many cases, the bad guy might have been stopped sooner by a civilian with a gun.

Second, the moral problem with the "just call the police" fallacy, is that it's at odds with the right of self-preservation. Even if police *could* arrive to protect you in every instance, you still have the right to take matters into your own hands if threatened. As you recall, this is the single most fundamental right of human existence—the ability to keep existing.

In other words, even if police could tap into some kind of psychic ability to foresee and prevent crimes a la *Minority Report*, you would still have the right to defend yourself before they arrive. Of course, police don't have this ability. In the real world, you're often on your own, and there's no guarantee the police will arrive before you're injured (or worse) by a violent criminal.

The bottom line is that as a human being, you have the right to protect your own life and a responsibility to protect the lives of others, even if the state pays other people (police) to help when they can. As a corollary, you also have the right to use the most effective tools—guns—for protecting yourself and those around you from violence.

Do Americans Only Have the Right to Own Muskets?

Some people say that if the Founders could have predicted the destructive power of modern guns, they never would have entrusted them to civilians. Instead, they argue, the Second Amendment only applies to the kinds of weapons available when it was created—muskets.

The main thing that bothers these people about modern guns isn't necessarily their range, accuracy, or killing power, but their rate of fire, or how many bullets they can fire in a short period of time. This, they say, is why mass shooters and murderers are able to kill so many people—they can fire a lot more bullets without reloading.

Many gun control advocates claim that if the Founders had known that in just a few centuries civilians would be able to buy an AR-15, AK-47, or Glock 17, they never would have written the Second Amendment. This is a particularly common refrain among pro gun-control media personalities and celebrities. For example:

"The 2nd amendment was devised with muskets in mind," tweeted British television host Piers Morgan, "not high-powered handguns & assault rifles. Fact."

"This is what they had in mind when they wrote the Second Amendment: a single shot firearm that takes a bit of work to reload," said Lawrence O'Donnell, host of *The Last Word with Lawrence O'Donnell*, and someone who describes themselves as a "practical European socialist."

"I think the Second Amendment is in the Constitution so that we can have *muskets* when . . . when the British people come [sic] over in 1800," remarked Rosie O'Donnell while interviewing the actor Tom Selleck.

"The Second Amendment is for muskets" makes a good soundbite, but it's a specious argument for several reasons.

First, if you assume that the Founding Fathers wouldn't have wanted modern guns protected under the Second Amendment, you'd also have to assume that they didn't want other "inalienable rights" protected when they were exercised with new technologies.

For example, you'd have to assume that the right to free speech—protected under the First Amendment—isn't protected on smartphones, the Internet, or social media websites, technologies that didn't exist when the First Amendment was created. Note that all of the quotes from gun control advocates shared a moment ago were collected from television clips, YouTube videos, and Tweets. You could make an argument that because these new technologies allow people to publish and manipulate information far more easily than anything available at the time of the Founding Fathers, they pose a danger to society. After all, American patriots did limit free speech during the American Revolutionary War, even burning down printing presses and newspapers that supported the British.

Thus, if gun-control advocates believe the Second Amendment doesn't protect your right to own an AR-15, gun rights advocates could just as easily argue that the First Amendment doesn't protect your right to promote misinformation about the Constitution on an iPhone. Of course, this is absurd, and both positions would be grossly unconstitutional.

This isn't just a thought experiment, either—the Supreme Court directly addressed this issue in the case of *D.C. v. Heller* and came to the same conclusion. As Justice Antonin Scalia wrote in the court's final opinion, "Some have made the argument, bordering on the frivolous, that only those arms in existence in the 18th century are protected by the Second Amendment. We do not interpret constitutional rights that way. Just as the First Amendment protects modern forms of communications, and the Fourth Amendment applies to modern forms of search, the Second Amendment extends . . . to all instruments that constitute bearable arms, even those that were not in existence at the time of the founding."

The Founding Fathers were also very specific with the words they used when drafting the Constitution and the Bill of Rights. According to American jurisprudence, the Supreme Court is supposed to assume that every word was chosen to communicate a particular message. The Framers chose the words *arms* instead of *muskets*, *blunderbuss*, or, if they wanted to be technical, *smoothbore small arms*, to describe what guns Americans had the right to own. They intentionally kept the wording vague and inclusive, probably because they knew that it would be impossible to enumerate every kind of gun Americans might own in the future.

This dovetails into the second problem with the "Second Amendment is for muskets" fallacy: The Founders may not have known exactly what kind of weapons would be developed after they drafted the Second Amendment, but they knew weapons technology would continue to advance at a rapid pace.

Why?

Because before, during, and after the American Revolutionary War, the Founders witnessed and took advantage of astounding advancements in firearms technology. Under ideal conditions, a well-trained soldier could fire about three shots per minute from a musket—maybe five in a pinch. Long before the American Revolutionary War, though, military engineers had been building guns that could shoot much faster than this. Here are a few examples:

- In 1630, the Kalthoff family designed the Kalthoff repeating rifle, which could fire up to thirty rounds per minute and was used during several wars in the late 1600s.
- In 1718, James Puckle invented a small cannon that could fire up to nine shots per minute, and fired sixty-three shots in seven minutes in a test in 1722.
- In 1750, John Crookson invented the Crookson repeater, a rifle that could fire nine shots in a matter of seconds (based on gun designs from 1690).
- In 1776, only a year after the American Revolutionary War began, Patrick Ferguson patented the Ferguson rifle, which could fire six to ten shots per minute. The British also used this rifle in several battles against the Americans.
- In 1777, Joseph Belton patented a design for the Belton Flintlock, which would have been able to fire thirty to sixty rounds per minute. Congress was so impressed with the design, they immediately placed an order for one hundred of these rifles, although they later cancelled it, deeming the rifles too expensive.
- In 1779, Bartolomeo Girardoni invented the Girardoni Air Rifle, which could shoot twenty-two to thirty bullets in thirty seconds at ranges of up to 150 yards. It was so effective that the Austrian Army used it for several decades, and Lewis and Clarke brought at least one on their expedition to the Pacific Coast.
- The same year, James Wilson invented the Nock gun for the British Navy, which could fire seven shots with a single pull of the trigger.
- As far back as 1481, shortly after gunpowder was introduced to Europe, Leonardo da Vinci had designed a multi-barreled, water-cooled, rapid-fire cannon over three centuries before the Second Amendment was written.

Several other wrinkles in weapons technology occurred around the time of the American Revolutionary War. More and more gunsmiths began cutting spiral grooves into musket barrels, an invention known as *rifling*, that drastically improved accuracy and range. While muskets were effective at about fifty to seventy-five yards, rifling allowed marksmen to shoot British officers hundreds of yards away. Flintlock rifles had also recently replaced matchlocks. Instead of using a burning piece of rope (a "match") to ignite the powder in the gun barrel, flintlocks ignited the powder using sparks from a piece of flint scraped against steel by a small hammer. This allowed for much faster and more reliable shooting, especially in damp conditions. Around the same time, bayonets became standard issue among most armies, giving soldiers the benefits of both a gun and a spear in a single weapon.

In summary, muskets were not the only weapons available at the time the Second Amendment was written. Muskets were popular because they were cheap, reliable, easy to produce, and could hold a bayonet (which rifles could not). This made them the best choice for the battle tactics of the day—marching close to the enemy, firing two or three volleys, and then finishing them off with bayonets, hatchets, and sabres.

This changed rapidly after the war, though, and once again the Founding Fathers saw firearms technology advance by leaps and bounds. In 1807, when many of the Founding Fathers were still alive, the percussion cap was invented, and a year later, the paper cartridge, which held the gunpowder, bullet, and percussion cap together and allowed shooters to reload much faster. In 1836, the same year James Madison died, Samuel Colt patented his famous design for the first revolver and Johann Nikolaus von Dreyse created the Dreyse Needle Gun, which could fire six to twelve bullets per minute.

Many of the Founding Fathers were also avid shooters, gun collectors, and amateur firearms engineers. George Washington owned several guns, and Thomas Jefferson bought firearms from France, Turkey, and Africa, owned a double-barrel shotgun as well as two Girardoni Air Rifles, and tinkered with gun parts in his spare time.

The Framers of the Constitution were not fools. They had seen military technology advance at a lightning pace and would have had no reason to think guns would not become increasingly sophisticated over the coming centuries. They knew that muskets would eventually be replaced by guns that could shoot faster, because many such guns existed before the Second Amendment was written. If the Founding Fathers were concerned about Americans owning these guns, there isn't a single scrap of evidence to prove it.

The Founding Fathers were also fine with private citizens owning far more than just rifles and pistols. On December 2, 1812, President James Madison signed a *letter of marque and reprisal*—an official document authorizing a private citizen to use his own warships to attack enemy vessels. Almost all of these ships were armed with privately owned cannons, and the *privateer* in charge of the ship was allowed to keep the enemy vessels and weapons he captured.

Although many documents have been lost, Congress signed at least 1,700 letters of marque during the American Revolutionary War, and nearly 800 ships were commissioned as privateers, including the twenty-six-gun *Caesar*. Through the course of the war, they destroyed or captured around 600 British vessels. Thus, it would seem the Founders were not only okay with private citizens owning guns, but also cannons and battleships.

At bottom, the Second Amendment is just as important now as it ever was, perhaps even more so.

On the one hand, we live in a world so peaceful and plentiful it's hard for many people to understand why Americans need guns. That's good. On the other hand, history proves that pride, complacency, and a false sense of security are the precursors of conflict, discord, and collapse. As long as there are people in this world who wish to take advantage of, rule over, and oppress others, the right to bear arms must never be relinquished.

10
3 Things You Can Do Right Now to Defend Your Second Amendment Rights

"... only a virtuous people are capable of freedom. As nations become corrupt and vicious, they have more need of masters."
—Benjamin Franklin, 18th century polymath, scientist, statesman, and signer of the Declaration of Independence, 1787.

"Politics is when you say you are going to do one thing while intending to do another. Then you do neither what you said nor what you intended."
—Saddam Hussein, fifth President of Iraq believed to be responsible for the deaths of at least 250,000 Shias and Kurds in his own country, and hundreds of thousands more in Kuwait and Iran, 1979.

You now know more about the Second Amendment than most people ever will.

You know the origins of the right to self-preservation, consensual government, and civic militarism that sprung from ancient Greece and Rome. You appreciate the bloody sacrifices made by ancient English soldiers, American settlers, and early American Patriots, and the indispensable role firearms played in the formation of the United States. You understand the moral, philosophical, and historical reasons the Founding Fathers created the Second Amendment, and what it was meant to protect. And you've cottoned on to the greatest political and legal threats to your Second Amendment rights.

That's all well and good, you may be thinking, but what's little ol' me supposed to do about any of this? What can *I* do to protect and practice my Second Amendment rights?

A lot, actually.

First, you've already taken the first and most important step in defending the Second Amendment: Educating yourself. Big ups to you, but remember that knowledge isn't much good to you or anyone else if you don't use it. After informing yourself, it's time to roll up your sleeves and march to the coalface, where the real work is done.

Here's a game plan for protecting the Second Amendment:

1. Continue learning your rights.
2. Be an ambassador for gun rights.
3. Support people who support the Second Amendment.
4. If you liked this book, please tell a friend.

Let's start at the top.

Step 1: Continue Learning Your Rights

We know we *should* understand and take part in the political process, but it can seem Byzantine, boring, and unproductive. Here's the rub: Politicians are counting on this. Most would prefer you don't learn how government works, how you can affect it, and what your rights are.

After all, the fewer people who can hold them accountable, the more leeway they have to do what they want (which usually means making whatever promises and passing whatever policies will improve their odds of reelection).

Chapter 10

The only solution to this problem is to peel back the curtain and take a hard look at what's going on behind the scenes of government. This book helped you understand your gun rights, but to truly understand your rights as an American and how you can protect them, you have to continue learning about your other rights and responsibilities.

"I consider knowledge to be the soul of the republic," wrote John Jay, "and as the weak and the wicked are generally in alliance, as much care should be taken to diminish the number of the former as of the latter. Education is the way to do this..."

If you want to understand politics, your best angle of attack is to first understand history.

A quote often attributed to Mark Twain says that, "History doesn't repeat itself, but it often rhymes." That is, events never play out exactly the same way twice, but if you look closely at the past, you can find lessons that enhance your understanding of the present. And if you want to change the way things are now and will be in the future, you also must look back before you can look forward.

In a perfect world, our leaders would spend more time attempting to understand history than how to get votes, but that's clearly not the case and unlikely to change any time soon. Ironically, though, it's more important that the voter understands history. Like using a piece of cheese to lure a mouse through a maze, we can use our votes to entice politicians in the right direction, even if they don't understand why they're turning left or right. Even better would be to *tell them* why you're voting the way you are, so they can more fully bend their energy and attention to protecting your rights (more on this in a moment).

So, the first step in protecting the Second Amendment is to continue what you've started by reading this book—to further hone your grasp of history. Luckily, educating yourself about history isn't expensive or even all that difficult. Here's what I recommend.

Read at least one book or document about history, politics, or government every one to two months.

If that seems daunting, make it a goal to read at least one book a year about these topics. Anything is better than nothing.

Here are a dozen of the best books to kickstart your knowledge:

- *The Lessons of History* by Will Durant
- *Common Sense* by Thomas Paine
- *Origins of the Bill of Rights* by Leonard Levy
- *The Know Your Bill of Rights Book* by Sean Patrick
- *The Founder's Second Amendment* and *That Every Man be Armed* by Stephen P. Halbrook
- *Deadly Force: Understanding Your Right to Self Defense* by Massad Ayoob
- *Democracy in America* by Alexis De Tocqueville
- *The British Are Coming* by Rick Atkinson
- *Carnage and Culture* by Victor Davis Hanson
- *The History of the Peloponnesian War* by Thucydides (There's also an abridged, simplified version called *How to Think About War*).

In addition to reading great books, it's also wise to apprise yourself of the writings of America's Founders and our chief liberty documents. You can find all of these documents for free online (and sometimes even in audio format), and aside from the odd word or grammatical twist, they're far more readable than many people realize. Here are five to start you off on the right foot:

- The Constitution of the United States
- The Bill of Rights
- The Declaration of Independence
- The Federalist Papers
- The Gettysburg Address

If you like listening in addition to reading, I recommend you check out the various lecture series' from Hillsdale College. They're thoroughly researched, well produced, free lectures that are on par with (or better than) what you'd get at many Ivy League colleges (especially when it comes to history and politics). Take advantage of them!

Here are five of their best lectures for quickening your understanding of history, politics, and government:

- Constitution 101: The Meaning and History of the Constitution
- Constitution 201: The Progressive Rejection of the Founding and the Rise of Bureaucratic Despotism
- Congress: How it Worked and Why It Doesn't
- The U.S. Supreme Court
- Public Policy from a Constitutional Viewpoint

Catch up on relevant current events once every two to four weeks.

If you're reading this book, you probably do a better job of keeping your finger on the pulse of politics than most, but all the same, allow me to offer a few pieces of advice:

At least once every two or four weeks, look at what's happening in politics, and especially gun rights, in America. You don't need to do it more often than this because most news is little more than clickbait, with relatively few consequential stories; most important stories will stay in the news for at least a week or two; and if a story is emerging, such as a new court case or proposed bill, allowing a few weeks to pass gives reporters time to produce better content and present a more comprehensive view of the facts.

Here's what I do and recommend:

1. Open up your preferred web browser and search for "second amendment," "gun rights," and "gun control."

2. Scroll through the results to see if any headlines catch your eye.
3. Open what seem to be the most important articles in new tabs in your browser.
4. Skim through each article to see if the story is worth reading in detail.
5. Thoroughly read the articles that cover the most important stories. If there's a particularly important story emerging (such as the renewed interest in red flag laws in 2019), read several articles to ensure you get a more balanced and complete understanding.

When time permits, read a few articles from news organizations that typically aren't sympathetic to Second Amendment rights: *The New York Times*, *The Atlantic*, *The Wallstreet Journal*, *Vox*, *CNN*, and so forth. This ensures you're aware of the main arguments against the Second Amendment and allows you to ponder how their reporting squares with what you're seeing from other outlets and your understanding of history, and then make up your own mind.

A helpful hack for getting a more complete perspective on the news is to check the website allsides.com/topics/guns, which presents news articles from media outlets regarded as left-, center-, and right-leaning, so you get a panoramic picture of the narrative.

In addition to checking traditional media outlets and popular articles, it's also wise to check a few websites that cover firearms news, such as the following:

- thetruthaboutguns.com
- opensourcedefense.com
- pewpewtactical.com
- tactical-life.com/

All in all, this process shouldn't take more than about thirty minutes per month.

Chapter 10

Step 2: Be an Ambassador for Gun Rights

This more or less boils down to being a good role model for others. While this may seem like an odd way to support your Second Amendment rights, it's one of the most important and effective.

Why?

Although it may not be obvious at first glance, we "elect" leaders among our family, friends, and coworkers all the time with our thoughts, behaviors, and actions. We're naturally receptive to people we respect, and if you want others to respond well to your message about the Second Amendment, it helps if they know, like, and trust the messenger.

In other words, if you want people to listen to, understand, and maybe even agree with your opinions, you need to get your own house in order first. Ask yourself, who are the people you admire, who do you want to emulate, who do you look to for leadership, support, and inspiration? Who has successfully changed your mind about a key issue in your life? And did their ideas appeal to you solely because they made a logical, evidence-based argument, or was it also because you respected them and were thus interested in what they had to say?

There's another reason to do what you can to produce and present the best version of yourself to the world: One of gun control advocate's favorite red herrings is to caricature gun owners as unsophisticated, untutored, uncouth, schlumpy, selfish, small-minded hayseeds. "Look at these silly peasants, clinging to their guns," is the insinuation.

For example, every few months, a news organization will write a "definitive" article on some aspect of gun control. To give the article some semblance of fairness, it'll feature arguments from people who are both for and against gun control. In the corner for gun control, they'll typically feature several suave PhDs, researchers, or politicians who parrot the usual potted talking points about gun control. In the corner for gun rights, though, they'll feature a few words from an unkempt, overweight gun owner that fits the stereotype they want to convey.

A perfect example of this selection bias is a 2017 article published in

Scientific American titled "More Guns Do Not Stop More Crimes, Evidence Shows," which featured input in favor of gun control from a criminologist at the University at Albany, S.U.N.Y.; another at the University of Maryland; an epidemiologist from the F. Edward Hébert School of Medicine at the Uniformed Services University; a physician from the University of California; an economist from Stanford University; and another from Duke University. In favor of gun rights, they featured input from two sheriffs, a firearms instructor, a pawnshop owner, an anonymous quote from a National Rifle Association representative, and a jot of data from the prominent pro-gun criminologist, John Lott.

The thrust of this and similar articles is subtle but unmistakable: people who don't like guns are urbane, learned intellectuals, and people who like guns are unenlightened rustics.

It's time we break this mold, and here are several actions you can take right now to help:

1. Get in shape. You don't need six-pack abs or a flat stomach, but the home truth is that people do tend to look at you more positively and be more receptive to what you have to say if you're in decent physical shape. If you aren't sure where to start, check out the books *Bigger Leaner Stronger* (for men) and *Thinner Leaner Stronger* (for women). Likewise, kicking unhealthy habits like excessive drinking or smoking can go a long way in making a good first impression.
2. Think before you speak. This is easier said than done, but people are generally much more interested in what you have to say if you listen attentively first, and then offer a thoughtful and respectful response. Don't get defensive, emotional, or antagonistic when people present contradictory or outrageous viewpoints. Often, the best way to handle conversations with people who disagree with you on fundamental issues is to use the Socratic method—continually asking questions about their argument, trying to get at the essence of their beliefs. Not only does this usually diffuse strong emotions (you're just probing, not prodding), it also tends to be

the most effective way of helping the other person come to their own realization of the truth. For example, if you keep asking people why they want guns to be banned, you'll often find the argument simply boils down to "I'm scared of guns and don't want others to have them," which even the speaker sometimes realizes isn't a good argument for banning them.
3. Learn the main arguments for and against the Second Amendment and gun ownership. Not to beat a dead horse, but educating yourself about the history, meaning, and legal significance of the Second Amendment, and sharing this information with others, is one of the best ways to be a good role model for your fellow citizens.

Step 3: Support People Who Support the Second Amendment

This means supporting politicians, companies, and organizations that champion your Second Amendment rights, and shunning those who wish to take them away.

Now, if you tend to have a rather dark view of politicians, I don't blame you (especially after reading this book). That said, you don't want to paint with too broad of a brush. While many (maybe even most) politicians are more concerned with securing reelection and feathering their nests than upholding their oaths to defend the Constitution, that's not always the case.

Remember, even the most venal, corrupt baby-kissers still need people like you to elect them. If enough people give their votes to candidates who support the Second Amendment, and don't give their votes to those who won't, sooner or later lawmakers will grasp that they better not pass gun laws that infringe on your right to bear arms.

Despite all of the hand-wringing in the West about the sacrosanct importance of the right to vote, about 40 percent don't vote in presidential elections and 60 percent don't vote in midterm elections. Don't be one of these rabble. Although voting may seem like a pointless enterprise, it's still one of the easiest and most vital ways to protect your right to bear arms.

When you vote, don't just vote down the party line. While it's true that Republicans generally have a better track record than Democrats when it comes to gun rights, this isn't always the case. Using tools like govtrack.us, you can see how Senators and members of Congress have voted on bills and resolutions dating back to 1789. If a politician has consistently voted to support aggressive gun-control measures like magazine restrictions, "assault weapon" bans, or gun registration, you should think twice about helping to keep them in office.

Aside from just voting, you can take things a step further by writing to politicians, letting them know why you're voting the way you are both before and after elections. You can find the contact information for Members of Congress (both the House and Senate) at contactingcongress.org.

In addition to voting for or against particular politicians, try to support companies that support the Second Amendment whenever possible, and try not to support those that don't. Some people say that you should only judge companies by their products and merits, and leave politics out of purchasing decisions, but I disagree for two reasons: First, it's rare that a company makes a product that's *so* spectacular that you can't get something of similar quality from someone else, so why not buy from companies that share your politics? Second, many people in charge of and employed by companies make political donations to organizations and candidates, some of whom may be working to undermine your Second Amendment rights. I don't want my dollars to fund the election of anti-gun apparatchiks.

You can see what politicians, political parties, and organizations companies have donated to by going to opensecrets.org, entering the name of the company in the search bar, and looking at where the company's owners or employees have donated money over the years.

For example, many of the people who work at the popular knife manufacturer Benchmade have donated thousands to Democratic candidates, several of whom are rabidly anti-gun, such as Ron Wyden and Mark Udall, and have exclusively donated to Democrats since 2012. In addition to determining what companies are fifth columns against the Second Amendment, you can also use this data to "exonerate" companies that might be suspect. For example, in 2018, the CEO of Daniel Defense, a popular AR-15 manufacturer, voiced support for a controversial piece of gun control legislation. He made a retraction and mea culpa upon further reflection, but many gun owners turned on him and his company. If you pull up the company on opensecrets.org, though, you'll see that 80 to 100 percent of donations from Daniel Defense employees and managers go to Republican candidates who oppose gun control. Thus, writing off the company because the CEO made a perfunctory nod toward a piece of gun legislation (that didn't get passed) would be silly.

Again, just because a company has donated prodigiously to Democrats isn't proof positive they're anti-gun, but it gives you a good indication of where their sympathies lie. The point of this exercise isn't to "cancel" or shame these companies out of business—everyone has the right to support whatever party and policies they choose—but to vote with your dollars. Businesses and people respond to incentives, and a decrease in sales is a strong incentive to stop meddling with your constitutional rights.

As a corollary, you can further amplify your vote and political opinions by donating to politicians and candidates that do support the Second Amendment. While it may seem unfair that you should have to pay to protect your inalienable rights, that's the reality. And for my part, if I can afford a cup of coffee or a few boxes of ammo, then I can cough up a few dollars to support my legal right to bear arms. The bottom line is that if you won't open your wallet on occasion, you very well may lose your guns.

Now, you should never donate more than you can safely manage (debt is a debilitating ulcer you should avoid as much as possible), but even if you're living in straitened circumstances, you should donate what little you can.

That raises the question, who should you donate to?

This is a touchy subject among gun owners. The largest gun-rights advocacy group in the US, the NRA, has been mired in controversy of late due to its leader's mismanagement and tepid support for key legal cases like *D.C. v. Heller*, and its decision not to oppose several new firearms laws, such as the bump stock ban. This has led many gun owners to turn away from the NRA, which is understandable. However, this is probably a case of throwing the baby out with the bathwater. While some of the NRA's actions have been questionable, it's also been one of the most stalwart defenders of Second Amendment rights, and it's probably not worth abandoning it quite yet.

If you don't feel comfortable supporting the NRA, though, there are other gun-rights organizations worthy of your support. For instance, one of my personal favorites, and the one I donate to monthly, is the Firearms Policy Coalition (FPC), which is a relatively new non-profit organization with a sterling track record of fighting gun control laws. They've filed legal actions against bans on bumpstocks, high-capacity magazines, and assault weapons, and in support of individuals whose constitutional rights have been violated. What's more, they've also worked on dozens of cases involving violations of the rights to free speech, due process, and equal protection. You can learn more about the organization at firearmspolicy.org.

There's one more thing you can do to help support the Second Amendment. If you feel that this book has helped improve your understanding of the Second Amendment—why it was created, why it's worth preserving, and what you can do to protect it—then please do both of us (and your fellow Americans) a favor, and tell a friend about it.

This is partly self-serving as I do make my living as a writer, but I didn't write this book to become wealthy (that would have been better accomplished by writing a steamy billionaire vampire romance). I wrote it because I believe all of our rights pivot on the right to bear arms. If the Second Amendment is neglected or legislated out of existence, the rest of our rights will truly become "parchment barriers."

So, if you know someone who might benefit from reading this book, please tell them about it.

11

The Civilian's Guide to Buying (and Safely Using) Guns, Ammo, and Other "Military" Arms

> "Despotic governments can stand 'moral force' till the cows come home; what they fear is physical force."
> —George Orwell, English novelist, essayist, and author of the book *1984*, 1942.

> "If the opposition [to the Bolsheviks] disarms, all is well and good. If it refuses to disarm, we shall disarm it ourselves."
> —Joseph Stalin, Soviet dictator responsible for the deaths of ~5 to 10 million of his countrymen, 1927.

If you're comfortable owning and using a gun, you should get one ... or two ... or five (hey, it's a free country). If you aren't comfortable owning and using a gun, keep reading, and you may change your mind.

First things first: What kind of gun should you get? The answer depends on how you plan to use it.

If you're primarily concerned with self defense, and you intend on carrying the gun on your person or in your car, then a small, semiautomatic pistol (often called a "concealed carry" or "subcompact" pistol) that fires nine millimeter bullets is the way to go. Most of these hold between six to twelve cartridges, are about the size of a large cell phone, and weigh a little more than a can of soda, which makes them easy to conceal in a holster on your waist, in a purse, or in a glovebox or console in your car.

Some good models in this category:

- Smith and Wesson M&P9 Shield ($350)
- Walther PPS M2 ($450)
- Glock 43X, 43, or 26 (~$530)
- SIG P365 ($530)*
- Springfield Hellcat ($580)
- Heckler and Koch VP9SK ($650)

(Note: I've organized each list of recommended products from least to most expensive, but not necessarily from worst to best or best to worst. In cases where I have a favorite product from those listed, I've put an asterisk next to it).

There are countless other models to choose from, too, but unless you have a specific preference for one, go with a Glock or SIG. They have the best reputation for reliability, offer good value for the money, are usually in stock at local stores, and are compatible with many different holsters and other accessories.

If you plan on primarily carrying a pistol in a backpack or keeping it in your car, but also occasionally carrying it on your waist, look at another category of pistols known as *compact* pistols, which are slightly larger than subcompact ones. This makes them easier to grip, reduces their "kick" when shooting, and allows them to hold more cartridges. The downside is they're heavier and bulkier, which makes them harder to conceal and less comfortable to wear for long periods of time.

Some good models in this category:

- CZ P-10 C ($499)
- FN 509 ($580)
- Glock 19, 19X, 45, or 48 (~$650)*

- Heckler and Koch VP9 ($770)
- SIG P229 or P226 (~$1,000)

If you plan on keeping your pistol in your car, house, or backpack, and don't plan on carrying it on your waist, look at full-size pistols. These are typically too heavy and bulky to carry on your person, but also hold the most cartridges, are the easiest to learn how to shoot, and have the least recoil.

Some good models to consider:

- CZ P-10 C F ($524)
- SIG P320 ($549)
- Smith & Wesson M&P9 M2.0 ($599)
- Glock 17 Gen 5 ($647)*
- Walther PPQ M2 5" ($749)

If you're primarily concerned with self defense, but don't plan on taking the gun outside your home, consider buying a 12-gauge shotgun. It's going to maximize your chances of hitting your target, subdue an attacker with very few shots, and depending on the kind of ammo you use, is less likely to penetrate through a wall and hit something you don't want to harm (like your neighbor's dog).

Some good options include the following:

- Winchester SXP Defender (~$350)
- Weatherby PA-08 (~$350)
- Benelli Nova ($399)
- Mossberg 500, 590, 590A1, or Maverick 88 (~$500)
- FN P-12 ($669)
- VEPR-12 ($1,149)*
- Benelli M4 ($1,999)

If you're primarily concerned with defending yourself, your community, and your country against civil unrest or a tyrannical government, you probably don't need me to tell you what you should buy, but I will anyway—an AR-15. For a variety of reasons, the AR-15 is the perfect all-around rifle for almost any situation, which is probably one of the reasons politicians have tried (and succeeded) in banning it in the past.

When buying an AR-15, there are a few features you want to look for:

- It should be chambered in 5.56, .223 Remington, or .223 Wylde.
- It should have either an M-Lok (preferred) or Keymod (still good) handguard for attaching accessories.
- It should have a *picatinny rail* on the top of the gun to mount accessories (the top of the gun will look flat).
- It should *not* have any flashy or ostentatious frippery attached or built into it. This means shiny silver or metal parts (which look cool but also reflect light) or holes cut into the receiver (which lighten the gun but also allow dirt and grime inside).

If you're new to guns, you don't need to spend more than $1,000, but also shouldn't spend less than $500, for a good AR-15. If you spend more than $1,000, you're getting significantly fewer additional benefits for your money. If you spend less than $500, you'll probably get something of doubtful quality.

There are many, many different brands of AR-15, but here are some of the best options at different price points:

- Palmetto State Armory 16" AR-15 with M-Lok Handguard ($740)
- Smith & Wesson M&P15 Sport II ($752)
- Ruger AR-556 with Free-Float Handguard ($819)
- SIGM400 Tread ($949)
- Aero Precision M4E1 Complete Rifle (~$1,000)
- Bravo Company Manufacturing RECCE-16 MCMR Carbine ($1,400)
- Daniel Defense DDM4 V7 ($1,729)

- Radian Weapons Model 1 (~$2,600—the Rolls Royce of AR-15s)*

Alternatively, you can also buy a semiautomatic AK-47 variant (there are many different versions that fall under this umbrella, including the AKM, WASR-10, and others). I recommend an AR-15 instead of an AK-47 because they both cost about the same, but AR-15s have less recoil, are generally more accurate, are just as reliable (if well-maintained), are lighter, and are more easily customizable, should you want to upgrade parts of your gun later.

If you're interested in my recommendations for AK-47s and other AR-15 variants, like AR-15 pistols, check out the gear guide that came with the bonus material for this book at secondamendmentmanifesto.com/bonus.

In an ideal scenario, you'd have one kind of gun from each category: A pistol for concealed carry, a shotgun for home defense, and an AR-15 or AK-47 rifle for anything and everything fate throws at you. That said, if you're just getting into guns and look at them more as tools than collector's items, here's a piece of advice you can take to the bank—after you buy your first gun, it's much better to spend the rest of your budget on ammunition and professional training than getting another blaster (more on this in a moment).

Before you learn where to buy guns, how to store them, and what other gear you should get, it's worth learning the four simple but important rules of gun safety.

The Four Rules of Gun Safety

The four rules of gun safety, as defined by "the father of pistol shooting," Jeff Cooper, are as follows:

1. All guns are always loaded (you should treat every gun as if it's loaded at all times, even if you think it's unloaded).

2. Never let the muzzle cover anything you are not willing to destroy (or as my brother says, "Never point the noisy end at anything you care about").
3. Keep your finger off the trigger until your sights are on the target (the rest of the time, your finger should be off the trigger and resting on the side of the gun).
4. Be sure of your target and what is beyond it (bullets have a tendency to go through things, so make sure you know what's behind your target).

If you keep these four simple canons (harhar) in mind, you'll avoid ninety-nine percent of the potential accidents you might otherwise have with a gun. Although these four rules are the basis of effective gun safety, there are a few more pointers worth remembering, too:

1. When you pick up a gun, always check to see if it's loaded before doing anything else.
2. Keep your gun pointed at the ground until you're ready to shoot (except at indoor shooting ranges, where the gun should always be pointed downrange).
3. Always warn the people around you before you start shooting (again, except at a gun range, where this is impractical and unnecessary).
4. Only trust people to hold, borrow, or shoot guns if they've demonstrated that they know what they're doing or are under your direct supervision (so you can make sure they follow the Four Rules).
5. Wash your hands after handling a gun or ammunition. When you shoot a gun, small particles of lead from the bullet and the primer collect on the outside of the gun and your hands, face, and clothes. Even if you just touch a gun, but don't shoot it, lead particles from previous shooting sessions can get on your hands. Most cartridges also have traces of lead on the outside left over from manufacturing. Although the amounts are miniscule, it's still wise to do what you can to minimize lead exposure.

Chapter 11

Where to Buy Guns and Ammo

When it comes to buying guns, spend some time poking around online to see what guns will fit your budget. Then go to a local gun store, talk to the people who work there about your needs, and handle several different guns. Then buy one.

Don't waste too much time bargain hunting or trying to find the absolute "best" model. A well-made, well-maintained gun will probably last longer than you will, so prioritize quality over price. Guns also hold their value better than most gimcracks like cars, clothes, and furniture, so if you want to sell them in the future, you'll probably get a good chunk of your money back. As when shopping for anything, you'll also encounter a lot of marketing lingo pushing glittery features of dubious benefit. Don't get snookered. If you stick to the guns I recommended earlier in this chapter or others at a similar price point, you'll get the best value for your money.

What about online shopping? You can't have guns shipped directly to your house (c'est la vie), but you can buy guns online and have them shipped to your local gun store, where you can pick them up.

If you've never purchased a gun before, here's what to expect: You'll ask to buy a gun, the seller at the gun store will ask to see your ID and hand you a piece of paperwork called a Firearms Transaction Record, or Form 4473. This form asks you to answer a number of questions that determine whether or not you're eligible to buy a firearm, and to record your personal details so the seller can conduct a background check. In some states you'll also be asked to fill out another form for the state police which is used to conduct the background check.

The seller will conduct a background check, and if you pass, you can buy the gun. Sometimes, a background check can be delayed, usually when your name is similar to someone else's. In these cases you can either wait at the store or come back later to pick up the gun once the background check is completed (assuming you pass). In some states you may also have to wait several days to pick up your gun after you pass the background check. The main reasons people are prohibited from purchasing guns are due to serious criminal violations like felonies or violent misdemeanors. If you don't have any of these on your record, you're probably eligible to buy a gun.

When you're filling out a form 4473, you may come across a question you aren't sure how to answer. If so, don't get offended if the seller doesn't offer you any advice on how to answer the question—they aren't allowed to by federal law. The ATF wants to ensure that you're answering the questions truthfully, and will sometimes conduct undercover operations to make sure gun sellers are following the law.

The specifics of this process vary from state to state, so you may have to jump through a few additional hoops depending on where you live. The people at your local gun store will help guide you through the process.

How to Store Guns Safely

When most people, especially politicians, say "safe gun storage," they usually mean storing guns in a way that makes them as difficult to access as possible—locked in a safe, unloaded, and in some cases, disassembled.

While this kind of "safe" gun storage more or less eliminates the possibility of a child (or childish adult) accidentally hurting themselves or someone else with your guns or of a criminal stealing your guns, it also makes it much more difficult for you to access your guns in an emergency. And there's nothing "safe" about trying to load a gun or find the key to your gun safe while an armed intruder is stalking through your home.

What "safe gun storage" really means is striking the right balance between gun accessibility and security for your specific circumstances—a decision only you can make. You need to ask yourself, which scenario is more likely: someone stealing or improperly using my guns, or me needing to use a gun against a home-invader?

For example, I have one friend who lives alone in a one-room house in the middle of nowhere in the Texas desert. While the chances of someone breaking into his home are slim, it would also take the police at least half an hour to arrive—far too long to be of much help. Since he doesn't have any children or roommates, the risk of someone accidentally firing his gun is basically zero. Thus, he feels comfortable keeping a loaded AR-15 beside his bed. On the opposite extreme, I have another friend who lives in a fifth-floor apartment in San Francisco, a city with notoriously high rates of theft and burglary (something he's well aware of, being an ex-cop). He feels the risk of someone breaking into his home while he's away and stealing his guns is higher than the risk of a violent intruder attacking him in his home, and so he keeps all of his guns locked in a safe. And then, I have another friend who lives in a suburban neighborhood outside of Washington D.C. While crime rates are fairly low in his area, he also lives with two small children. Thus, he keeps most of his guns unloaded and locked in a safe, and one loaded pistol in a small push-button safe in a drawer next to his bed.

While only you can decide the best way to store your guns, here are a few guidelines that will work for most people in most circumstances.

Keep your guns unloaded and locked unless you plan on using them for self defense.

While every loaded gun could be an asset in an emergency, and it's easy to think that "more is better," remember that every loaded gun can also be a liability in the wrong hands. Thus, while it's fine to keep more than one gun loaded and ready to use, keep any guns you don't plan on using in a self-defense situation unloaded and, ideally, locked in a safe or secured with a trigger lock.

Keep your loaded self-defense gun(s) in a secure, easily accessible location.

If you feel the risk of someone stealing or misusing your guns is low, this could be as simple as keeping a loaded pistol in a bedside drawer. No matter where you live, though, it's a good idea to store your guns in a way that someone looking through a window wouldn't be able to see them. If you feel the risk of someone stealing or misusing your guns is high, you should keep your guns in a locked drawer, locked room, or, ideally, a safe.

If you carry a gun for self defense, keep it chambered and ready to shoot.

A "chambered" gun is one that has a cartridge loaded into the chamber and is ready to fire when you pull the trigger. Some people think that keeping a gun loaded but unchambered is safer, because you have to "cock" the gun before it can fire, but this is wrongheaded. In a life-threatening situation, you probably won't have time or the presence of mind to chamber a cartridge before shooting. Instead, you want to be able to draw, aim, and fire in one smooth motion. (Self-defense instructors often speak of a "rule of three," which states that most shootings involve three shots, at about three feet of distance, in about three seconds.)

Keep your guns in a safe or cabinet (if you can afford one).

Not everyone needs to store their guns in a safe, but it's a good idea if you live in a high-crime area or with small children or roommates. Even if these circumstances don't apply to you, though, it's a good idea to keep your guns in a safe or locked metal cabinet for peace of mind.

If your main concern is preventing family members, children, and guests at your house from accessing your guns, you don't necessarily need a safe—a locking metal storage cabinet will work just fine. If you want to protect your guns from theft, flooding, or fire damage, though, you'll need to get a safe.

When it comes to what kind of safe to get, the most important thing is that it can be opened using a push-button combination. While you can find many other opening methods nowadays (fingerprint scanner, Wi-Fi, Bluetooth, and RFID), and many safes use a mix of different methods, a push-button combination is the most reliable. The main drawback of push-button combination safes is that you have to remember the combination and then quickly enter it, but both of these problems can be overcome with training. Use a four-to-six character code that you can remember and then set a reminder on your phone or calendar to practice entering the code quickly once a day for a month. After that, practice once per week. You should practice until you can quickly enter the code and draw your gun in the dark, without looking at the keypad.

Here are some of the best safes for holding pistols:

- Vaultek VR10
- Vaultek VT20i (larger version with a fingerprint scanner)*
- Fort Knox FTK-PB

Here are some of the best safes for holding rifles and shotguns:

- Moutec 5-Gun Rifle Safe
- Liberty Centurion 12-, 18-, or 24- Gun Safe*
- SecureIt Agile Ultralight: Model 52 Plus

At this point you may be wondering, should you still buy a gun if you can't afford a safe?

Yes.

Even if you live in a high-crime area or with small children or roommates, you can still safely store a gun without buying a gun safe by following these steps:

1. Store any loaded guns in a locked drawer, closet, or room that only you have access to.
2. Store unloaded guns using a cable or trigger lock. A cable lock is a small loop of metal cable that you can push through the inside of the gun and then lock with a key, making it inoperable. All pistols sold in the U.S. come with a cable lock, and you can buy one for your rifle or shotgun for about $5. This won't prevent someone from stealing your gun if they break into your home, but it will prevent someone from accidentally or intentionally shooting your gun without your permission. A trigger lock works much the same way, except it blocks the trigger from being pulled.
3. Keep all of your guns—loaded and unloaded—out of sight.
4. Don't keep any of your guns in your car (cars are too easy to break into).

5. If you have children or roommates, teach them the four rules of gun safety you learned a moment ago.

How to Shoot a Gun Accurately

Before you ever go to the range, spend some time "dry-firing" your guns. Dry-firing is the practice of simulating the shooting of a gun but without any ammunition, so you can practice good shooting technique without needing to go to the range multiple times per week.

Dry firing involves charging the gun so the trigger is ready to be pulled, holding your gun the same way you would when shooting ammunition, aiming at something (such as a sticker on the wall), lining up your sights, and pulling the trigger. This may seem silly or pointless, but it's actually one of the most effective ways to quickly learn proper shooting technique, and it pays significant dividends when you practice with live ammunition.

The main things you want to focus on in your dry-fire practice are as follows:

Grip

This depends on the kind of gun you're using, but for modern semiautomatic pistols, it involves gripping the gun firmly with your "shooting hand" (the one pulling the trigger), and even firmer with your "support hand" (the one holding the other side of the pistol). If you shoot right-handed, your right hand is your shooting hand, and your left hand is your support hand. You should rest your support hand thumb as high as possible on the side of the pistol without touching the slide (which will move back and forth as the pistol fires).

Sight Alignment

This involves quickly pointing your gun at a target, lining up your sights on that target, and pulling the trigger without disturbing the alignment of the sights. You want to focus on putting the front sight on your target and then using your peripheral vision to manipulate the gun so that the rear sight lines up with the front sight.

Trigger Pull

This involves pulling the trigger of the gun quickly but smoothly—not jerking your finger back (which jars the gun and decreases accuracy). Many people have a tendency to flinch—gripping the gun and squeezing the trigger harder as they anticipate the noise and recoil of the gunshot. Instead, you want to maintain a firm, consistent grip on the gun, pull the trigger steadily backward, and let the gunshot "surprise" you.

After you get the hang of proper grip, sight alignment, and trigger pull, you want to start practicing other skills such as . . .

Fixing Malfunctions

Guns are machines, and like any machine, they can fail. Luckily, most failures are minor problems that are easily fixed in a matter of seconds, often without even putting the gun down.

For example, a common malfunction is known as *failure to eject* (FTE), where the casing is removed from the chamber but doesn't exit the gun, preventing the next cartridge from loading properly and "jamming" the slide or bolt open. In most cases, this is fixed by a little procedure known as "tap, rack, target." You "tap" the bottom of the magazine to make sure it's fully inserted into the gun, you "rack" the slide (on a pistol) or charging handle (on a rifle or shotgun) back to allow the empty cartridge to fall out and insert a new one, and you get back on "target" as quickly as possible. There are other malfunctions you should learn how to address eventually, but this little drill will fix most of them.

You can safely simulate these kinds of malfunctions and practice clearing them at home by buying some "snap caps," small pieces of plastic shaped like real cartridges but without any bullet, propellant, or primer. With these, you can intentionally cause your gun to fail and then practice quickly and efficiently fixing that failure. I like the Tipton 9mm snap caps for 9mm pistols and the St Action Pro .223 snap caps for .223 rifles.

Reloading

Reloading involves ejecting the empty magazine, grabbing a full one, inserting it into the gun, and releasing the slide or bolt of the gun to load a new cartridge from the full magazine. Ideally, you'd buy a shooting belt with magazine pouches to make reloading faster and easier, but you can also practice good reloading technique by putting a magazine in your pocket or on a table next to you. Do this on a carpeted floor—not hardwood or concrete—as the magazines can scratch your floor and vice versa as they fall out of the gun.

Drawing and Transitioning Between Targets

If you have a pistol with a holster, you should practice drawing and reholstering it until it's second nature. Remember that most violent encounters are over in a matter of seconds, so you want to be able to quickly draw your pistol, aim, fire, and then reholster if you need your hands for something else. You should also set up multiple targets and practice quickly moving your sights from one target to the next, while keeping your front and year sights aligned properly.

Chapter 11

Two 20-Minute Dry-Fire Routines You Can Do At Home

If you want to improve your shooting skills as fast as possible, try to practice dry-firing your guns at least three times per week for twenty or so minutes at a time (at least an hour per week). This is particularly important for improving your pistol technique, as it's much harder to learn how to shoot a pistol than it is to shoot a rifle. And if you're really gung-ho and want to progress even faster, dry-fire every day.

Here are two dry-fire routines that will help you get up to speed on the basics of rifle and pistol shooting. Each routine takes about twenty minutes to complete and touches on all three of the most important fundamentals—grip, sight alignment, and trigger pull. I recommend you schedule your dry-fire "workouts" ahead of time the same way you would any other important meeting. For example, you could schedule pistol dry-fire practice on Monday, rifle dry-fire practice on Wednesday, and pistol dry-fire practice again on Friday.

Before Every Dry-Fire Practice . . .

1. Check to make sure the chamber and magazine of your gun are empty of ammunition.
2. Attach a target to a wall that's about the size of a playing card and about chest height off the floor.
3. Stand about 10 to 15 feet in front of the target—your feet about shoulder-width apart and your chest facing the target.
4. "Cock" the gun by pulling the slide (on a pistol) or charging handle (on a rifle or shotgun) back, so that the trigger clicks when you squeeze it (again, make sure the gun isn't loaded). Since you aren't using live ammunition, you'll need to re-cock the gun each time after you pull the trigger.

Pistol Dry-Fire Routine

Drill #1: Using a proper, firm, two-handed grip, line up the sights on the target and hold them there for 5 seconds (make sure you really grip the gun hard, as if you were about to shoot), and then pull the trigger after your 5 seconds are up. The goal is to keep the sights lined up and within the edges of the target for the whole 5 seconds. After your 5 seconds are up, point the pistol at the ground and relax for about 30 seconds. Repeat a total of five times.

Drill #2: Hold the pistol with a proper grip directly in front of your chest, pointing toward your target. Quickly push the pistol forward so your arms are extended in front of you, line up the sights on the target, and hold them there for 3 seconds. After your 3 seconds are up, point the pistol at the ground and relax for about 30 seconds. Repeat a total of five times.

Drill #3: Do the same thing, except pull the trigger after your 3 seconds are up, making sure you keep the sights lined up on the target as you "fire" the gun. Repeat five times.

Rifle or Shotgun Dry-Fire Routine

Drill #1: Line up the sights on the target and hold them there for 5 seconds (make sure you really grip the gun hard, as if you were about to shoot), and then pull the trigger after your 5 seconds are up. The goal is to keep the sights lined up and within the edges of the target for the whole 5 seconds. After your 5 seconds are up, point the gun at the ground and relax for about 30 seconds. Repeat a total of 5 times.

Drill #2: Hold the rifle in what's known as the "low ready" position, with the stock braced against your shoulder and the barrel of the gun pointed down toward the floor at about a 30-degree angle. Quickly bring the rifle up to eye level, line up the sights on the target, and hold them there for 3 seconds, keeping the sights within the edges of the target. Return the rifle to the low ready position and rest about 30 seconds. Repeat 5 times.

Drill #3: Do the same thing, except pull the trigger after your 3 seconds are up, making sure you keep the sights lined up on the target as you "fire" the gun. Repeat 5 times.

As your skills improve, you can make these drills more difficult by . . .

- Using a smaller target
- Standing farther away from your target
- Doing more repetitions
- Doing the same drills faster
- Doing more complex drills to practice clearing malfunctions, reloading, drawing, and transitioning between targets

If you want to further burnish your ballistic skills, check out the following YouTube channels, which are a wealth of information on proper shooting technique:

- T. Rex Arms (secondamendmentmanifesto.com/trex)
- Garand Thumb (secondamendmentmanifesto.com/garandthumb)
- Greyhive (secondamendmentmanifesto.com/greyhive)
- Chris Sajnog (secondamendmentmanifesto.com/chris)
- National Shooting Sports Foundation (secondamendmentmanigesto.com/nssf)

While dry-fire practice will improve many aspects of your shooting technique, there's no replacement for shooting live ammunition, also known as "live firing." Live fire training tests and polishes the skills you develop while dry-firing and teaches you how to control recoil and not flinch while pulling the trigger (and it's fun).

Once you have some experience shooting live ammo, the next best thing is to take a shooting class. You can learn a lot from trained instructors, and most classes are not terribly expensive ($100 to $300 for a two to eight hour class). Search for "shooting classes" or "pistol/rifle classes" near you in any search engine, and ask your local gun store for recommendations. There are also a number of excellent training companies who offer classes around the United States as well, including:

- Baer Solutions
- Capable Incorporated
- Haley Strategic Partners
- Rune Nation
- Centrifuge Training
- Tactical Response
- Dark Angel Medical
- Viking Tactics

If you want to further enhance your skills, here are several good books on proper shooting technique:

- *How to Shoot Like a Navy SEAL: Combat Marksmanship Fundamentals* by Chris Sajnog
- *Green Eyes & Black Rifles: Warrior's Guide to the Combat Carbine* by Kyle Lamb
- *DryFire Reloaded* by Ben Stoeger
- *The Long Range Shooting Handbook* by Ryan Cleckner (In case you want to explore long-range precision shooting).

You can also find links to videos demonstrating all of the techniques in this chapter by downloading the free bonus materials that came with this book at secondamendmentmanifesto.com/bonus.

Chapter 11

How to Legally Carry a Gun in Public

Thanks to court cases like *D.C. v. Heller*, you're allowed to have a gun inside your home in nearly every state in the U.S. (though the kind of guns you're allowed to own and the storage requirements still vary).

If you want to carry your gun when you're out and about, though, things get more complicated. There are basically two options for carrying a gun: "concealed" carry and "open" carry. Concealed carry is exactly what it sounds like: The practice of carrying a concealed firearm on one's person in public. Typically, the firearm needs to be hidden under clothing so that someone looking at you couldn't easily tell you're carrying a gun. In most states, you need to obtain a concealed weapons permit before you can legally concealed carry. This typically involves taking an online or in-person test to prove you know basic gun laws and safety practices, filling out some paperwork, paying a fee, and waiting a few weeks (or years, in the case of California). In some states, like Connecticut, Maryland, and Hawaii, you have to convince state authorities that you have a compelling reason to carry a gun before they'll grant you a concealed weapons permit (known as "may issue" states). In other states, like Nevada, Virginia, and Montana, you're automatically entitled to a concealed-carry permit if you meet the criteria and properly submit the application (known as "shall issue" states).

Open carry is also exactly what it sounds like: The practice of carrying a gun openly on your person, such as in a holster on your hip in the case of a pistol or slung across your shoulder in the case of a rifle.

Whether you're allowed to open or concealed carry and what guns you're allowed to carry depends on your state and local laws. What's more, many states and counties have differing rules about whether you can carry a gun in your car or into a bar, whether you're required to notify a police officer that you have a gun on you if you interact with police, whether you can legally ignore "no weapons" signs posted outside businesses, and other specific restrictions. These laws often change, too, so it's important to look up the regulations in your area before you open or concealed carry.

Another wrinkle is that getting a concealed weapons permit in one state doesn't automatically mean you can carry a gun in other states. Although many states have reciprocity agreements, where they'll honor concealed weapons permits from other states, not all states do. Thus, if you want to carry a weapon outside of the state where your permit was issued, you need to carefully check the gun laws of any other states you'll be visiting.

Some of the best resources for finding this information include:

- gunstocarry.com

    This website features a clickable map of the United States that shows you the specific gun laws for each state and which states honor concealed-carry permits from other states.

- usconcealedcarry.com

    This website is more or less the same as gunstocarry.com, although it also shows you stats for concealed weapons permits for each state.

- usacarry.com

    This website has detailed information about the process of getting a concealed-carry permit in every state.

Gun Accessories Worth Buying

In addition to purchasing a gun, there are two "need to have" and eleven "nice to have" accessories you should consider buying.

The "need to have" accessories are:

1. Ammunition
2. Ear and eye protection

And the "nice to have" accessories are:

1. Rifle and pistol sights
2. Holster
3. Cleaning kit
4. Gun bag or case
5. Medical supplies
6. Extra magazines
7. Rifle sling
8. Weapon light
9. Belt
10. Magazine pouches and carriers
11. Body armor

Ammunition

When you buy your gun, you'll also want to get some ammunition ("ammo"). You can roughly divide ammunition into two categories:

- "Fancy" ammo, which is expensive, high-quality, very reliable ammo that's typically used for competitions, self-defense, hunting, and the like.
- "Cheap" ammo, which is more affordable, lower-quality, reasonably reliable ammo that's typically used for target practice, training, and fun.

You should get some of both. Specifically, you should get at least one box (usually 25 to 50 cartridges) of the fancy ammo. This kind of ammo tends to be very expensive (at least $1 to $2 per cartridge), but it's worth the cost. It's exceptionally reliable, slightly more accurate, and causes far more damage (and thus eliminates the threat more quickly) than cheap ammo. You don't need to buy very much, though, because you just need enough to keep your self-defense gun (or guns) loaded.

Some good options include:

- Hornady Critical Defense*
- Federal Personal Defense HST
- Speer Gold Dot
- Magtech Guardian Gold
- Fiocchi Shooting Dynamics

Most of these brands make ammunition for rifles as well as pistols. If your local store or online shop doesn't have these in stock, ask their customer support team for help in picking something comparable. When picking pistol and rifle ammunition, make sure the bullets are what are known as *jacketed hollow points*, which are much more effective than regular bullets. When picking shotgun ammunition, get buckshot, preferably "double-aught" buckshot.

You should also buy a few hundred cartridges of cheap ammo to practice with. This will usually cost around twenty to forty cents per cartridge, making it much more affordable to shoot than fancy ammo.

Some good options include:

- CCI Blazer
- Aguila
- Brown Bear, Silver Bear, and Golden Bear
- Tulammo
- Armscor
- PMC Bronze

In most respects, you won't be able to tell any difference between cheap ammo and fancy ammo. You may get more jams or misfires (the cartridge doesn't fire when it should) with cheap ammo, but these should be pretty rare regardless of what ammo you buy. The one exception is the Winchester USA Forged ammo, often sold in bulk. It's coated in a powdery wax-like substance that causes jams in many different kinds of pistols (almost everything except Glocks, in my experience). Don't buy it.

One thing to keep in mind is that cheap ammo tends to "kick" a little less than fancy ammo, because manufacturers use less gunpowder to save money, so it's worth firing a few cartridges of fancy ammo every few months so you're familiar with how it feels when shooting.

You may be wondering, why not use cheap ammo instead of fancy ammo even "when it counts?" Several reasons:

1. Although most kinds of cheap ammo are fairly reliable, fancy ammo almost never jams or misfires when used in a well-maintained, modern gun, like the ones listed earlier in this chapter. When you're in a life or death situation, the last thing you want to hear is "click" when you pull the trigger (and it could be the last thing you hear).
2. Fancy ammo tends to be a little more accurate. The difference is small, but any little advantage helps.
3. Most importantly, fancy ammo is *much* more lethal. Typically, the bullets are designed to expand, break apart, or tumble after entering the target, which causes much more damage to the person you're shooting at. While this sounds grisly, it's exactly what you want. If you're in a situation where shooting someone makes sense—when your life or someone else's is at stake—you want to subdue the attacker with as few shots as possible to eliminate the threat as quickly as possible and minimize the chances of hitting an innocent bystander. That means using the deadliest ammo you can.

When weighed in the balance, the best solution is to practice with cheap ammo, which allows you to shoot more often and more affordably, thus allowing you to become a better shot, and always keep your self-defense gun (or guns) loaded with fancy ammo.

When it comes to buying ammo, try to find the best deal you can, then buy a bunch at one time. It's much better to get a bit more than you'll think you need than realize halfway through your first day at the range that you're about to "go Winchester," as Airforce pilots say. A good minimum would be 500 cartridges per rifle or pistol, and about half that for shotguns. That's enough to last you a few trips to the gun range, assuming you have multiple guns and aren't just blasting away the whole time.

Follow the Warren Buffet strategy of investing when purchasing ammo: Buy when demand and prices are low, and don't buy when demand and prices are high. Ammo prices often rise and fall based on major political elections and the degree of civil unrest in the country. For example, ammo and gun prices skyrocketed around the time of Obama's election in 2008 (due to fears of new gun laws), at the beginning of the COVID-19 pandemic, and during the George Floyd riots, with many guns and ammo types doubling in price or going out of stock. It's much better to spend a few hundred bucks and "lock in" a good price on a large stash of ammo that you can use over the course of several months to a year, than pay twice as much for the same ammo in a crisis—or be unable to buy ammo at all.

Local gun stores and gun shows often have good prices on common ammo types such as 9 mm, .223 Remington, 12-gauge shotgun, and .308 Winchester. Although you can often find good deals on ammo when shopping online, make sure you reckon shipping costs, too, which can be high.

Here are several helpful websites for finding the best prices on ammo:

- wikiarms.com/deals/ammo
- ammopile.com/
- ammoseek.com/

Ear and Eye Protection ("Ears and Eyes")

If you don't wear hearing protection while shooting, you *will* get hearing damage. Any cheap over-the-ear protection will work (the same kind you might wear while mowing the lawn).

In-ear foam earplugs are fine if you're using a relatively quiet gun like a .22 rifle or 9 mm pistol, but you should use over-the-ear protection for maximum hearing protection and always when shooting high-powered rifles and shotguns like AR-15s, AK-47s, and Mossberg 500s. If you plan on shooting regularly, invest in a pair of electronic ear protection. These block loud noises like gunshots or explosions, but allow you to hear quieter noises like a person's voice. The most popular entry-level model is the Howard Leight Impact Sport electronic earmuffs, which you can get for about $50 on Amazon.

Personally, I like to use both in-ear foam earplugs and electronic hearing protection over my ears. This means my ears are fully insulated against noise from high-powered rifles, but I can also dial up the volume if I'm using quieter guns and want to communicate with the people around me.

Eye protection is also a must when shooting. Although most modern guns and ammunition are well made and accidents are rare, they can happen. Burning gunpowder or hot gun oil from an overpowered cartridge can fly back in your face; dirt or dust blown up in the air could stick in your eye; or a metal fragment from a bullet or target could come back and hit you (very, very rare, unless you're standing right in front of the target, but a possibility nonetheless).

You don't need to buy anything fancy. If you're shooting outside in bright conditions, you can use any pair of sunglasses. If you're shooting inside, though, you'll need to get a pair of clear plastic eyeglasses, which usually cost around $10 to $20. I like the Howard Leight Uvex Acadia shooting glasses. And if you wear prescription glasses, just wear those (contacts don't count!).

Rifle and Pistol Sights

A sight is a device that helps you accurately aim a gun, and you can broadly divide sights into two categories:

1. *Iron sights*, which consist of a front sight and a rear sight that you

align over the target.
2. *Optics*, which is a loose term that includes more or less everything that isn't an iron sight, including scopes, red dot sights, holographic sights, thermal scopes, and more.

There are several different variations of iron sights, with the main ones being:

- Night sights, which incorporate small fiber optic rods or vials of a radioactive substance called *tritium* that glow in the dark so you can accurately shoot with minimal ambient light. They're designed so that only you can easily see the sights, so they won't give away your position to an attacker. (And don't worry—the amount of radiation released from these little tritium vials isn't nearly enough to harm you).
- Folding sights, which are just like regular iron sights except they can be folded down when you aren't using them and quickly flipped back up when you need them. These are usually used on rifles as a backup in case your red dot or holographic sight breaks or runs out of battery. You'll often see these marketed as *backup iron sights* (BUIS).

Most pistols come with regular iron sights installed, but I recommend you replace these with night sights as soon as you can. Night sights not only allow you to accurately shoot at night, they're easier to see during the day, better made than most factory iron sights, and aren't terribly expensive. Some companies, like SIG, Glock, and CZ, also offer pistols with night sights pre-installed.

Go with tritium night sights if you can afford them—they're more durable than fiber optic ones. Here are some of the best brands of tritium night sights, all of which cost between $60 and $130:

- Trijicon
- Ameriglo

- Meprolight
- XS DXT2
- TRUGLO

(I would recommend specific models, but which night sights you should buy depends on your pistol, as not all manufacturers make night sights that are compatible with every pistol brand).

Most rifles don't come with sights, as people generally prefer to buy their own. I recommend you get a red dot or holographic sight as your main sight, and get a pair of folding iron sights as a backup. Some of the best folding iron sights are:

- Magpul MBUS Front and Rear Sight ($98)
- Magpul MBUS Pro Front and Rear Sight ($190, almost the same as their MBUS Sights, but made of metal instead of plastic)*
- Geissele Folding Front and Rear BUIS ($200)
- Ultradyne C4 Folding Front and Rear Sight ($249)

When it comes to optics, you have a few options to choose from:

- Red dot sights, aka "red dots," which are electronic sights that reflect a red or green light onto a tiny mirror inside the sight, creating a small dot (known as a *reticle*), that you line up with the target.
- Holographic sights, aka "holographic weapon sights (HWS)," which use a laser and series of prisms to project a reticle onto a piece of glass in front of your eye.
- Low-powered variable optics (LPVOs), which use a series of lenses to magnify your target and make it easier to see.

Red dot sights are simpler and lighter than holographic sights or LPVOs, and are known for their exceptional durability and battery life (generally 50,000 hours, or about 5 years of continuous use). Holographic sights provide a wider window through which you can see your target (known as "field of view"), reticle designs that make it easier to get on target, and most importantly, allow you to see the reticle even if your eye isn't lined up with it perfectly (which isn't the case with red dot sights). That said, which one you choose comes down to your personal preferences. For my part, I feel that the light weight, durability, and battery life of red dot sights outweighs the advantages of holographic sights, but I like, use, and trust both designs.

Both red dot and holographic sights are what's known as 1x sights, which means they don't magnify the target at all. When you look through the sight, the target appears to be at exactly the same distance as it would when viewed with your naked eye. This makes these sights ideal for shooting targets within about 150 meters, or one-and-a-half football fields away.

But what if you want to "reach out and touch someone," as the cool kids say? That's where LVPOs come into play. These are basically very durable rifle scopes that make it easy to adjust the magnification up or down as needed, usually from one to six magnification (usually written as 1-6x). For example, when adjusted to its maximum setting, a 1-6x scope will make the target appear six times closer than it really is. Most LVPOs also feature an illuminated reticle, just like a red dot, which makes it easy to quickly get on target.

The advantage of LPVOs is that they allow you to shoot targets at close range, just like you would with a red dot or holographic sight, but also accurately shoot targets several hundred meters away, using your gun like a sniper rifle. The downsides of LPVOs are that they're much heavier and bulkier than red dot or holographic sights, they're much more expensive, and the batteries don't usually last as long. (That said, most LPVOs also have a reticle etched into the glass of the scope, so you can still use them if the battery dies.) And although they work well at close range, it usually takes longer to get on target with an LPVO than it does with a red dot or holographic sight.

So, what should you buy? If you're new to shooting, get a red dot or holographic sight. If you have some experience shooting, want to use your rifle for long-range shooting, or have moolah burning a hole in your pocket, get an LPVO.

Some of the best red dot sights are:

- Bushnell TRS-25 ($147)
- Sig Sauer Romeo5 1x20 mm ($180)
- Holosun HS403C ($242) or HS403C-GR ($259, if you want a green reticle)
- Trijicon MRO ($579)
- Aimpoint Micro T-2 ($869)*
- Aimpoint Comp M5S ($991)

Some of the best holographic sights are:

- EoTech EXPS2 ($599, not night vision compatible)*
- EoTech EXPS3 ($699, night vision compatible)
- Vortex AMG UH-1 Gen II ($800)
- Leupold Carbine Optic ($910)

And some of the best LPVOs are:

- Primary Arms SLx 1-6x24 ($290)
- Burris R-T6 1-6x24 ($419)
- Vortex Razon HD Gen-II 1-6x24 ($2000)
- Kahles K16i 1-6x24 ($2,000)*
- Swarovski Z6i 1-6x24 ($2,254)
- Nightforce ATACR 1-8x24 ($2,800)
- Leupold Mark 6 1-6x20 ($2,860)
- Vortex Razor HD Gen-III 1-10x24 ($2,900)
- Schmidt Bender 1-8x24 PM II ($4,390)

While holographic sights usually come with a mount to attach it to your rifle, that's not always the case with red dot sights or LPVOs. If you need to buy a mount, here are some of the best for red dot sights:

- Reptilia Dot Mount ($95)
- Geissele Super Precision T1 Mount ($120)
- Scalarworks LEAP Red Dot Mount ($149)*

And here are some of the best mounts for LPVOs:

- Badger Ordnance Condition One Modular Mount ($305)
- Geissele Super Precision AR15/M4 Scope Mount ($325)
- Scalarworks LEAP Scope Mount ($400)*

You can also get red dot sights for pistols, but unless you're already very skilled using iron sights, I don't recommend you get one. High-quality pistol red dot sights are expensive, and you're better off spending that money on ammunition, training, or any of the other gear listed in this chapter first. That said, if you either already have all of this stuff or want to ignore my advice, here are some good options:

- Vortex Viper ($350)
- Leupold Deltapoint Pro ($400)
- Holosun HE508T-RD V2 ($435)
- Trijicon RMR Type 2 ($550)
- Trijicon SRO ($530)*
- Aimpoint ACRO P-1 ($667)

Holster

If you plan on carrying a pistol on your person or in your vehicle, you should buy a holster.

While modern pistols have multiple safety mechanisms to ensure that the gun only fires when the trigger is pulled, you still need to keep the trigger covered when you aren't using the gun. If you throw your pistol into your pocket with your keys, for instance, it's possible that the keys could press against the trigger of the gun, resulting in a very, very unpleasant experience. The same thing is true of throwing a gun into a glove compartment, backpack, or crowded bedside table. As a general rule, if you have a pistol, it should be in a case or holster whenever it's not in your hand.

When it comes to what kind of holster you buy, I recommend you buy a holster made out of a hard plastic called Kydex. It's durable, cheap, and most importantly, allows holster manufacturers to perfectly fit the holster to your gun. The downside is this means you need to place a custom order from a holster manufacturer and wait a few days or weeks for it to arrive, but it's worth it. Most good holsters will cost around $50 to $100—be wary of anything that costs less than this, as cheaper models often won't fit your gun properly or hold up over time.

Before you buy a holster, you'll also need to decide what kind of holster you want to buy. Broadly speaking, there are two categories of holsters:

1. Inside the waistband (IWB) holsters
2. Outside the waistband (OWB) holsters

An inside the waistband holster is designed to fit between your underwear and the inside of your pants, and typically fastens to your belt using a small plastic or metal clip. You can wear an IWB holster in a variety of positions, but most experts recommend the *appendix* position. Basically, the holster goes right above your naughty bits. While this sounds dangerous, if you're using a modern pistol with a good holster (like the ones listed in this chapter), the risk of shooting yourself in the nethers or anywhere else is basically zero. This makes the pistol easy to conceal and draw and allows you to comfortably sit down in a chair (not easy if you wear the pistol on the back side of your waist).

An outside-the-waistband holster is designed to be worn hanging from the outside of your belt, typically resting against the side of your hip or thigh. These are useful for practicing at a shooting range or taking a class, but if you plan on open-carrying a pistol in public, you'll want to make sure you get a holster that also has some form of *active-retention*. This means there's a mechanism inside the holster that holds the pistol in place, only allowing it to be drawn when you press a small lever on the holster. This prevents other people from snatching your pistol out of your holster while still allowing you to quickly draw your gun.

There's an entire cottage industry of high-quality holster manufacturers to choose from, but here are some of my favorites:

- T-Rex Arms
- Tier 1 Concealed
- ANR Design
- Dara Holsters
- Vedder Holsters

Specifically, here are some of the best inside-the-waistband holsters:

- T. Rex Arms Raptor ($65)* or Sidecar ($105)
- Tier 1 Concealed Xiphos ($65)
- ANR Design Appendix Lightbearing with Claw ($85)

Here are some of the best outside-the-waistband holsters:

- Tier 1 Concealed Optio ($65)
- T. Rex Arms Ragnarok ($70)*
- ANR Design Tactical Lightbearing ($100)

And if you plan on openly-carrying a pistol, do yourself a favor and buy a Safariland ALS holster (~$200). These are by far the best on the market and are widely considered *the* standard among the military and law enforcement. They won't work with every pistol model, but they're compatible with most of the pistol brands listed earlier in this chapter.

If you insist on keeping a gun in your pocket (not recommended) and don't want to use a hard plastic holster, you can also buy a padded holster,

Chapter 11

which is better than nothing. Sticky Holsters is a good company if you want to go down this route.

Cleaning Kit

You don't need to buy a cleaning kit when you purchase a gun, but you'll probably want one eventually, so it's best to get one at the same time you buy a gun. At minimum, a gun cleaning kit should contain the following items:

- Gun oil
- Solvent
- Cleaning rod(s)
- Cleaning patches
- Instructions

Some good cleaning kits and tools are the:

- Hoppe's M-Pro 7 ($12) or #9 ($10) Gun Cleaner
- Hoppe's #9 Gun Lubricant ($2.5)
- Hoppe's .22 Rifle Cleaning Kit ($15)
- Real Avid Gun Boss Handgun Cleaning Kit ($27)
- Allen Co Toolbox Cleaning Kit ($65)
- The Otis Elite ($149)

If you don't want to buy the full kit right away, you can also make do with just a bottle of gun oil and some paper towels. Wipe off any obvious crud and apply a few drops of oil to any moving parts inside your gun after each time you shoot, and call it a day.

Gun Bag or Case

A gun bag or case protects your guns from damage, makes them easier to store, and reduces the chances of a passerby making a fuss about you carrying a gun. Many shooting ranges also require you to keep your guns in a case or holster until you're ready to shoot.

I recommend you buy a soft case for rifles and shotguns and a hard case for pistols.

Some good soft rifle cases:

- Bulldog Extreme Rectangle Discreet Rifle Case, 35-inch ($78)*
- Savior Equipment American Classic Tactical Double Rifle Case, 36" to 55" ($69 to $105)
- Haley Strategic Incog Rifle Carbine Bag ($170)

And some good hard rifle cases:

- Plano Pro-Max® Contoured Rifle Case ($35)
- Plano Rusticator AW2 36" Rifle Case ($120)
- Pelican V730 Vault Tactical Rifle Case ($190)*

Most pistols comes with a hard case, but if yours didn't, some good ones are the:

- Plano Protector Series® Single Pistol Case ($10)
- Pelican V200 Vault Medium Pistol Case ($58)*
- Plano AW2™ Two-Pistol Case ($60) and Four-Pistol Case ($80)

Medical Supplies

If you own a gun, and especially if you carry one, then you're probably the kind of person who likes to be prepared. And whether you own guns

Chapter 11

or not, accidents happen. You get into a car accident; you slip on an icy sidewalk; you try to take a selfie with a bison ... you get the idea. And as you've learned in this book, there are people in the world who may try to harm you or those around you, and one day they may succeed.

Whether you're injured accidentally or intentionally, you'll want to have a first-aid kit close at hand. A *real* first-aid kit—not the little bags of band-aids and antibacterial cream you'll find in the camping aisle at Walmart. While these "boo-boo" kits are worth having, they aren't going to save your life if you nick an artery or puncture a lung. Luckily, there are medical kits that will do just that.

Before we go over what you want in your medical kit, though, it's important to understand that none of what follows is a substitute for hands-on first-aid training, which I recommend you get. This is particularly true of some of the more complex tools, like decompression needles. That said, it's still wise to have these supplies on hand even if you haven't received first-aid training for two reasons:

1. It's always possible someone who *does* have medical training could put your first-aid kit to good use.
2. Although professional medical training will improve your ability to use these tools effectively, some of them are pretty straightforward and using them imperfectly is still often better than not using them at all.

Here are the five "must have" tools you want in your first-aid kit:

- Tourniquet
- Hemostatic bandage
- Wound dressing
- Chest seal
- Surgical gloves

One more thing: Remember that if you're seriously injured, first aid is just the *first* step in saving your life. The tools and techniques in this section are meant to keep you alive long enough to make it to a hospital where a doctor can patch you up. After you take the preliminary steps described below to save yourself, call 911 or get someone else to do so ASAP.

Tourniquet

A tourniquet is a small loop of cloth that's designed to be tightened around a limb to stop bleeding through a severed vein or artery. The goal is to reduce blood loss so you can survive long enough to make it to a hospital, where doctors can use other methods to staunch the bleeding and keep you alive. Most tourniquets are made of a strap of plastic webbing with a small plastic lever attached that you can use to tighten the webbing around a limb.

You only need to use a tourniquet in cases where major arteries in your arms or legs have been severed, but if that happens, you *need* to use a tourniquet. For example, if your femoral (thigh) or brachial (upper arm) arteries are punctured, you can bleed to death in a matter of minutes. By wrapping a tourniquet around the limb three to four inches above the wound and cinching it down, you can stop the bleeding and save your own life. (If you get shot in the chest, belly, groin, or head, a tourniquet won't help you, but the other items on this list will).

The two most popular kinds of tourniquets are the Combat Application Tourniquet (CAT) and the SOFTT-W, both of which have been used extensively by the military. They're durable, affordable, and most importantly, can be tightened and secured with one hand (in case your other one is hors de combat). Get whichever one you can find, read the instructions, and practice on yourself a few times to make sure you know how to use it. Both of these cost about $30.

Hemostatic Bandage

A *hemostatic* substance reduces bleeding, so a hemostatic bandage is a cloth bandage that's been impregnated with a hemostatic (the most common hemostatic is *kaolin*, a kind of clay). Hemostatic bandages not only reduce bleeding by blocking the wound, they also promote the blood's natural clotting ability, which reduces bleeding much faster than regular bandages.

The most well-known and highly-rated brand of hemostatic bandage is QuickClot. Their products are expensive, but if you're ever injured badly enough to warrant using one of their bandages, you probably won't regret the $40 you spent on one. I recommend their Combat Gauze Z-fold, which comes in pre-sealed foil packages.

To use a hemostatic bandage, you should follow the instructions on the package, but the gist is this: You rip open the package, unravel the bandage, push it directly into the wound, using all of the gauze, and then hold it there with firm, consistent pressure for at least three minutes. Then, you wrap a wound dressing around the hemostatic bandage to keep it in place.

Wound Dressing

Also known as a pressure dressing, this is simply a roll of elastic cloth, usually with a sterile gauze pad attached in the middle, which is designed to be wrapped around a wound to apply pressure and reduce bleeding. Typically, wound dressings are designed to be used in conjunction with a hemostatic bandage like QuickClot. The hemostatic reduces bleeding by encouraging clotting, and the wound dressing holds the hemostatic in place and provides consistent pressure, so clotting can continue and the wound doesn't reopen. These usually cost about $5 to $10. I recommend the Flat Emergency Trauma Dressing (ETD) from North American Rescue, which costs $7.

Chest Seal

A chest seal is a thin sheet of plastic with a strong adhesive on one side that's used to seal a gunshot wound (or any other kind) to the chest. Basically, it's like a tire patch for your torso.

When someone is shot in the chest, this often creates what's called a *sucking chest wound*. What this means is that when the person breathes in, some air enters the chest through the bullet hole instead of the mouth, which prevents the lungs from properly inflating. This can quickly cause a condition known as *tension pneumothorax*, where air inside the chest cavity interferes with proper lung function (more on this in a moment). This causes a rapid decrease in oxygen to the brain, and eventually, death.

One of the simplest ways to avoid this problem is by quickly sealing the puncture wound in the chest with an airtight, plastic bandage—a chest seal. These typically cost $10 to $15 and are sold as a pair: One for the entry wound, and one for the exit wound (if there is one). I recommend the Hyphin Vent Chest Seal Twin Pack, which costs $12.

Surgical Gloves

Your hands are one of the germiest parts of your body, and if you're touching someone with an open wound, wearing a pair of gloves ensures your grubby paws don't infect them. These usually cost a few cents per pair.

In addition to these five essentials—a tourniquet, hemostatic bandage, wound dressing, chest seal, and surgical gloves—there are eight more "nice to have" items worth including in your medical kit if you don't mind spending a little more money.

Nasopharyngeal Airway (NPA)

Also known as a "nose hose," this is a small, flexible plastic tube that can be inserted into someone's nose to ensure they can breathe even if they lose consciousness.

When someone zonks out, the muscles in their jaw relax, which could allow their tongue to flop backward and seal off their pharynx (the part of your throat that leads to the stomach and lungs), suffocating them. An NPA ensures the tongue can't block this essential passageway so that the person is still able to breathe even if they're out cold.

Unlike all of the other items you've learned about so far, you can't use this on yourself. The reason for carrying it is so you can use it on someone else who passes out or, if you pass out, so someone can use it on you. These usually cost about $5 to $10. I recommend the Nasopharyngeal Airway with Lubricant from North American Rescue.

Decompression Needle

Let's say someone has a puncture wound in their chest. You've applied the chest seal, but maybe some air already snuck into their chest and deflated one of their lungs. What do you do now? In this case, you need to release the air from inside their chest cavity so their lung can properly inflate, and the best way to do this is with a device known as a *decompression needle*. This is a long, thin needle that's inserted into the chest which acts like a little escape valve, allowing the excess air to leave the chest cavity so the lung can inflate.

Although you shouldn't use a decompression needle unless you're trained to use it, having one is still beneficial in case someone you're with knows how to use it. I recommend the SPEAR decompression needle from North American Rescue, which costs $46.

Medical Tape and Duct Tape

Medical tape is useful for bandaging small cuts that don't warrant a wound dressing, and for securing a wound dressing so it doesn't come undone. Duct tape is helpful for all of the same reasons. It's less comfortable and doesn't breathe as well as medical tape, but it's also more water resistant and can be used to fix anything from ripped pants to the fender of the Lunar Rover on the Apollo 17 expedition (seriously).

Frog Tape is a popular brand of medical tape because it comes in small, pre-cut strips that lie flat and don't take up much space, but any kind of medical tape will do. In the case of duct tape, make a small roll about a half inch to an inch in diameter instead of bringing along an entire roll. You can buy a roll of duct tape or a few strips of Frog Tape for about $5.

Burn Dressing

It's easy to burn your leg or hand on a hot gun barrel (or lawnmower engine, stove, and so forth). While most of us probably just shrug it off and accept that we're going to have an ugly, painful patch of skin for a few days, there are medicines that can reduce the pain, damage, and scarring caused by burns.

A burn dressing is a bandage that's been impregnated with one of these medicines so you can easily apply it to burned skin. While burn dressings don't make burned skin heal faster, they help reduce scarring and allow the skin to quickly repair itself without being disturbed. They're also designed to let the wound breathe while protecting it from infection.

You don't need to apply burn dressing to small, minor burns (like if a hot cartridge casing lands on your arm), but it's a good idea to carry at least one burn dressing for large, severe burns (like if someone accidently brushes a hot gun barrel against your leg). I recommend the Burntec Burn 4x4-inch dressing, which costs about $5.

Trauma Shears

If someone has a serious injury, you can't treat it if it's hidden under several layers of clothing. Taking the time to undress the person wastes precious seconds and can disturb the wound, so it's best to cut the clothing away from the wound with a pair of trauma shears—scissors that are designed for exactly this purpose. These usually cost about $10. I recommend the North American Rescue Trauma Shears, which cost $11.

Antibiotic Ointment

It's easy to get small cuts, nicks, and pricks doing just about anything, whether it's making dinner or loading a pistol magazine. When this happens, putting a little antibiotic ointment on the cut is a good insurance policy against infection. You don't need to be a hypochondriac and apply this to every papercut or cracked cuticle, but a good rule of thumb is that if the cut is bleeding, it's worth using antibiotic ointment. You can buy antibiotic ointment as a spray or a gel, but I recommend the Neosporin Neo To Go spray, which costs about $5.

Band-Aids

The main reasons to use band-aids aren't to stop a wound from bleeding or to help it heal faster—they don't do either job well. Instead, the main reasons to use band-aids are to prevent dirt from getting in the wound, protect the wound while a scab forms, and to soak up blood and plasma that escapes from the wound so it doesn't get on your clothes or gross out your friends.

First-Aid Pouch

In terms of how you store all of this gear, most people "in the know" like to organize it in a small cloth pouch that you can carry on your belt or throw in a backpack or glovebox. The main benefit of these medical pouches is they're easy to carry and won't burst if you drop them or smoosh them under other gear. The downside is they can be bulky and are more expensive than other options. If you don't want to buy a cloth medical pouch, you can use a gallon-size Ziploc bag instead.

I recommend the following pouches:

- T. Rex Arms Med1 Pouch ($45)*
- Blue Force Gear Micro Trauma Kit NOW! Pouch ($69.95)
- North American Rescue Ocho Mesh Aid Pouch ($24.99)

Where to Buy Medical Supplies

You can buy all of these items separately, or you can buy them as a pre-assembled kit. You may be able to save a few dollars by buying everything separately, but I recommend you buy a kit. Most pre-assembled medical kits come in a custom-fit pouch that's easy to carry and can be opened quickly with one hand. Most medical kits don't include a tourniquet, because tourniquets tend to be bulky and many people like to store them outside their medical kit for easier access.

Here are some of the medical kits I recommend:

- T. Rex Arms Individual Trauma Response Kit ($62)
    This kit includes a hemostatic bandage, wound dressing, two chest seals, and surgical gloves, and is meant to be a minimalist kit that you can keep in a pocket, gun bag, and glovebox, and so forth. It comes in a vacuum-sealed plastic pouch.

- T. Rex Arms Med1 Kit ($145)*
    This kit includes a hemostatic bandage, wound dressing, NPA, Burntec burn dressing, two chest seals, gauze, and a CAT tourniquet, and comes in a compact cloth pouch that's easy to carry on your belt. Unlike most medical kits, this also includes two small straps so you can easily attach your tourniquet to the outside of the pouch for rapid access.

- Blue Force Gear Advanced Micro Trauma NOW Kit ($199.95)
    This kit includes a hemostatic bandage, wound dressing, NPA, two chest seals, decompression needle, gauze, two strips of Frog Tape, and medical gloves, all of which comes in a compact cloth pouch that's easy to carry on your belt. It doesn't come with a tourniquet, so you'll need to buy that separately.

- North American Rescue Advanced Ocho IFAK ($174.99)
    This kit includes a hemostatic bandage, wound dressing, NPA, two chest seals, gauze, decompression needle, surgical gloves, and a CAT tourniquet, all of which comes in a lightweight nylon pouch that's easy to carry on your belt. This kit is less "tacticool" looking than the other options, but is a good option for keeping in your car, backpack, desk, and so forth.

Extra Magazines

Most of the time you'll get one to three magazines when you buy a rifle or pistol, but there are three reasons to buy more:

1. If you only have a few magazines, that means you'll need to reload them at the range. This wastes time and money (since you're paying for the range time). Instead, it's much more time efficient to load up all of the ammunition you plan on shooting in magazines beforehand

so you can spend your time at the range shooting, not loading.
2. Magazines wear out, break, and get misplaced, so it's nice to have several backups.
3. Gun control advocates are constantly agitating to ban high-capacity magazines (the kind of magazines used by most rifles and pistols), so it's always possible you won't be able to buy more in the future. Better to stock up now so you don't get caught in a bind should high-capacity magazines get banned.

When it comes to pistol magazines, it's best to buy from the same brand that manufactured the pistol. You can sometimes buy aftermarket pistol magazines that work, but they often cause malfunctions. If you're using a pistol for concealed carry, you should always use magazines made by the same company that manufactured your pistol (Glock magazines in a Glock pistol, for instance).

You have a bit more flexibility when it comes to rifle magazines. A few good brands include Magpul, Lancer, and Brownells. Check out gunmagwarehouse.com to find good prices on magazines, which usually cost about $10 to $20 for rifle magazines and $20 to $50 for pistol magazines.

Rifle Sling

A rifle sling is a strip of leather or cloth that allows you to easily carry a rifle or shotgun and to secure a rifle or shotgun against your body if you need your hands for something else. It also makes it harder for someone to pull your gun away from you in a fight. You want to buy what's known as a two-point sling, which attaches to the rifle or shotgun in two places. These are more secure than single-point slings (which attach to the gun in one place), and prevent the gun barrel from hitting you in the family jewels should you need to let go of it for whatever reason.

There are many good brands of rifle slings to choose from including Ferro Concepts, T. Rex Arms, and Blue Force Gear, but my personal favorite is the ESD Rifle Sling by Edgar Sherman Designs, which costs $45 to $50 and is worth every penny. It's light, durable, allows for very fast transitions between your rifle and pistol, and is easily adjusted on the fly thanks to some clever engineering by its creator (Edgar Sherman).

Weapon Light

A weapon light is a flashlight that's designed to be attached to a rifle, pistol, or shotgun. The main reason for owning a weapon light is that most crimes are committed at night, and thus it's helpful to be able to quickly identify whether or not someone is a threat and to see where you're walking.

There are many good brands to choose from, but these are some of the best pistol-mounted weapon lights…

- Streamlight TLR1-HL ($145)
- SureFire X300 Ultra ($299)*
- SureFire XC1-B ($270)

and some of the best rifle- or shotgun-mounted weapon lights.

- SureFire M600DF Scout ($269)
- ModLite OKW or PLH* Weapon Light ($289)
- Cloud Defensive REIN ($280)

Pro tip: Most weapon lights are attached close to the muzzle of the gun, and so tend to get covered with particles of burned gunpowder that can block the light. A simple workaround is to smear some chapstick on your gun light's glass before you shoot. When the burned powder residue builds up on the lens, you can wipe off the soiled chapstick, leaving the lens clear.

Belt

Whether you choose to conceal or open carry a pistol, you'll need a sturdy belt. If you're concealed carrying, any good nylon or leather belt will work fine. If you're open carrying, though, you're probably carrying a heavier pistol and maybe spare magazines and other gear, so you'll want to use a more robust belt.

In this case, you have two options:

- Regular belts
- Battle belts (aka "duty belts")

Regular belts are usually 1.5 to 1.75 inches wide and made of nylon or leather. These will support the weight of a concealed-carry pistol and an extra magazine, and are small and stylish enough that they're comfortable to wear and don't scream "military." Some good regular belts are the:

- Arc'teryx Conveyor Belt ($39)
- Bison Designs Box Canyon Leather Belt ($50)*
- T. Rex Arms NOVA Belt ($70)
- Ferro Concepts Every Day Carry Belt (EDCB2) ($80)
- Magpul® Tejas Gun Belt 2.0 ($85)

Battle belts usually consist of a narrower inner belt about 1.5 to 2 inches wide that goes through your belt loops, and a wider outer belt about 2 to 3 inches wide that attaches to the inner belt. You then mount all of your equipment on the outer belt. Battle belts allow you to carry more gear on your waist and avoid the hassle of threading multiple pouches and your holster on and off your belt every time you gear up. The downside is they're heavy, bulky, and often not comfortable to wear for long periods of time. This makes them well suited for shooting classes, trips to the range, or combat, but not useful for everyday concealed carry. Some good battle belts are the:

- Stormrider Overlord ($90) and Underlord ($47) ($137 total)
- T. Rex Arms Orion Outer ($110) and Inner ($50) Belt ($160 total)
- Ronin Task Force Belt ($190)
- Ferro Concepts Bison Belt ($215)*

Magazine Pouches and Carriers

There are three reasons to carry extra magazines for your rifle or pistol:

- Guns are useless if you run out of ammo.
- Most gunfights are won by shooting more bullets accurately at the enemy than they're shooting at you.
- Some gun malfunctions are easiest to fix by ejecting the magazine in your gun and inserting a fresh one.

That said, sometimes carrying extra magazines is more trouble than it's worth. For example, I rarely carry an extra magazine when concealed carrying, because it adds a lot of weight to my belt and is one more thing to conceal. In almost every other situation, though, you should carry extra magazines for whatever gun you have on you. If you want to carry an extra magazine while concealed carrying, the easiest way is usually to buy a holster with a built-in magazine carrier, like the:

- ANR Design Master Blaster with Claw ($80, only works with concealed carry pistols)
- T. Rex Arms Sidecar ($105)*
- Tier 1 Concealed AXIS Elite ($135)

If you prefer to keep an extra magazine in your pocket, you can also buy a little magnetic clip that holds the magazine at the top of your pocket for easier access called the NeoMag ($50).

If you're open carrying, you'll want magazine pouches that are attached to your belt (ideally the front or side for quick access). Magazine pouches come in all shapes, sizes, and designs, with some being made of elastic, nylon, or cordura cloth, others hard plastic like Kydex, and others a combination of the two. As a general rule, cloth magazine pouches are quieter and more durable and comfortable to wear, while hard plastic magazine carriers allow you to reload faster.

Some of the best belt-mounted magazine pouches and carriers for both pistols and rifles are:

- Esstac Kywi*
- HSGI Taco
- T. Rex Arms MARS
- Blue Force Gear Ten-Speed
- Velocity Systems Helium Whisper
- G-Code Scorpion Softshell

(Prices vary depending on whether you're buying rifle or pistol pouches or carriers).

There's a limit to how many magazines you can carry on your waist (most people prefer two pistol and one rifle magazine), and so the next best place to carry them is on your chest—specifically, using a set of magazine pouches attached to a chest rig or plate carrier.

A chest rig is a cloth harness that you strap to your torso that's custom designed to carry magazines on your chest (hence the name). Usually, these are designed to hold anywhere from three to eight rifle magazines, and some can hold a combination of pistol and rifle magazines.

Some of the best chest rigs:

- Viking Tactics VTAC Assault Chest Rig ($156)
- Spiritus Systems Microfight Mk4 (~$160 to $200, depending on the configuration)*
- Haley Strategic D3CRX ($185)

You'll learn more about plate carriers in a moment, but they work more or less the same way as chest rigs when it comes to carrying ammo. Typically, it's best to buy magazine pouches from whatever company made your plate carrier.

Body Armor

Body armor refers to any kind of clothing worn to protect against gunshots, usually in the form of a vest that covers your most important organs—your heart and lungs. If you think there's any possibility that someone could shoot at you, it's worth buying body armor if you can afford it.

Now, body armor is one of the more controversial pieces of kit you can buy, and there's an ongoing effort by many left-leaning politicians and activists to ban its sale to civilians. Why?

As you learned earlier in this chapter, most violent encounters occur in a matter of seconds. In most cases where you're forced to defend yourself with a gun—home invasions, attempted robberies, assaults, and so forth, you probably won't have time to don body armor beforehand. Thus, the main reason for owning it is to protect yourself in situations where you *expect* to be shot at, such as if an armed gang or violent anarchists take over your neighborhood (as happened in Seattle in 2020) or wayward police officers or soldiers threaten you, your family, or your community. And, as is their wont, leftists typically don't want citizens to own equipment that would allow them to stand up to the police and military (or, apparently, violent rioters).

Of course, it's also possible that violent criminals could use body armor to protect themselves from police bullets, but this is an extremely rare occurrence. Good body armor is too expensive for most criminals to afford; felons and violent criminals are already prohibited from owning it; and most people don't know how to use it properly, reducing its effectiveness. Plus, body armor doesn't make you immune to bullets—it just improves your odds of surviving a gunshot to your chest or back. What's more, the media often reports that criminals are wearing body armor when they really aren't. For example, there are still articles from CNN, the *Washington Post*, the *New York Times*, *USA Today*, the *LA Times*, and other media outlets claiming the Aurora Colorado shooter wore body armor when he killed twelve people in a movie theater in 2012. In reality, he wore a nylon vest with pockets for holding magazines, which offers about as much protection as a thick t-shirt.

Body armor is legal in all fifty states, but there are some restrictions on who can purchase it and how it can be used. Many states have laws that make it illegal for felons or people with a history of violent crime to buy or own body armor, and other states have laws that make it illegal to wear body armor while committing any crime (violent or otherwise). In most states, you can purchase body armor online or in person. The state with the strictest body armor laws is Connecticut, where it's illegal for civilians to buy body armor online or out of state. You can still buy it in state in face-to-face transactions, though. Finally, the federal government also prohibits taking body armor outside of the US without their permission.

What Kind of Body Armor Should You Buy?

When buying body armor, the first thing you want to consider is the material. You can roughly divide body armor into "hard" and "soft" varieties. Hard body armor is made of materials like steel, high-strength plastic, or ceramic, and usually consists of a front and a back plate held in place with a cloth vest. Soft body armor is made of woven layers of ultra-tough plastic fibers like Dyneema, Kevlar, and Spectra, and usually comes in the shape of a vest.

Soft body armor tends to be cheaper and more comfortable and concealable than hard body armor, making it less conspicuous when worn under clothing (which is why it's often worn by undercover police). Unfortunately, most forms of soft body armor are only able to stop pistol bullets, and won't stop most kinds of rifle ammunition. Thus, while any body armor is better than none, it's best to get hard body armor if you can afford it, as it will stop much more powerful bullets. The main downsides of hard body armor are that it's bulkier and more expensive than soft body armor. That said, when worn properly, it's just as comfortable as soft body armor (if not more so, depending on how it's worn).

In terms of what kind of hard body armor you should buy, you have three options:

Steel armor is the cheapest, but comes with two major downsides: It's much heavier and usually less safe than high-strength plastic or ceramic armor. When bullets hit a steel plate, they disintegrate into many small metal fragments that fly across the surface of the plate. These metal fragments, called *spall*, act as tiny bullets that can embed themselves in your stomach, groin, legs, arms, throat, and head. Thus, you should only buy steel body armor that's coated with an anti-spall coating, and even then, this may not trap all of the spall. Most steel plates weigh around 5 to 8 pounds, cost around $50 to $150, and will stop most kinds of common rifle and pistol bullets.

High-strength plastic armor is usually made of layers of pressed, heated, high-strength plastic fibers called u*ltra-high molecular weight polyethylene* (UHMWPE). Most UHMWPE plates weigh around 2 to 5 pounds, cost around $400 to $1,400, and will stop most kinds of common rifle and pistol bullets. UHMWPE plates are lighter than steel and ceramic ones, but are also usually weaker, bulkier, and significantly more expensive than the other options. The best plates are usually a combination of UHMWPE and ceramic, but they also tend to be the most expensive and are unnecessary for most people.

Ceramic armor is made of extremely strong minerals that are bonded together under pressure. Most plates weigh around 3 to 6 pounds, cost around $200 to $400 each, and will stop most kinds of common rifle and pistol bullets. The main downsides of ceramic armor are that it's slightly more expensive than steel (though still cheaper than UHMWPE) and less durable than both steel or UHMWPE. Since it's made of ceramic, it can crack if it's hit hard enough. That said, most ceramic plates are designed so that they won't break if dropped from a few feet off the ground, stepped on, or subject to normal wear and tear.

All in all, ceramic plates offer the best combination of protection, weight, comfort, and affordability. Even if you're on a budget, I recommend you save up and get ceramic body armor instead of steel or soft body armor. It's not *that* much more expensive, but it's much lighter and offers better protection.

You may have also heard that you should have some kind of "ballistic pad," "trauma pad," or "ballistic insert" behind your hard body armor. While this is necessary to catch bullet or plate fragments on some kinds of armor (especially steel), it's not necessary on most modern ceramic and UHMWPE plates. Most modern, high-quality plates are what are known as "stand-alone" plates, which already feature a cloth backing that will catch bullet and plate fragments. If you're unsure of whether or not you need a ballistic pad, contact the company you're considering buying from.

How Much Protection Do You Need?

After deciding what kind of armor you want to buy, you need to decide what "level" of protection is right for you. Despite what many people think, "bulletproof vests" are not bulletproof, at least against all bullets. Instead, body armor is graded on a scale according to the most powerful kind of bullets it will stop, based on rigorous tests from the National Institute of Justice (NIJ). Higher levels of protection will stop more powerful bullets, and lower levels will stop weaker bullets.

There are five levels of protection on the NIJ scale, which you can see on the following chart:

	NIJ Level	Protects Against . . .	Description
Soft Body Armor	Level IIA	9 mm .40 S&W	Easily concealed, but only protects against weak pistol bullets
	Level II	9 mm .40 S&W .357 Magnum	Also easily concealed, but protects against most kinds of pistol bullets
	Level IIIA	.357 SIG .44 Magnum	Bulkier and less concealable, but protects against almost all kinds of pistol bullets
Hard Body Armor	Level III	7.62x39 Ball 5.56 M193 7.62x51 M80 Ball	Lightweight, thin, and protects against most kinds of non-armor-piercing rifle bullets (there are also soft versions of Level III armor, but most are hard)
	Level IV	5.56 M855 ("green tip"), M855A1, and SS109 7.62x39 PS and API 7.62x54R AP 7.62x51 M61 AP ("black tip") 30-06 M2 AP ("black tip")	Heavier, bulkier, and protects against almost all rifle bullets, including armor-piercing ones

So, what level of protection should you get?

While Level IV armor offers the most protection against the widest range of projectiles, it's also heavier, bulkier, and more expensive than everything else, making it overkill for most people (pardon the pun). That is, unless there's a reasonable possibility that you might get shot with a high-powered, armor-piercing bullet, you probably don't need Level IV armor, and will be better served by getting a set of Level III or, even better, *special threat plates.*

Special threat plates are basically "upgraded" Level III plates which are designed to "defeat" very specific kinds of bullets—usually armor-piercing variations of common rifle calibers like 5.56 or 7.62x39. The catch is they aren't usually able to stop high-powered rifle bullets like 30-06, 7.62x51, or 7.62x54R. That is, most special threat plates will protect you from armor-piercing bullets from most modern assault rifles like the AR-15 and AK-47, but won't protect you from bullets fired by high-powered "battle rifles" like the M14 or G3, or "sniper rifles" like the Dragunov or AR-10. Special threat plates give you protection from the most common kinds of bullets you're likely to encounter, without the extra weight, bulk, and expense of Level IV plates. You'll often see special threat plates marketed as "Level III+," "Level III++," "Level IIIX," or "specialty" plates.

Here are a few more things to keep in mind when interpreting this chart and determining how much protection you need:

- If body armor stops one kind of bullet, such as a .357 Magnum, it will also stop any bullet that is less powerful, like 9 mm and .40 S&W, and bullets that aren't listed on the chart like .38 Special and .45 Auto. (In this case, "power" is defined as the energy of the bullet when it leaves the barrel of the gun.)
- Bullet caliber isn't the only thing that determines how powerful a bullet is or how well it penetrates body armor. Bullet velocity, weight, and construction also have a major impact on a bullet's penetrating power, and different kinds of the same caliber bullet can have different penetrating abilities. For example, a normal 7.62x39 (AK-47) bullet will not penetrate Level III body armor, but a steel-core 7.62x39 bullet usually will.
- Body armor tests typically involve shooting a vest or plate multiple times in different places—not shooting it repeatedly in the same spot. While most kinds of body armor can stand up to many shots, if you shoot it enough, in the same spot, eventually a bullet will get through. Bullets don't just bounce off, after all.
- Although any kind of body armor will help slow or even stop stabbing weapons like knives, soft body armor is much less effective than hard body armor in this regard.
- Body armor is very durable, long-lasting, and doesn't "go bad," unless it's left in extremely hot or humid conditions for long periods

of time. Most plates come with a five-year warranty, but will probably last decades if you take care of them.
- If you get hard body armor, make sure it's either single-curve (nice) or multi-curve (ideal). This just means the plates are contoured to match the shape of the human torso, making them more comfortable.

So, with all of this in mind, here are the plates I recommend:

- Hesco L210 Specialty Plate ($370 per pair)*
- Hesco 3810 Level III+ Specialty Plate (~$1,200 per pair)
- DFNDR Level III X Plate (~$1,100 per pair)

And if you're a baller and want the best protection money can buy, check out the Hesco Level IV 4800 Plate (~$2,600 per pair).

If, despite reading all of this, you still want soft body armor, a good option would be the Safe Life Defense Concealable Multi-Threat Vest Level IIIA ($450).

Next, you need to make sure you get the right size armor plates. You want the top of the plate (or pad, in the case of soft body armor) to be at about the level of your sternal notch—the little indentation at the top of your chest where your two collar bones meet, and the bottom of the plate or pad to be at or slightly above your belly button.

You can also choose between different shapes, or "cuts," of plates, with the two most common being SAPI cut plates and shooter's cut plates. SAPI cut plates provide slightly more protection but are also a little heavier and more cumbersome, and shooter's cut plates offer a little less protection but are more comfortable to wear. Which one you choose mostly boils down to personal preference, but in most cases, a shooter's cut plate is probably the way to go.

So, all in all, you'll want to buy two (front and back) ceramic or UHMWPE, stand-alone, Level III or special threat plates that fit properly.

What Kind of Plate Carrier Should You Buy?

In addition to plates, you'll also need to buy what's known as a *plate carrier*, which is a specially designed vest that holds the plates comfortably against your body in the correct position. Most plate carriers are also designed to carry other equipment such as magazine pouches, medical kits, hydration bladders, radios, and so forth.

As with armor, it's worth investing in the nicest plate carrier you can afford. Cheaper carriers will fall apart faster, may not hold the plates properly against your body, and likely won't be as comfortable or customizable. Luckily, plate carriers are much more affordable than body armor, with most costing around $150 to $300.

Some of the best plate carriers include:

- Ferro Concepts Slickster ($158)
- Crye Airlite SPC ($169)
- Crye JPC 2.0 ($240)
- Spiritus Systems LV119 (~$250, depending on the configuration)*
- First Spear Strandhögg™ ($519)

As with any expensive avocation, there are *many* other gun-related gadgets you could buy, but when you're starting out, stick with the items on this list. Prioritize practicing with what you have rather than gathering more gear.

If you're the kind of person who likes to stay on top of the latest and greatest equipment, the following YouTube channels and websites break down the ins and outs of everything from night vision to silencers to rucksacks, and everything in between.

YouTube channels:

- Garand Thumb (secondamendmentmanifesto.com/garandthumb)
- Kit Badger (secondamendmentmanifesto.com/badger)
- Honest Outlaw (secondamendmentmanifesto.com/outlaw)

- Vickers Tactical (secondamendmentmanifesto.com/vickers)
- Hickok45 (secondamendmentmanifesto.com/hickok45)
- Mrgunsngear (secondamendmentmanifesto.com/mrgunsngear)
- Warrior Poet Society (secondamendmentmanifesto.com/warrior)
- Iraqveteran8888 (secondamendmentmanifesto.com/iraqveteran8888)
- TWANGnBANG (secondamendmentmanifesto.com/twangnbang)
- Military Arms Channel (secondamendmentmanifesto.com/militaryarmschannel)

Websites:

- Everyday Marksman (everydaymarksman.co)
- Kit Badger (kitbadger.com)
- Mil-Spec Monkey (milspecmonkey.com)
- Pewpew Tactical (pewpewtactical.com)
- Tactical Life (tactical-life.com)

Well, this chapter was a door stopper. There's quite a bit of information to process and implement, so to make your life easier, I created a list of all of the gear recommended in this chapter along with links to videos demonstrating how to use and where to buy each item. To download this gear guide and the other free goodies that come with this book, go to secondamendmentmanifesto.com/bonus.

12
The Fight Ahead

"More inhumanity has been done by man himself
than any other of nature's causes."
—Samuel von Pufendorf, German philosopher, historian, and legal scholar, 1673.

"It may be true that you can't fool all the people all the time, but
you can fool enough of them to rule a large country."
—Anonymous

First of all, congratulations, and thank you.
    Congratulations, because you now know more about the Second Amendment, the Bill of Rights, and the Constitution than most politicians, lawmakers, and citizens of the United States.

Thank you, because you took the time out of your life to educate yourself about one of the most important issues in America.

This isn't the end, though, but the beginning.

Remember that being a citizen of the United States doesn't just mean you have certain rights and privileges; it also means that you have certain responsibilities and obligations.

Don't make the mistake of thinking that the liberties, values, and institutions of America will endure without your active support. We aren't forever guaranteed the world we inherited from our Founding Fathers; instead, it must be earned anew each generation, each year, and each day.

"When one is deprived of one's liberty," wrote Thucydides, "one is right in blaming not so much the man who puts the shackles on as the one who had the power to prevent him, but did not use it."

As you've learned in this book, a free society like ours is the *exception*, not the rule. The history of the human race has been one of tyranny, oppression, and corruption—of a small elite controlling the fate of the masses for their own benefit, with no regard for the wellbeing, happiness, or liberty of those in their thrall. But the Founders of America chose a different path. As Abraham Lincoln proclaimed after the Battle of Gettysburg, ". . . our fathers brought forth on this continent a new nation, conceived in liberty and dedicated to the proposition that all men are created equal." Let those words sink in—*a new nation, conceived in liberty*.

This is what makes America different even today.

No country in Europe trusts their citizens with firearms the way the United States does. In most European countries, citizens don't even get to vote in primary elections to choose political candidates. And of course, we enjoy a level of freedom, opportunity, and prosperity that awes most of the inhabitants of Central and South America, Africa, and Asia, which prompts them to flock to our shores, not the other way around.

We have something special. We are different. And we should be proud of it.

We are a nation founded by free men, pioneers, and patriots, who prized individualism and liberty above subservience to and dependence on our leaders. We were willing to sacrifice the safe confines of serfdom for the dangerous wilds of freedom. Despite all that's changed since the American Revolution, you can see the echoes of this independent ethos even today.

According to a 2014 survey conducted by the Pew Research Center, 73 percent of Americans said that they believed it was possible to become successful if they worked hard, whereas only 35 percent of Europeans felt the same way. In the same survey, 58 percent of Americans said allowing citizens to pursue their goals without interference from the government is more important than the state providing basic needs for everyone. In

Europe, the majority of people in every country felt a state-run safety net was more important than individuals controlling their own destiny.

This great civilization in which we live is an anomaly in the annals of history, a single frame in the film of the human race, and we must not take it for granted.

Lord Byron once observed that, "The best prophet of the future is the past," and it's something all Americans should remember. Unless you take a stand against designing politicians; unless you defend your birthright from the tendrils of tyranny; and unless you are willing to fight hammer and tongs to preserve the world you now enjoy, then it will spiral into decay like all those that came before.

"If you want a vision of the future," warned George Orwell, "imagine a boot stamping on a human face—forever." The Founders glimpsed that same nightmare, which is why they created the Second Amendment. They knew that as long as Americans had a love for freedom in their hearts, an understanding of their rights in mind, and a gun in their hands, the future will be as the state flag of Virginia shows it: a free citizen resting their foot on the slaine corpse of a would-be tyrant.

Remember, too, that the story of the Second Amendment is not just about guns. It's the story of humankind's millennia-long crusade for freedom. It's the saga of humanity's escape from the cages of despotism. It's the tale of our species' continued fight for independence, prosperity, and the simple idea that our lives are our own, and no one else's. Simply put, those who do not trust you to be armed, do not trust you to think, to speak, and to act in ways that they don't control.

These ideals may seem unrealistic, high-minded, and impractical, especially when politicians can strip away your rights with impunity, criminals can burn and loot American cities under the aegis of equality, and law-abiding gun owners are fingered as culprits for mass shootings, murder, and mayhem.

When these thoughts creep into your mind, remember that the tides of history are often only turned by the cruel pressures of persecution, privation, and violence. "It's not *that* bad, let's wait and see" must turn into "it *is* that bad, and it's time to act," for free men and women to steer civilization away from tyranny and toward freedom.

This doesn't (necessarily) mean violent revolution, but it does mean becoming ferociously active in the political process. It means voting in every local, state, and federal election you can. It means voicing your opinions when challenged, and refusing to be browbeaten by bullies. It means donating what money and time you can to candidates and organizations who are working to protect your rights. And it means being armed and able to defend yourself, your family, and your civilization from oppression and chaos.

From the overthrow of the kings of Rome to the Glorious Revolution to the modern tempests of unrest across the United States, history proves that things may have to get much worse before they get better. And as things degenerate further, it will become all the more important for free men and women like you to embrace, nurture, and defend the fundamental liberties that form the bedrock of our culture: the rights of life, liberty, and property, which all depend on the right to bear arms as their shield.

Arms are the last defense against despotism, the gavel that will pound out the verdict of fate, and the pen that will write the version of history read by your ancestors.

Do you want your children, your grandchildren, and all of their descendants to remember you as one of the dithering, thoughtless, self-interested pawns who allowed their singular culture to crumble under the weight of a corrupt, unjust, venal government? To be pulled apart by parasitical anarchists?

Or do you want to be remembered like our ancestors? The lionhearted, learned, and virtuous partisans who walked into the cannon's mouth, so you could enjoy the abundance we now relish.

You may not need to make the same sacrifices they did, but you can fight for the same idea: that government is created by the people to protect their life, liberty, and property, its powers forever subordinate to these sacred rights.

Honor their genius, courage, and sacrifice by preserving the tree of liberty they planted for you, so it can continue to bear fruit for you and your children too.

Would You Do Me a Favor?

Thank you for reading *The Second Amendment Manifesto*—I hope it's helped you gain a deeper insight into, appreciation for, and understanding of your right to bear arms.

Now I have a small favor to ask of you.

Would you mind taking a minute to write a review on Amazon about this book? Even a few words helps, and while this only takes a moment, it means a lot to me because...

- My favorite part about writing is getting feedback from readers like you. I also carefully read every review, positive and negative.
- Amazon looks at each review as a little "vote" for or against a book, and the more votes this book gets, the more people will see it, read it, and possibly throw their support behind the Second Amendment.

To leave me a review, go to secondamendmentmanifesto.com/review, leave a rating and your thoughts, and click "Submit."

Or, you can...

1. Open Amazon on your web browser.
2. Search for "second amendment manifesto."
3. Click on the book.
4. Scroll down and click on the "Write a customer review" button.
5. Leave your thoughts.

Thanks again for reading my scribbles, and I look forward to reading and responding to your feedback!

Glossary: What "They" Don't Want You to Know About Your Second Amendment Rights

> "... the advancement & diffusion of Knowledge ...
> is the only Guardian of true liberty ..."
> —James Madison, author of the Bill of Rights and fourth
> President of the United States, 1825.

> "I actually don't know what a barrel shroud is, it's
> the shoulder thing that goes up."
> —Carolyn McCarthy, Democratic New York Congresswoman,
> when asked to define the word "barrel shroud" and explain why it should be
> regulated in a proposed assault-weapons ban, 2007.

First of all, you deserve a pat on the back.

By reading this book, you've taken the first step toward informing yourself about one of the most critical and contentious debates in the US: whether or not Americans have the right to own guns.

This probably isn't the first time you've dipped your toes into these turbulent waters. Maybe you see news stories pop up in your Facebook, Twitter, or YouTube feed, or pick up bits and pieces of the debate when you turn on the news, tune into a podcast, or read a blog article. Or maybe you've even read a few books about gun rights, gun control, and the Second Amendment. Despite your research, though, chances are good that you still don't feel like you have all of the facts.

On the one hand, you don't want to spend your free time trudging through complex legalese or digesting dusty historical documents to find the truth. On the other hand, you're also suspicious of the sanitized, simplified soundbites you hear from the media, politicians, and maybe even some of your friends and family members.

So, what's the solution? How can you educate yourself about the debate over guns without becoming a part-time legal scholar? While there are no shortcuts, the closest thing there is to a "hack" for understanding the debate over guns is hiding in plain sight:

Paying attention to the precise definition of words.

Seriously, that's it. The big reveal. The hidden barrier to understanding your constitutional rights. When the Founding Fathers wrote the Second Amendment, they chose words based on specific definitions in order to communicate their ideas as clearly as possible. If you don't share the same understanding of the words they used, you won't receive the information in the same light, and thus the concepts they were trying to convey will be garbled or lost.

Having an incomplete understanding of the words you're reading is particularly dangerous when it comes to historical documents like the Bill of Rights, because one of the easiest ways to manipulate their meaning is to apply new definitions to the words in these texts. Over time, these little changes accumulate, until the original meaning of the text bears little resemblance to what the authors intended. As you learned in chapter nine, this kind of modern mistranslation of words underlies the greatest legal threat to the right to bear arms. The misunderstanding of words is also one of the reasons some people argue that the Second Amendment is outmoded, obsolete, and at odds with civil society.

Perhaps no one in American history understood this peril more than Founding Father Noah Webster, a man who devoted his life to defining words. Starting in 1806, Webster began writing what would become the most widely used dictionary in America and learned twenty-eight different languages to ensure he had a complete understanding of the definition and etymology of as many words as possible. He also understood how accidental and intentional changes to the definitions of words could be used to control public opinion and twist facts.

"[I]n the lapse of two or three centuries, changes have taken place which ... obscure the sense of the original languages...," Webster wrote in 1833. "The effect of these changes is that some words are ... now used in a sense different from that which they had ... [and thus] present a wrong signification or false ideas. Whenever words are understood in a sense different from that which they had when introduced, mistakes may be very injurious."

Webster's contemporaries shared his belief that the specific definition of words was the bedrock on which the liberties of the United States were based. Without specific, standardized definitions of words, the new government would be like a castle built on quicksand—briefly brilliant, strong, and impressive, but ultimately crumbling into the mire of ignorance.

The Founding Fathers realized that misdefining words could plague future debates about the Constitution and they admonished their colleagues to cling to the original definitions of the words used when it was written. For example, in 1823, Thomas Jefferson urged Supreme Court Justice William Johnson to use the following method of interpreting the Constitution:

> "On every question of construction, carry ourselves back to the time when the Constitution was adopted, recollect the spirit manifested in the debates, and instead of trying what meaning may be squeezed out of the text, or invented against it, conform to the probable one in which it was passed."

The author of the Bill of Rights and the Second Amendment, James Madison, agreed with this approach, stating, "I entirely concur in the propriety of resorting to the sense in which the Constitution was accepted and ratified by the nation. In that sense alone it is the legitimate Constitution. And if that be not the guide in expounding it, there can be no security for a consistent and stable, more than for a faithful, exercise of its powers . . . What a metamorphosis would be produced in the code of law if all its ancient phraseology were to be taken in its modern sense."

"Do not separate text from historical background," Madison warned. "If you do, you will have perverted and subverted the Constitution, which can only end in a distorted, bastardized form of illegitimate government." Unfortunately, Madison's concerns became reality. One of the main reasons there's so much confusion about the meaning of the Second Amendment is that many people don't understand (or willfully distort) the meaning of the words written by the Founders.

In order to understand the true meaning of the Second Amendment, and thus what role the Founding Fathers intended guns to play in America, you have to understand the definition of the words in the Second Amendment, in the documents written about it, and in the laws that affect it.

In school, you were probably taught to *infer* the meaning of words by the surrounding text, making a guess based on the words and sentences before and after it. While this can work to some extent, especially for familiar synonyms, it produces the wrong definition as often as it produces the right one. Furthermore, this method all but guarantees you'll misunderstand new, complex, or archaic terms—like the ones used in the Second Amendment and by the generations of legal scholars who've attempted to interpret it. And when enough people don't understand the true definition of a word or phrase, it's easy for others to insert their own definitions, often for nefarious reasons.

A fuzzy understanding of key words also makes it hard to understand the debate surrounding new gun laws. For instance, do you know the real definition of an *assault rifle*? Or a *semiautomatic*? Or a *magazine*? If not, you'll never be able to fully comprehend the gun control debate in America or the meaning of the Second Amendment.

Now for the good news: If you learn the definitions of just a handful of key terms, you'll instantly be more informed about the Second Amendment than anyone else you know. You'll be able to piece together the historical puzzle that is the Second Amendment.

All definitions of the words used in the Second Amendment were sourced from historical dictionaries that were published before, during, and shortly after the Second Amendment was written, including the 1755 edition of Samuel Johnson's *A Dictionary of the English Language*, the 1771 edition of Timothy Cunningham's *A New and Complete Law Dictionary*, and the 1828 edition of Noah Webster's *An American Dictionary of the English Language*. To improve readability, I simplified the definitions based on input from modern dictionaries, including *The Oxford English Dictionary*, *The Oxford American Dictionary*, *The Merriam-Webster Online Dictionary*, and *The American Heritage Dictionary of the English Language*, without altering the original meaning of the word. I also used these modern dictionaries for the definitions of the other words in this glossary.

The Key Words of the Second Amendment

Understanding the following ten words will improve your grasp of the right to bear arms.

Arms
Weapons of offence, or armor of defence and protection of the body.

Bear
To carry something; to move something from place to place.

Infringe
To limit or reduce someone's legal rights or freedoms or break the terms of a law, agreement, etc., whether by intervention or by not fulfilling some duty.

Keep
To have in one's possession or retain for future use.

Militia
Citizens trained for military service who can join together to fight as a unit, as opposed to full-time professional soldiers.

People

The body of persons who compose a community, town, city, or nation; regular members of society as opposed to people of a special rank or position.

Regulate

To bring order, method, or uniformity to; to govern or direct according to rules or bring under control of law.

Right

A moral or legal freedom to have or obtain something or act in a certain way.

Security

The state of being free from danger or threat.

State

A nation or territory organized under one government.

The Key Words of Government

One of the reasons politics appears so perplexing is it seems to have its own language. Luckily, you only need to understand a handful of terms to make sense of it as a layman.

The main ones you need to know to understand gun laws—both past and present—are as follows.

Amendment

An article added to the US Constitution.

Article

A clause or paragraph of a legal document or agreement, typically one outlining a single rule or law.

Authority

1. Legal power or a right to command or to act.
2. A person or group of persons that are given the power to command or control, especially to enforce the law.

Bill

A draft of a proposed law presented to a legislature, but not yet passed and made law.

Clause

A part of a contract, agreement, will, or other writing.

Congress.

The legislative body of the United States, comprising the Senate and the House of Representatives.

For a bill to be passed and made law, it must be approved by a majority vote in both the House and the Senate, and then must be approved by the President. If the President rejects (vetoes) a bill, the Senate and House can override his decision and make the bill into law with a two-thirds majority vote in favor of the bill.

In theory, Congress is also the only government entity allowed to declare war on another country, although the specifics of how this process should occur are vague and disputed. The United States has only officially declared war five times in its history, and in each case, the President asked Congress to make the declaration, which they later signed.

The last time the US officially declared war was on June 5, 1942, when Franklin D. Roosevelt signed a declaration of war against Bulgaria, Hungary, and Romania—allies of Nazi Germany (war was already declared on Japan and Germany on December 8 and 11, 1941, respectively). In every war or major military engagement since—Korea, Vietnam, Panama, Grenada, Somalia, Bosnia, the two wars in Iraq, Afghanistan, and Syria—the US has never officially declared war and thus has not required direct approval from Congress.

Constitution

A document that outlines the basic laws, rules, and principles by which a country or organization is governed.

Draft

The first form of any writing, which may be changed.

Federal

Relating to or denoting the central government as distinguished from the separate units constituting a federation, such as the individual states that make up the United States of America.

Freedom

The ability to act, speak, or think as one wants without resistance or restraint.

Govern

Conduct the policy, actions, and affairs of a state, organization, or people.

Government

The group of persons that direct the actions of societies and states according to the established constitution and laws or by arbitrary decisions.

House of Representatives (the "House")

One of the two elected legislative bodies of the United States, comprised of 435 members with six additional members who can't vote.

The number of representatives for each state is determined by the population of the states (states with larger populations get more representatives in the House).

Law
1. A system of rules that a particular country or community recognizes as regulating the actions of its members that may be enforced by the use of penalties.
2. A rule of conduct or procedure as a part of such a system, enforceable by an authority.

Legislature
A group of people, usually elected, that has the authority to make, change, and repeal laws.

Liberty
Within society, the state of being free from oppressive restrictions imposed by authority on one's way of life, behavior, or political views; the power or scope to act as one pleases.

Principle
A fundamental idea or belief.

Petition
1. A formal written request appealing to an authority about a particular cause, typically one signed by many people.
2. To make or present a formal request to an authority about a particular cause.

Select Militia
A portion of the regular militia—typically those who are most able-bodied or most ideologically compatible with the government's aims—picked by the government to receive weapons, training, and often funding, and who receive orders from the government.

Senate
One of the two elected legislative bodies of the United States, comprised of 100 members (two from each state).

Society
An organized group of people united either for a temporary or permanent purpose, with laws and traditions that control how they behave toward one another.

Standing Army
A permanent army composed of full-time, professional soldiers who are paid, armed, and trained by the government, who typically do not have another profession outside the military, and can be deployed immediately.

Statute
A written law passed by a legislative body.

The Key Words of Guns

You don't need to be a soldier, weapons engineer, or gun geek to understand the Second Amendment, but you do need to have a rudimentary grasp of firearms lingo to understand modern gun laws, regulations, and rhetoric.

Many of the people who propose, write, and enforce gun laws have little to no understanding of how guns work. Not only does this mean many gun laws fail to achieve their intended purpose (making Americans safer), they also unnecessarily restrict the rights of law-abiding citizens.

By learning the definitions of these words, you can become part of the solution by holding lawmakers to higher standards.

AK-47

A lightweight semi-automatic rifle about three feet long that fires 7.62x39 mm ammunition, designed by Mikhail Kalashnikov in 1947, and adopted by the Russian military in 1949.

The letters "AK" are an initialism of the Russian words Avtomát Kaláshnikova, which translates to *Kalashnikov's automatic device*. The reason the AK-47 is the most produced and popular gun in the world is primarily due to its reliability. Kalashnikov designed the rifle with large, durable parts that fit loosely together, which allows it to function despite being clogged with gunk and grime and with minimal maintenance.

The reason the AK-47 is the most popular gun in the world (over 100 million made and counting) is due to its affordability and extreme reliability. For example, there are stories of AK-47s being lost in rivers, recovered decades later, and then firing without being cleaned.

AR-15

A style of lightweight semi-automatic rifle about three-and-a-half-feet long that fires .223 Remington ammunition, based on the ArmaLite AR-15 rifle design, which was adopted by the US military as the M-16 in 1959.

Although many people believe "AR" stands for "assault rifle," it's actually an initialism of the words "ArmaLite Rifle." The reason the AR-15 has become *the* rifle among first world countries is because in most ways, it truly is the perfect rifle: It's light, extremely accurate, infinitely customizable, and produces minimal recoil. Although some early models in the 1960s had reliability issues, these problems were quickly fixed, and it's fair to say that most modern AR-15s are almost as reliable as AK-47s when properly maintained.

Assault Rifle

A rifle that can be set to fire in both semiautomatic and fully automatic modes, fires a medium-size cartridge, and uses a detachable magazine.

A common source of confusion is that many "assault rifles," such as the AK-47 and M-16, are available in semiautomatic-only versions for civilians.

Although they are identical to assault rifles in other respects, these rifles are not assault rifles, as they cannot be set to fire on fully automatic. For example, the AR-15 is a semi-automatic version of the M-16, and thus not an assault rifle.

Assault Weapon

There is no consistent, standard, or official definition of what constitutes an "assault weapon," which is why firearm experts rarely use this term.

Typically, the term "assault weapon" is only used by legislators when creating a bill that would ban firearms that meet whatever definition was created for the bill.

For example, the now-expired Federal Assault Weapons Ban of 1994 loosely defined assault weapons as semiautomatic firearms with a large-capacity magazine with features often found on military-style rifles, which includes a wide variety of firearms often used by civilians for hunting, sport shooting, collecting, and self-defense.

As follows, the state of California applies a much broader definition which includes various kinds of rifles, shotguns, and pistols:

> A semiautomatic, centerfire rifle that has the capacity to accept a detachable magazine and any one of the following:
>
> - A pistol grip that protrudes conspicuously beneath the action of the weapon.
> - A thumbhole stock.
> - A folding or telescoping stock.
> - A grenade launcher or flare launcher.
> - A flash suppressor.
> - A forward pistol grip.
>
> A semiautomatic, centerfire rifle that has a fixed magazine with the capacity to accept more than 10 rounds.

A semiautomatic, centerfire rifle that has an overall length of less than 30 inches.

A semiautomatic pistol that has the capacity to accept a detachable magazine and any one of the following:

- A threaded barrel, capable of accepting a flash suppressor, forward handgrip, or silencer.
- (B) A second handgrip.
- A shroud that is attached to, or partially or completely encircles, the barrel that allows the bearer to fire the weapon without burning his or her hand, except a slide that encloses the barrel.
- The capacity to accept a detachable magazine at some location outside of the pistol grip.

A semiautomatic pistol with a fixed magazine that has the capacity to accept more than 10 rounds.

A semiautomatic shotgun that has both of the following:

- A folding or telescoping stock.
- A pistol grip that protrudes conspicuously beneath the action of the weapon, thumbhole stock, or vertical handgrip.

A semiautomatic shotgun that has the ability to accept a detachable magazine.

Any shotgun with a revolving cylinder.

In essence, California defines an assault weapon as almost any gun that isn't a hunting rifle.

Automatic

Now, the term "automatic" generally refers to fully automatic firearms—machine guns.

In the early 1900s, however, "automatic" was generally used as a synonym for "semiautomatic." For example, the semiautomatic Colt 1911 pistol was also referred to as the "Colt Automatic."

As fully automatic guns became more common in the 1920s, more people began to refer to them as "automatic," which created confusion. As a result, people began referring to rifles that fired a single bullet with every squeeze of the trigger as "semiautomatic," and guns that fired multiple bullets with every squeeze of the trigger as "automatic."

Background Check

The process a person or company uses to verify that an individual is who they claim to be, to determine whether or not they have committed a crime, and if so, the time, place, manner, and severity of the crime.

All gun stores and licensed sellers of firearms in the US are required to perform a background check on every person who wishes to purchase a gun and are severely penalized if they knowingly sell or give a gun to someone convicted of a crime that would make them ineligible to own one.

Barrel Shroud

A covering attached to the barrel of a firearm that partially or completely encircles the barrel, which prevents users from burning their skin against the hot barrel.

(It's not "the shoulder thing that goes up.")

Bureau of Alcohol, Tobacco, Firearms, and Explosives (BATFE) or "ATF"

A federal law enforcement organization within the United States Department of Justice responsible for enforcing firearms regulations.

This includes preventing the illegal use, manufacture, transportation, and possession of firearms and explosives. All gun stores and individual gun sellers in the United States who intend to sell guns on a regular basis must apply for a Federal Firearms License from BATFE and comply with all BATFE regulations.

(BATFE is often shortened to "ATF," which is an acronym that refers to the bureau's chief areas of interest: alcohol, tobacco, and firearms.)

Bullet

A metal projectile fired from a rifle, revolver, or other small firearm, typically cylindrical and pointed.

Cartridge

A type of preassembled firearm ammunition that contains a projectile (bullet, shot, or slug), a propellant (usually either smokeless or black powder), and an ignition device (primer) within a metallic, paper, or plastic case. Also referred to as a "round."

Although many people refer to cartridges as "bullets," in reality, "bullet" only refers to one kind of projectile used in some cartridges.

Concealed Carry

The practice of carrying a concealed firearm on one's person in public.

Concealed Carry Weapon (CCW)

A weapon, such as a pistol or knife, that is easily concealable on one's person.

The acronym "CCW" is also used to refer to the license that allows someone to possess this kind of weapon in public.

Flash Suppressor

A small metal cage fixed to the muzzle of a gun that disperses burning gasses as they escape from the barrel, reducing the flash or "fireball" that erupts from the muzzle immediately after the bullet leaves the barrel. Reducing the flash produced while firing serves two important roles: It allows the shooter to quickly refocus on the target between shots, and (in military situations) makes it more difficult for enemy combatants to locate the shooter. Flash suppressors do not affect the killing power of guns in any way.

Foregrip

An ergonomic piece of metal or plastic fixed to the front of a gun that makes it easier to hold, control recoil, and avoid burning one's hand on the hot barrel or barrel shroud.

Fully Automatic ("Full Auto")

A setting that causes a gun to continuously fire bullets as long as the trigger is being squeezed.

A machine gun generally refers to a gun that only fires on fully automatic, although some machine guns can be set to both semiautomatic or fully automatic modes.

Gun Buyback Program

A program that allows or forces citizens to sell their guns to the government for money.

This name is a misnomer, because the government never owned the guns it is supposedly buying "back" in these programs. Instead, a more accurate term would be a subsidized gun confiscation program.

Gun buyback programs are typically created after a particular kind of firearm has been made illegal or is about to be made illegal. The buyback program encourages citizens to comply with the law and gives them the opportunity to surrender their weapons without being prosecuted for a period of time.

Historically, governments have offered around $50 to $100 per firearm, or around 25 to 95 percent of the market value, depending on the specific program and the condition of the gun.

Large-Capacity Magazine

As with "assault weapon," there is no official, consistent definition of what constitutes a "large-" or "high-" capacity magazine, and the definition varies depending on what bill is being proposed.

For example, New York State defines a "high-capacity magazine" as any magazine that can contain more than seven cartridges, California as any that can hold more than ten, and Colorado sets the limit at fifteen cartridges.

Typically, though, large capacity magazines are defined as magazines that can contain more than ten cartridges.

Most semiautomatic pistols use magazines that contain fifteen or more cartridges, and most semiautomatic rifles use magazines that contain thirty or more cartridges. Thus, the standard magazines used in the majority of modern pistols and rifles are considered "high-capacity" magazines. (This is like calling a twenty-gallon gas tank a "high-capacity" gas tank, even though this is the standard size found in most modern sedans).

M-16

A category of military rifles that fires 5.56x45 NATO ammunition based on the ArmaLite AR-15 rifle design.

Most versions feature a 20-inch barrel and can be set to fire on semiautomatic, fully-automatic, or three-round-burst fire (firing three bullets for every squeeze of the trigger).

Machine Gun

A gun that fires multiple bullets with a single squeeze of the trigger.

The term "machine gun" generally refers to weapons that only fire on fully-automatic, although guns that can fire on both semiautomatic, three-round-burst, and fully automatic are all considered machine guns.

Due to the Firearm Owners Protection Act of 1986, machine guns manufactured after 1986 are illegal for civilians to own. Currently, there are roughly 600,000 machine guns that can be legally purchased in the United States, most of which cost at least $10,000 and are owned as financial assets or collectors items.

Magazine

A device for storing and feeding ammunition into a gun.

Most modern magazines are rectangular, spring-loaded, detachable boxes that can be inserted into a gun, which push a new cartridge into the gun after the previous one is fired and ejected. Once a magazine becomes empty, it can be removed, reloaded with more cartridges, and reused hundreds of times.

Some people mistakenly refer to magazines as "clips," which is incorrect. Clips only refer to metal strips that hold a group of cartridges together so they can be more easily inserted into a gun by hand.

Pistol

A small firearm designed to be held in one hand, also referred to as a handgun or sidearm.

Most pistols are either semiautomatic or revolvers.

Pistol Grip

An ergonomic handle found on some rifles and shotguns similar to the kind found on pistols.

Projectile

An object designed to be fired from a gun or rocket.

Bullets, shot, and slugs are examples of common projectiles fired from guns.

Recoil

The rearward thrust generated by a gun when it's fired. Also known as "kick."

Red Flag Law

A law that allows family members, household members, and law enforcement officers to petition a court to temporarily prevent someone from accessing firearms.

If a court decides that the person in question is a danger to themselves or others, the person must surrender their firearms to the police and is prohibited from buying, selling, or possessing firearms until the prohibition expires.

Red flag laws are also known as "firearms restraining orders" or "extreme risk protection orders" (ERPOs).

Revolver

A handgun that holds multiple cartridges in a revolving cylinder, one or more of which is aligned with the barrel when the gun is fired.

Rifle

A gun designed to be braced against the shoulder when fired that has spiral grooves (rifling) cut into the barrel to make the bullets more accurate.

Rifling

Spiral grooves cut into the inside of a gun barrel to make projectiles spin as they pass through the barrel, thus making them more accurate.

Safety

A mechanism that prevents the accidental firing of a gun.

Typically, safeties take the form of a small lever (called a "safety lever") that the user can switch "on" and "off" to allow or prevent the gun from firing.

Semiautomatic ("Semiauto")

A setting that causes a gun to fire a single bullet with every squeeze of the trigger.

Most guns owned by and sold to civilians are semiautomatic, whereas most guns used by the military can be set to semiautomatic or fully-automatic.

Short-Barreled Rifle (SBR)

A rifle with a barrel less than 16-inches long or a total length of less than 26 inches.

Due to the National Firearms Act of 1934 (NFA), SBRs are subject to an additional layer of federal regulation, as they were perceived as easier to conceal and thus more dangerous to society at the time. People who wish to purchase or make an SBR must pay a $200 tax to the government, submit fingerprints, photographs, and a completed application form to the BATFE, and typically wait six to twelve months for the government to approve the purchase or manufacture of the SBR.

The primary reasons many shooters prefer SBRs are they're lighter, easier to aim, carry, maneuver in confined spaces (such as in your home), and conceal in a car or backpack for self defense. Shortening a rifle's barrel also keeps the overall length manageable when a suppressor is attached (which adds about six to twelve inches to the total length of the rifle).

Short-Barreled Shotgun (SBS)

A shotgun with a barrel less than 18-inches long.

In some cases, shotguns are manufactured with short barrels to make them easier to aim, carry, and conceal, and in other cases, criminals illegally saw off the barrel of a shotgun for the same purposes. In this case, shotguns are referred to as "sawed-off" shotguns, although some people inaccurately refer to any shotgun with a barrel less than 18-inches long as a "sawed off."

SBSs are also subject to NFA regulations, and in order to purchase one, people must go through the same process as when buying or making a short-barrelled rifle (explained earlier).

Shot

A small, spherical metal projectile typically fired in large numbers from a single cartridge.

Shot is used instead of bullets for several reasons: to improve the chances of hitting the target, to ensure the projectiles don't travel farther than the shooter intends (shot doesn't travel as far as bullets), or to cause as much damage as possible to the target at close range.

Shotgun

A gun without rifling that fires shot. The primary advantages of shotguns over rifles and pistols are they increase the chances of hitting the target and cause massive damage at close range. Shotguns are primarily used for hunting birds and shooting clays (which are difficult to hit mid-air), and for self defense, because when loaded with high-powered ammunition, they can cause significantly more damage at close range than rifles or pistols.

Silencer

A device used to reduce the sound of a gun as it is fired.

Typically, silencers are cylindrical metal tubes that contain a series of hollow chambers which slow down the speed of burning gasses escaping from the barrel of the gun, reducing the sound of the gunshot. The main reasons civilians use silencers are to protect their hearing, avoid disturbing neighbors and wildlife, and more easily communicate with others while shooting. The main reasons soldiers use silencers are to protect their hearing, more easily communicate with other soldiers, and make it more difficult for the enemy to identify their position. Despite what some people believe, silencers do not make guns more or less deadly, accurate, or anything but quieter.

A more accurate term for these devices is *suppressors*, as they're designed to suppress, or muffle, the sound of a gunshot. For example, an AR-15 using a silencer is still about as loud as a jackhammer or ambulance siren (around 135 decibels). Despite this, "silencer" is the legal term used by the BATFE in official regulations.

Slug

A single, large-diameter projectile fired from a shotgun. Slugs are sometimes used by hunters to shoot targets farther than fifty meters away.

While shot tends to slow down considerably after traveling about fifty meters, reducing its killing power, slugs can be used to reliably kill wild game up to around one hundred meters away. Rifle bullets are almost always a better choice than shotgun slugs, and so most hunters only use shotgun slugs when local regulations prohibit the use of a rifle or if they don't own a rifle.

Stock

The rear portion of a rifle or shotgun that the shooter braces against the shoulder while firing to assist with aiming and controlling recoil.

The stock is also called a gunstock, shoulder stock, buttstock, or butt.

Select-Fire

A feature on some guns that allows the user to quickly switch between semiautomatic and fully-automatic settings.

Typically, this is part of the safety lever.

As you looked over these definitions, chances are good a few of them surprised you. Maybe some of these words were new to you, some of them had different meanings than you originally thought, and others had multiple meanings you weren't aware of.

If so, *good*.

This means you're going to have a much easier time understanding, appreciating, and forming your own opinions about everything you've learned in the previous chapters.

References

Chapter 1: Why You Should Read This Book

1. *debarred the use of arms."* "I. First Draft by Jefferson, [before June 1776]," Founders Online, National Archives, https://founders.archives.gov/documents/Jefferson/01-01-02-0161-0002. [Original source: The Papers of Thomas Jefferson, vol. 1, 1760–1776, ed. Julian P. Boyd. Princeton: Princeton University Press, 1950, pp. 337–347.]
2. *your AR-15, your AK-47."* Carter, Brandon. "Beto O'Rourke On Gun Control: 'Hell, Yes, We're Going To Take Your AR-15' : NPR." Accessed October 7, 2020. https://www.npr.org/2019/09/12/760386808/orourke-promises-to-take-your-ar-15-but-americans-are-split-on-buybacks.

Chapter 2: The Two-Thousand Year History of the Right to Bear Arms (In 15 Minutes)

1. *free man from a slave."* "Whether the Second Amendment Secures an Individual Right MEMORANDUM OPINION FOR THE ATTORNEY GENERAL," 2004. https://www.justice.gov/file/18831/download.
2. *all Americans to feel safe."* Bell, Larry. "Gun Control Misses Mark: Sen. Feinstein Shoots-off Mouth, Hits Foot." Accessed October 7, 2020. https://www.forbes.com/sites/larrybell/2013/03/26/gun-control-misses-mark-sen-feinstein-shoots-off-mouth-hits-foot/#20931e206e5e.
3. *their country's borders.* Gagarin, M. "Self-Defense in Athenian Homicide Law," 1978; Duncan, Mike. "The History of Rome: 1- In the Beginning." Accessed October 7, 2020. https://thehistoryofrome.typepad.com/the_history_of_rome/2007/07/1-in-the-beginning-.html.
4. *fight to defend it.* Hanson, V D. Carnage and Culture: Landmark Battles in the Rise to Western Power. Knopf Doubleday Publishing Group, 2007. p. 123

5. *defend themselves from violence.* Gagarin, M. "Self-Defense in Athenian Homicide Law," 1978; Hyde, Walter. "The Homicide Courts of Ancient Athens." University of Pennsylvania Law Review 66, no. 4 (June 1, 1918). https://scholarship.law.upenn.edu/penn_law_review/vol66/iss4/3.

6. *the world had ever seen.* Hanson, V D. Carnage and Culture: Landmark Battles in the Rise to Western Power. Knopf Doubleday Publishing Group, 2007. p. 9

7. *head of a household."* Bishop, Michael C. "Core of the Legion: The Roman Imperial Centuria." Ancient Warfare Magazine, 2010.

8. *cannot readily explain."* Tocqueville, Alexis de., Zunz, Olivier. Democracy in America. New York: Library of America, 2004. p. 33

9. *lance and iron helmet."* "Assize of Arms.," Source Problems in English History in Source Problems in English History, ed. Albert Beebe White and Wallace Notestein (New York: Harper & Brothers Publishers, 1915), 90–91. Original Sources, accessed October 7, 2020, http://www.originalsources.com/Document.aspx?DocID=4MJPU3F3L5GRLEX.

10. *other than a knife.* Levy, Leonard Williams. Origins of the Bill of Rights. United Kingdom: Yale University Press, 2001. p. 134

11. *the assault rifle of the middle ages.)* Chinn, George Morgan. The Machine Gun. United States: U.S. Government Printing Office, 1951.

12. *informally for centuries.* Kopel, David B. "THE 'POSSE COMITATUS' AND THE OFFICE OF SHERIFF: ARMED CITIZENS SUMMONED TO THE AID OF LAW ENFORCEMENT on JSTOR." Accessed October 7, 2020. https://www.jstor.org/stable/44113410?seq=1.

13. *the "hue and cry."* Sagui, Samantha. "The Hue and Cry in Medieval English Towns." Historical Research 87, no. 236 (May 1, 2014): 179–93.

14. *future Pope Pius II.* Henri Chandler, Jean. "A Brief Examination of Warfare by Medieval Urban Militias in Central and Northern Europe." Acta Periodica Duellatorum, Practical Section 1, no. 1 (2016): 106–51. http://actaperiodicaduellatorum.com/previous-issues-1/2016/12/7/a-brief-examination-of-warfare-by-medieval-urban-militias-in-central-and-northern-europe-jean-henri-chandler-apd12013.

15. *maintain their power."* Giorgini, Giovanni. "Five Hundred Years of Italian Scholarship on Machiavelli's Prince." The Review of Politics 75, no. 4 (2013): 625–40. doi:10.1017/S0034670513000624.

16. *within his domain . . ."* Machiavelli, Niccolò. Discourses on Livy. United States: University of Chicago Press, 2009. p. 374

17. *disciplining men properly..."* Ibid. p. 29
18. *provide them with arms."'* Ibid. p. 373
19. *the youth in the country..."* Machiavelli, Niccolò., Lynch, Christopher. Art of War. United Kingdom: University of Chicago Press, 2009.
20. *nor in no part elsewhere..."* Cramer, Clayton E. "The Statute of Northampton (1328) and Prohibitions on the Carrying of Arms." SSRN Electronic Journal, September 23, 2015. https://doi.org/10.2139/ssrn.2662910.
21. *strike or cast at another."* Encyclopaedia Londinensis, Or, Universal Dictionary of Arts, Sciences, and Literature. United Kingdom: n.p., 1810.
22. *than carrying weapons.* Cramer, Clayton E. "The Statute of Northampton (1328) and Prohibitions on the Carrying of Arms." SSRN Electronic Journal, September 23, 2015. https://doi.org/10.2139/ssrn.2662910.
23. *coffers were almost empty.* Verduyn, Anthony. "The Politics of Law and Order during the Early Years of Edward III." English Historical Review 108, no. CCCCXXIX (October 1, 1993): 842–67. https://doi.org/10.1093/ehr/CVIII.CCCCXXIX.842.
24. *bear arms in public.* Woolrych, Humphry William. A Practical Treatise on Misdemeanor. 221-2 (1842).

Chapter 3: Guns, Money, and Religion: The Bloody War that Created the English Right to Bear Arms

1. *an offense to keep arms."* Story, Joseph. A Familiar Exposition of the Constitution of the United States: Containing a Brief Commentary on Every Clause, Explaining the True Nature, Reasons, and Objects Thereof, Designed for the Use of School Libraries and General Readers, with an Appendix Containing Important Public Documents, Illustrative of the Constitution. United States: Harper & Brothers, 1840.
2. *wrong people is intolerable."* Brufke, Juliegrace. "Ohio GOP Rep Announces Support of Military-Style Weapon Ban | TheHill." Accessed October 7, 2020. https://thehill.com/homenews/house/456416-ohio-gop-rep-announces-support-of-military-style-weapon-ban.
3. *the god of war."* Morrill, J S. "The Army Revolt of 1647 BT - Britain and the Netherlands: VolumeVI War and Society Paper Delivered to the Sixth Anglo-Dutch Historical Conference." edited by A C Duke and C A Tamse, 54–78. Dordrecht: Springer Netherlands, 1977. https://doi.org/10.1007/978-94-009-9674-8_3.

4. *"meek, temperate, and quiet man."* Hutchinson, Lucy. "Memoirs of the Life of Colonel Hutchinson." Memoirs of the Life of Colonel Hutchinson. London : New York: J.M. Dent; E.P. Dutton, 1913. file://catalog.hathitrust.org/Record/101687302.

5. *militia leader within one week.* Firth, Charles Harding., Rait, Robert Sangster. Acts and Ordinances of the Interregnum, 1642-1660. United Kingdom: H.M. Stationery Office, 1911.

6. *none are seized."* Library., Bodleian, F J Routledge, William Henry Bliss, William Dunn Macray, Octavius Ogle, C H Firth, H O Coxe, and Edward Hyde Clarendon. "Calendar of the Clarendon State Papers Preserved in the Bodleian Library." Oxford: Clarendon press, 1869. file://catalog.hathitrust.org/Record/001596156.

7. *and wealthy followers.* Pepys, Samuel, 1633-1703. Samuel Pepys' Diary. New York : De Luxe Editions, 1932.

8. *contradiction or gainsaying."* Malcolm, Joyce Lee. To Keep and Bear Arms: The Origins of an Anglo-American Right. United Kingdom: Harvard University Press, 1996.

9. *to protect him."* Debates of the House of Commons: From the Year 1667 to the Year 1694. United Kingdom: D. Henry and R. Cave, and J. Emonson, 1763.

10. *mean they should."* Ibid.

11. *army for the war."* Ibid.

12. *gun parts into England.* Ibid.

13. *watched, arrested, and disarmed.* By the King. A proclamation, prohibiting the seizing of any persons, or searching houses without warrant, except in time of actual insurrections. England and Wales. Sovereign (1660-1685 : Charles II), Charles II, King of England, 1630-1685.

14. *weapons were rarely returned.* Walker, James. The Yorkshire Plot, 1663. United States: Society, 1934.

15. *law-abiding, loyal Englishmen.* Lee Malcolm, Joyce. "Charles II and the Reconstruction of Royal Power." The Historical Journal 35, no. 2 (1992): 307–30. doi:10.1017/S0018246X00025814.

16. *or any other weapons.* Malcolm, Joyce Lee. To Keep and Bear Arms: The Origins of an Anglo-American Right. United Kingdom: Harvard University Press, 1996.

17. *rebel strongholds demolished.* Malcolm, Joyce Lee. To Keep and Bear Arms: The Origins of an Anglo-American Right. United Kingdom: Harvard University Press, 1996.

18. *within their control."* Hutton, Ronald. The Restoration: A Political and Religious History of England and Wales, 1658-1667. United Kingdom: Oxford University Press, 1993. p. 289
19. *would ever recover.* Shirley, Evelyn Philip. Some Account of English Deer Parks: With Notes on the Management of Deer. United Kingdom: J. Murray, 1867. p. 67
20. *forest and game laws."* Blackstone, William. Commentaries on the Laws of England. United Kingdom: Clarendon Press, 1768.
21. *requirement for voting.* Ibid.
22. *other Engines aforesaid."* Statute of the Realm, 1660-1671, CII, c22-23, 24-25, p.745 https://www.nationalarchives.gov.uk/education/candp/crime/g04/g04cs6s2.htm
23. *'idle and disorderly.'"* Malcolm, Joyce Lee. To Keep and Bear Arms: The Origins of an Anglo-American Right. United Kingdom: Harvard University Press, 1996.
24. *one-third, involved guns.* Ibid. p. 80
25. *gunpowder to Irish Catholics.* Ibid. p. 96
26. *Irish Army was Catholic.* Ibid. p. 97
27. *candidates and voters.* Ibid. p. 98
28. *he himself wished for."* Burnet, Gilbert. Bishop Burnet's History of His Own Time. vol. 1 edited by Gilbert Burnet, second son of the Bishop, and others; vol. 2 edited, with a life of the author, by Sir Thomas Burnet. L.P.. Ireland: J. Hyde, 1724.
29. *with Catholic officers.* Miller, John. "Catholic Officers in the Later Stuart Army." The English Historical Review LXXXVIII, no. CCCXLVI (January 1, 1973): 35–53. https://doi.org/10.1093/ehr/LXXXVIII.CCCXLVI.35.
30. *monarchs of all time.* Malcolm, Joyce Lee. To Keep and Bear Arms: The Origins of an Anglo-American Right. United Kingdom: Harvard University Press, 1996.
31. *avoid its clutches."* Ibid. p. 107
32. *across the country.* Childs, John Charles Roger., Childs, John. The army, James II, and the Glorious Revolution. Manchester: Manchester University Press, 1980.
33. *almost without restraint."* Ibid.
34. *legion of troops.* Ibid.
35. *become dead letters.* Malcolm, Joyce Lee. To Keep and Bear Arms: The

Origins of an Anglo-American Right. United Kingdom: Harvard University Press, 1996.

36. *till further order."* Ibid.
37. *their fellow citizens.* Ibid.
38. *J.R. Western put it.* Ibid.
39. *his empty promises.* Ibid.
40. *in the House of Commons."* Ibid.
41. *only 4,000 remained.* Ibid.
42. *threw up in a day."* Ibid.
43. *dread of military rule."* Ibid.
44. *a standing army."* Ibid.

Chapter 4: America's Love Affair with Guns Is Older than America

1. *of their arms."* Aristotle. Politics. United States: Dover Publications, 2012.
2. *go to prison."* Loesch, Dana. Hands Off My Gun: Defeating the Plot to Disarm America. United States: Center Street, 2014.
3. *against their interests.* Galiani, Sebastian, and Gustavo Torrens. "Why Not Taxation and Representation? A Note on the American Revolution." Cambridge, MA, October 2016. https://doi.org/10.3386/w22724.
4. *under any circumstances.* The Charter or Fundamental Laws, of West New Jersey, Agreed Upon - 1676 (1676). https://avalon.law.yale.edu/17th_century/nj05.asp
5. *they were armed.* Allen Candler, By D. The Colonial Records of the State of Georgia, Vol. 19: Part I. Forgotten Books, 2018.
6. *guns in America.* Lindgren, James, and Justin L Heather. "Counting Guns in Early America." Vol. 43, 2001. https://scholarship.law.wm.edu/wmlr.
7. *our Founding Fathers.* "The Demographics of Gun Ownership in the U.S. | Pew Research Center." Accessed October 8, 2020. https://www.pewsocialtrends.org/2017/06/22/the-demographics-of-gun-ownership/.

Chapter 5: Everything You Know About the American Revolution Is Wrong

1. *the cartridge box."* Van Auken, Robin., Hunsinger, Louis E.. Williamsport: Boomtown on the Susquehanna. United States: Arcadia, 2003. p. 57

2. *to command the Party."* Tse-Tung, Mao. Selected Works of Mao Tse-Tung: Vol. II. Second Pri. Foreign Languages Press, 1967. https://www.marxists.org/reference/archive/mao/selected-works/volume-2/index.htm.

3. *million of his countrymen, 1938.* "HOW MANY DIED? NEW EVIDENCE SUGGESTS FAR HIGHER NUMBERS FOR THE VICTIMS OF MAO ZEDONG'S ERA - The Washington Post." Accessed October 8, 2020. https://www.washingtonpost.com/archive/politics/1994/07/17/how-many-died-new-evidence-suggests-far-higher-numbers-for-the-victims-of-mao-zedongs-era/01044df5-03dd-49f4-a453-a033c5287bce/.

4. *American Revolutionary War.* Phaedo. N.p.: U.P., 1875.

5. *and the Netherlands.* Lindert, Peter H, and Jeffrey G Williamson. "Unequal Gains: American Growth and Inequality since 1700." Juncture 22, no. 4 (March 1, 2016): 276–83. https://doi.org/10.1111/j.2050-5876.2016.00874.x.

6. *one shilling per year.* Galiani, Sebastian, and Gustavo Torrens. "Why Not Taxation and Representation? A Note on the American Revolution." Cambridge, MA, October 2016. https://doi.org/10.3386/w22724.

7. *various colonies in 1765.* Walton, Gary M.., Shepherd, James F.. The Economic Rise of Early America. United Kingdom: Cambridge University Press, 1979.

8. *and political lobbying.* Galiani, Sebastian, and Gustavo Torrens. "Why Not Taxation and Representation? A Note on the American Revolution." Cambridge, MA, October 2016. https://doi.org/10.3386/w22724.

9. *big scheme of things.* McCusker, John J., and Russell R. Menard. 2014. The Economy of British America, 1607-1789. North Carolina: University of North Caroline Press.

10. *the nation's GDP.* "2. Estimates as a Percentage of Gross Domestic Product." Accessed October 8, 2020. https://www.ssa.gov/OACT/TR/2017/VI_G2_OASDHI_GDP.html.

11. *French and Indian War).* Galiani, Sebastian, and Gustavo Torrens. "Why Not Taxation and Representation? A Note on the American Revolution." Cambridge, MA, October 2016. https://doi.org/10.3386/

w22724; Atkinson, Rick. The British Are Coming: The War for America, Lexington to Princeton, 1775-1777. United Kingdom: HarperCollins Publishers, 2019. p. 8

12. *the Atlantic coast.* Brewer, John. 1988. The Sinews of Power: War, Money and the English State, 1688-1783. Cambridge, Massachusetts: Harvard University Press; Atkinson, Rick. The British Are Coming: The War for America, Lexington to Princeton, 1775-1777. United Kingdom: HarperCollins Publishers, 2019. p. 8

13. *on the colonists' behalf.* Middlekauff, Robert, 2007. The Glorious Cause: The American Revolution, 1763-1789 (Oxford History of the United States). 2nd Revised ed. Edition. Oxford, UK: Oxford University Press.

14. *plummeted 48 percent.* McCusker, John J., and Russell R. Menard. 2014. The Economy of British America, 1607-1789. North Carolina: University of North Caroline Press.

15. *a world to come.* Atkinson, Rick. The British Are Coming: The War for America, Lexington to Princeton, 1775-1777. United Kingdom: HarperCollins Publishers, 2019. p. 26

16. *much they produced.* Galiani, Sebastian, and Gustavo Torrens. "Why Not Taxation and Representation? A Note on the American Revolution." Cambridge, MA, October 2016. https://doi.org/10.3386/w22724

17. *in the 19th century.* Ibid.

18. *not when we must."* Atkinson, Rick. The British Are Coming: The War for America, Lexington to Princeton, 1775-1777. United Kingdom: HarperCollins Publishers, 2019. p. 20

19. *almost to madness."* Ibid.

20. *than the two last."* Atkinson, Rick. The British Are Coming: The War for America, Lexington to Princeton, 1775-1777. United Kingdom: HarperCollins Publishers, 2019. p. 22

21. *to join Parliament.* Galiani, Sebastian, and Gustavo Torrens. "Why Not Taxation and Representation? A Note on the American Revolution." Cambridge, MA, October 2016. https://doi.org/10.3386/w22724

22. *all of the colonies.* Atkinson, Rick. The British Are Coming: The War for America, Lexington to Princeton, 1775-1777. United Kingdom: HarperCollins Publishers, 2019. p. 8

23. *with the crown.* Ibid.

24. *instead of profit."* Atkinson, Rick. The British Are Coming: The War for America, Lexington to Princeton, 1775-1777. United Kingdom: HarperCollins Publishers, 2019. p. 13

25. *called English liberties."* Atkinson, Rick. The British Are Coming: The War for America, Lexington to Princeton, 1775-1777. United Kingdom: HarperCollins Publishers, 2019. p. 29
26. *them short of hanging."* Atkinson, Rick. The British Are Coming: The War for America, Lexington to Princeton, 1775-1777. United Kingdom: HarperCollins Publishers, 2019. p. 13
27. *"my deluded subjects."* Atkinson, Rick. The British Are Coming: The War for America, Lexington to Princeton, 1775-1777. United Kingdom: HarperCollins Publishers, 2019. p. 14
28. *view to homicide."* Zobel, Hiller B.., Adams, John., Wroth, L. Kinvin. Legal Papers of John Adams. United States: Belknap Press of Harvard University Press, 1965.
29. *pound of bullets by him . . ."* William Gerard Hamilton to Gerard Calcraft, February 1767, Chatham Correspondence, in Frank A. Mumby, George III and The American Revolution. London: Constable & Co., 1924. p. 173
30. *the Russian Empire.* "Population in the Colonial and Continental Periods." Accessed October 8, 2020. https://www2.census.gov/prod2/decennial/documents/00165897ch01.pdf: Morton, Rogers CB. "Historical Statistics of the United States: Colonial Times to 1970," 1975.
31. *the ancient Catepulta."* Shalhope, Robert E. "The Ideological Origins of the Second Amendment." The Journal of American History 69, no. 3 (1982): 599-614. Accessed October 8, 2020. doi:10.2307/1903139.
32. *three times per week.* Atkinson, Rick. The British Are Coming: The War for America, Lexington to Princeton, 1775-1777. United Kingdom: HarperCollins Publishers, 2019. p. 47
33. *the militia's response.* Kopel, David B. "How the British Gun Control Program Precipitated the American Revolution." SSRN Electronic Journal, January 5, 2012.
34. *the American militia.* Lord Dartmouth to Thomas Gage, February 1774 https://www.nps.gov/mima/learn/education/upload/Lord%20Dartmouth%20to%20General%20Thomas%20Gage.pdf
35. *Masters of the Country."* Kopel, David B. "How the British Gun Control Program Precipitated the American Revolution." SSRN Electronic Journal, January 5, 2012.
36. *war in 1783.* Ibid.
37. *the ships of war."* Frothingham, Richard. Life and Times of Joseph Warren. United States: Little, Brown, 1865. P. 381

38. *Virginia state militia.* "The Rise of Virginia's Independent Militia - Journal of the American Revolution." Accessed October 13, 2020. https://allthingsliberty.com/2014/09/the-rise-of-virginia-independent-militia/.
39. *are coming out!"* Revere, Paul. Paul Revere's Three Accounts of His Famous Ride. United States: Massachusetts Historical Society, 1961.
40. *let it begin here."* Coburn, Frank Warren. The Battle of April 19, 1775: In Lexington, Concord, Lincoln, Arlington, Cambridge, Somerville, and Charlestown, Massachusetts. United States: Lexington historical society, 1922.
41. *England is in earnest."* Atkinson, Rick. The British Are Coming: The War for America, Lexington to Princeton, 1775-1777. United Kingdom: HarperCollins Publishers, 2019. p. 47
42. *into Parker's men.* Maj. John Pitcairn to General Gage, April 26, 1775. www.digitalhistory.uh.edu/active_learning/explorations/revolution/account3_lexington.cf, accessed October 13, 2020.
43. *renew the attack.* Fischer, David Hackett., Fischer, Harmondsworth Professor of American History and Fellow David Hackett. Paul Revere's ride. United Kingdom: Oxford University Press, 1994.
44. *killing them without mercy . . ."* Massachusetts Spy (Worcester), May 3, 1775, at 3, col. 2.
45. *by some Officers."* Barker, Lt. John. The British in Boston. Being the Diary of Lieutenant John Barker of the King's Own Regiment from November 15, 1774 to May 31, 1776. Cambridge, MA: Harvard University Press, 1924.
46. *the Rubicon crossed."* Jennings, Francis. The creation of America: through revolution to empire. United Kingdom: Cambridge University Press, 2000. p. 158
47. *in his choice?"* Washington, George., Ford, Worthington Chauncey. The Writings of George Washington. United Kingdom: G.P. Putnam' Sons, 1889.
48. *stockpile of weapons.* Frothingham, Richard. History of the Siege of Boston, and of the Battles of Lexington, Concord, and Bunker Hill: Also an Account of the Bunker Hill Monument. United States: Little, Brown, & Company, 1903.
49. *possessions in Boston.* Meyer, H. H. B. Documents Illustrative of the Formation of the Union of the States, H.R Doc. No. 398, 69th Cong. 1st Sess. 14-15, 1927

50. *dominion in America."* Clinton, Henry. The American Rebellion: Sir Henry Clinton's Narrative of His Campaigns, 1775-1782, with an Appendix of Original Documents. United Kingdom: Yale University Press, 1954.
51. *son in the streets.* Plutarch, The Parallel Lives
52. *the American trenches.* Atkinson, Rick. The British Are Coming: The War for America, Lexington to Princeton, 1775-1777. United Kingdom: HarperCollins Publishers, 2019. p. 61

Chapter 6: Why Does the United States Have a Bill of Rights?

1. *the killer's hands."* Seneca, Letters from a Stoic, Letter LXXXVII: Some arguments in favor of the simple life
2. *hands of everyday people."* "Tucker Presses Bill de Blasio: NYC Is Dirty, and Getting Dirtier - YouTube." Accessed October 13, 2020. https://www.youtube.com/watch?v=WejRt8DZ1gE&feature=emb_title.
3. *makes war upon him."* Locke, John. Two Treatises of Government. United Kingdom: C. and J. Rivington, 1824.
4. *a Bill of Rights."* George Washington to Lafayette, April 28– May 1, 1788. https://founders.archives.gov/documents/Washington/04-06-02-0211. Accessed October 13, 2020.
5. *shape of a motion."* Levy, Leonard Williams. Origins of the Bill of Rights. United Kingdom: Yale University Press, 2001. p. 13
6. *a Bill of Rights."* Hamilton, Alexander, The Federalist Papers, No. 84
7. *right is abandoned?"* Levy, Leonard Williams. Origins of the Bill of Rights. United Kingdom: Yale University Press, 2001. p. 29
8. *not expressly reserved."* Ibid, p. 30
9. *in a monarchy."* Ibid.
10. *be of disservice."* Bowling, Kenneth R. "'A Tub to the Whale': The Founding Fathers and Adoption of the Federal Bill of Rights." Journal of the Early Republic 8, no. 3 (1988): 223.
11. *no Bill of Rights."* Wood, Gordon S.. Empire of Liberty: A History of the Early Republic, 1789-1815. United Kingdom: Oxford University Press, 2009.

Chapter 7: What the Second Amendment Was *Really* Meant to Protect

1. *all of them imaginary."* Mencken, Henry Louis. In defense of women. United States: Dover Publications, 2004.

2. *death and horror."* Spitzer, Eliot. "Gun Control: Obama and Bloomberg Could Limit Semi-Automatics by Using Government Purchasing Power." Accessed October 14, 2020. https://slate.com/news-and-politics/2012/08/gun-control-obama-and-bloomberg-could-limit-semi-automatics-by-using-government-purchasing-power.html.

3. *violence from others.* Curran, Eleanor, and Eleanor Curran. "The Full Right to Self-Preservation and Sovereign Duties." In Reclaiming the Rights of the Hobbesian Subject, 103–22. Palgrave Macmillan UK, 2007.

4. *with the People."* Locke, John. Two Treatises of Government. United Kingdom: C. and J. Rivington, 1824.

5. *violence of oppression."* Blackstone, William. Commentaries on the Laws of England. United Kingdom: n.p., 1862.

6. *with ammunition suitable."* Konig, David Thomas. "The Second Amendment: A Missing Transatlantic Context for the Historical Meaning of 'the Right of the People to Keep and Bear Arms.'" Law and History Review 22, no. 1 (2004): 119–59.

7. *slave for life."* Burgh, James. Political Disquisitions: Or, An Inquiry Into Public Errors, Defects, and Abuses. Illustrated By, and Established Upon Facts and Remarks, Extracted from a Variety of Authors, Ancient and Modern.... United States: Robert Bell, in Third-street; and William Woodhouse, in Front-street., 1775.

8. *my own Life."* John Adams to Thomas Jefferson, February 3, 1812. https://founders.archives.gov/documents/Jefferson/03-04-02-0361

9. *Milo at Rome."* Madison, James., Elliot, Jonathan. The Debates in the Several State Conventions on the Adoption of the Federal Constitution as Recommended by the General Convention at Philadelphia, in 1787: Together with the Journal of the Federal Convention, Luther Martin's Letter, Yates's Minutes, Congressional Opinions, Virginia and Kentucky Resolutions of '98-'99, and Other Illustrations of the Constitution. United States: Lippincott, 1888.

10. *Founding Fathers themselves:* Cicero, Selected Political Speeches, Translated by M. Grant, p.222, 1969

11. *revolution was justified.* Maier, Pauline. From Resistance to Revolution.

United Kingdom: Knopf Doubleday Publishing Group, 2013.

12. *they are accustomed."* Thomas Jefferson, et al, July 4, Copy of Declaration of Independence. -07-04, 1776. Manuscript/Mixed Material. https://www.loc.gov/item/mtjbib000159/.

13. *"Woe to the vanquished."* In 390 BCE, an army of Gauls led by the Brennus, chieftain of the Senones, swept through what is modern-day France, crossed the Alps, routed a Roman Army at Allia, and then sacked Rome. Well, almost all of Rome. A small force held out on the Capitoline Hill in the west of the city and were able to broker a peace agreement with the barbarians: they would pay Brennus to leave. As the Romans weighed their ransom—1,000 pounds of gold—they complained that the scales were loaded in Brennus's favor. In response, Brennus threw his sword on the scales (increasing the amount of gold the Romans would have to pay), and snarled, "Vae victis." "Woe to the vanquished."

14. *occupying New Jersey.* Atkinson, Rick. The British Are Coming: The War for America, Lexington to Princeton, 1775-1777. United Kingdom: HarperCollins Publishers, 2019. p. 497

15. *for multiple terms.* Stout, S.E. "Training Soldiers for the Roman Legion on JSTOR." Accessed October 14, 2020. https://www.jstor.org/stable/3288082?seq=4#metadata_info_tab_contents.

16. *citizens grew complacent.* Gibbon, Edward. The History of the Decline and Fall of the Roman Empire. United Kingdom: R. Priestley, ... J. Offor, ... W.H. Reid, ... Priestley and Weale, ... M. Doyle, ... and D.A. Talboys, Oxford, 1821.

17. *power on our side . . ."* Atkinson, Rick. The British Are Coming: The War for America, Lexington to Princeton, 1775-1777. United Kingdom: HarperCollins Publishers, 2019. p. 21

18. *company of Connecticut militia.* Ibid. p. 107

19. *hungry or grew impatient.* Ibid. p. 84

20. *a broken staff."* George Washington to John Hancock, September 25, 1776. https://founders.archives.gov/documents/Washington/03-06-02-0305#:~:text=To%20place%20any%20dependance%20upon,resting%20upon%20a%20broken%20staff.&text=These%20Sir%2C%20Congress%20may%20be,%2C%20%26%20that%20is%20the%20expence.

21. *massive foreign armies.* Atkinson, Rick. The British Are Coming: The War for America, Lexington to Princeton, 1775-1777. United Kingdom: HarperCollins Publishers, 2019. p. 563

22. *of regular troops."* Webster, Noah. An Examination Into the Leading Principles of the Federal Constitution Proposed by the Late Convention Held at Philadelphia. With Answers to the Principal Objections That Have Been Raised Against the System. By a Citizen of America. United States: Creative Media Partners, LLC, 2018.

23. *may have a gun."* Henry, Patrick. The Founders' Constitution. Volume 3, Article 1, Section 8, Clause 16, Document 10. The University of Chicago Press, 1788. http://press-pubs.uchicago.edu/founders/documents/a1_8_16s10.html

24. *a free country."* Hamilton, Alexander, The Federalist Papers, No. 29

25. *a free people."* Hamilton, Alexander, The Federalist Papers, No. 28

26. *of regular troops."* Madison, James. The Federalist Papers, No. 46

Chapter 8: Are Guns Only for People in the Military? Here's What the Founders Wanted . . .

1. *creed of slaves."* Pitt, William, speech at House of Commons (18 November 1783), in Oxford Essential Quotations. Vol. 1., Ratcliffe, Susan, ed. Oxford University Press, 2016. https://www.oxfordreference.com/view/10.1093/acref/9780191826719.001.0001/q-oro-ed4-00008337

2. *these [assault] weapons."* Press Release 'ATF data', Nov 5, 2003

3. *idea as collectivists.* This isn't meant to imply these people are communists, socialists, or "collectivists" in the broader sense, but calling them "supporters of the collective-theory of the Second Amendment" would have been too wordy.

4. *age of forty-five years . . ."* Militia Act of 1792, May 8, 1792, art. I

5. *the National Guard."* "Implementing the National Defense Strategy 3 CNGB EXECUTIVE OVERVIEW 19 FIGHTING AMERICA'S WARS," n.d.

6. *people who elected him.* S. 2766 (109th): John Warner National Defense Authorization Act for Fiscal Year 2007

7. *the federal government.* Farrand, Max. The Records of the Federal Convention of 1787, vol. 2 [1911]; Friedman, Leon. Conscription and the Constitution, 67 MICH. L. REV. 1493, 1537-38 (1969).

8. *denied and denounced.* Yassky, David. "The Second Amendment: Structure, History, and Constitutional Change." Pace Law Faculty Publications, December 1, 2000. https://digitalcommons.pace.edu/lawfaculty/928.

References

9. *historian David Yassky.* Ibid.

10. *in the US war machine.* This is not a criticism of the men and women who serve in the National Guard (which would include the author's brother), but a criticism of the concentration of military power under federal control.

11. *aged 17 to 45.* "[USC02] 10 USC Ch. 12: THE MILITIA." Accessed October 14, 2020. https://uscode.house.gov/view.xhtml?path=/prelim@title10/subtitleA/part1/chapter12&edition=prelim.

12. *it deems proper."* Charles, Patrick J.. The Second Amendment: The Intent and Its Interpretation by the States and the Supreme Court. United Kingdom: McFarland, Incorporated, Publishers, 2009.

13. *the American Bar Association."* Kates, Don B. "Handgun Prohibition and the Original Meaning of the Second Amendment," April 15, 1983. https://papers.ssrn.com/abstract=2953447.

14. *4.6 million to 13 million.* Lott, John R., John E Whitley, and Rebekah C. Riley. "Concealed Carry Permit Holders Across the United States." SSRN Electronic Journal, July 22, 2015. https://doi.org/10.2139/ssrn.2629704.

15. *support for gun control.* Pew Research Center." Accessed October 14, 2020. https://www.pewresearch.org/politics/2010/03/23/public-divided-over-state-local-laws-banning-handguns/; "Despite More Shootings, Americans Are Less Supportive of Tougher Gun Control HuffPost." Accessed October 14, 2020. https://www.huffpost.com/entry/shootings-guns-and-public_b_8065682.

16. *half supporting less.* "Stricter Gun Laws Have Gained Support in U.S. since 2017 | Pew Research Center." Accessed October 14, 2020. https://www.pewresearch.org/fact-tank/2019/10/16/share-of-americans-who-favor-stricter-gun-laws-has-increased-since-2017/.

17. *private gun ownership.* "Americans Prefer Living in Neighborhoods With Guns - Rasmussen Reports®." Accessed October 14, 2020. https://www.rasmussenreports.com/public_content/politics/current_events/gun_control/americans_prefer_living_in_neighborhoods_with_guns.

18. *40 percent opposed it.* "Guns | Gallup Historical Trends." Accessed October 14, 2020. https://news.gallup.com/poll/1645/guns.aspx.

19. *in Article 1, Section 8.* U.S. Const. art. I,§8. https://www.law.cornell.edu/constitution/articlei

20. *bear their private arms.* Halbrook, Stephen P.. That Every Man be Armed: The Evolution of a Constitutional Right. United States: University of New Mexico Press, 2013.

21. *First Congress was meeting.* Hardy, David T. "The Rise and Demise of the Collective Right Interpretation of the Second Amendment." Accessed October 14, 2020. https://engagedscholarship.csuohio.edu/clevstl-revhttps://engagedscholarship.csuohio.edu/clevstlrev/vol59/iss3/4.
22. *the heads of household.* George Mason, 3 Elliot, Debates at 425-426
23. *of powder and ball."* Militia Act of 1792, May 8, 1792, art. I
24. *wrote in 1891 that:* Siegel, Stephen A. "Historism in Late Nineteenth Century Constitutional Thought," July 31, 1990. https://papers.ssrn.com/abstract=1322161.
25. *law for the purpose."* Cooley, Thomas McIntyre. The General Principles of Constitutional Law in the United States of America. United States: Lawbook Exchange, 2000.
26. *life, liberty, chastity . . ."* Spooner, Lysander. The Unconstitutionality of Slavery. United States: B. Marsh, 1845.
27. *paper it consumed."* Tiffany, Joel. A Treatise on the Unconstitutionality of American Slavery: Together with the Powers and Duties of the Federal Government in Relation to that Subject. United States: J. Calyer, printer, 1850.
28. *Second Amendment was written.* Johnson, Samuel. A Dictionary Of The English Language: In Which The Words are Deduced from Their Originals, And Illustrated in Their Different Significations By Examples from the Best Writers, To Which Are Prefixed, A History of the Language, And An English Grammar : In Two Volumes. United Kingdom: Knapton, 1755.
29. *armour of defence."* Ibid. https://johnsonsdictionaryonline.com/arms/
30. *or strike another."* Cunningham, Timothy. A New and Complete Law-dictionary: Or, General Abridgment of the Law : on a More Extensive Plan Than Any Law-dictionary Hitherto Published : Containing Not Only the Explanation of the Terms, But Also the Law Itself, Both with Regard to Theory and Practice. Very Useful to Barristers, Justices of the Peace, Attornies, Solicitors, &c. United Kingdom: Law printers to the King's Most Excellent Majesty, 1765.
31. *with his bare hands.* Beowulf. Translated by Lesslie Hall. The Project Gutenberg. Part 7, Line 65. https://www.gutenberg.org/files/16328/16328-h/16328-h.htm
32. *manner of Weapon . . ."* Cramer, Clayton E, and Joseph Edward Olson. "What Did 'Bear Arms' Mean in the Second Amendment?" Accessed October 14, 2020. http://ssrn.com/abstract=1086176.

References

33. *abroad in the Fields...*" 1 Geo. 1, c. 54 (1715).
34. *violation of the statute.* Cramer, Clayton E., and Joseph Edward Olson. "What Did 'Bear Arms' Mean in the Second Amendment?" Accessed October 14, 2020. http://ssrn.com/abstract=1086176.
35. *their own defence."* The London Magazine, or Gentleman's Monthly Intelligencer. October, 1780, at 467-68
36. *official state militia.* Pennsylvania Const. XIII. September 28, 1776. https://avalon.law.yale.edu/18th_century/pa08.asp
37. *their state constitution.* Verment Const. XV. July 8, 1777. https://avalon.law.yale.edu/18th_century/vt01.asp
38. *the British government."* Tucker, St. George., Christian, Edward., Blackstone, William. Blackstone's Commentaries: With Notes of Reference, to the Constitution and Laws, of the Federal Government of the United States; and of the Commonwealth of Virginia. In Five Volumes. With an Appendix to Each Volume, Containing Short Tracts Upon Such Subjects as Appeared Necessary to Form a Connected View of the Laws of Virginia, as a Member of the Federal Union. United States: William Young Birch, and Abraham Small ... Robert Carr, printer, 1803.
39. *not be infringed...*" Nunn v. State, 1 Ga. 243 (1846).
40. *Supreme Court of Kansas in 1905.* Salina v. Blaksley, 72 Kan. 230, 83 P. 619, 3 L.R.A. (N.S.) 168, 115 Am. St. Rep. 196, 7 Am. & Eng. Ann. Cas. 925 (1905).
41. *as practicable observed."* Bishop, Joel Prentiss. Commentaries on the Law of Statutory Crimes: Embracing the General Principles of Interpretation of Statutes; Particular Principles Applicable in Criminal Cases; Leading Doctrines of the Common Law of Crimes, and Discussions of the Specific Statutory Offenses, as to Both Law and Procedure. United States: Little, Brown,, 1873.
42. *drills and parades."* Commonwealth v. Murphy, 166 Mass. 171, 44 N.E. 138 (1896).
43. *violated the Second Amendment.* Hardy, David T. "The Rise and Demise of the Collective Right Interpretation of the Second Amendment." Accessed October 14, 2020. https://engagedscholarship.csuohio.edu/clevstlrevhttps://engagedscholarship.csuohio.edu/clevstlrev/vol59/iss3/4.
44. *to commit crimes.* "John Dillinger — FBI." Accessed October 15, 2020. https://www.fbi.gov/history/famous-cases/john-dillinger.

45. *and still are).* Cummings, Homer. Selected Papers of Homer Cummings: Attorney General of the United States, 1933-1939. United States: Literary Licensing, LLC, 2013.
46. *Second Amendment rights.* Frye, Brian L. "The Peculiar Story of United States v. Miller." NYU Journal of Law & Liberty 3, no. 48–82 (2008).
47. *decision—not guilty.* United States v. Miller, 26 F. Supp. 1002 (W.D. Ark. 1939) https://law.justia.com/cases/federal/district-courts/FSupp/26/1002/2593592/#:~:text=The%20court%20is%20of%20the,%2C%20shall%20not%20be%20infringed.%22
48. *cherished American right.* Frye, Brian L. "The Peculiar Story of United States v. Miller." NYU Journal of Law & Liberty 3, no. 48–82 (2008).
49. *bolster the NFA.* Ibid.
50. *personal friend of mine."* Letter from Heartsill Ragon, Judge, W.D. Ark., to John J. Cochran, US Representative, Mo. (April 10, 1939) (on file with the University of Arkansas at Little Rock Archives and Special Collections).
51. *relation to the militia."* Supreme Court Bars Sawed-Off Shotgun, N.Y. TIMES, May 16, 1939, at 15.
52. *guarding German prisoners.* Crowell, Benedict. America's Munitions 1917-1918: Report of Benedict Crowell, the Assistant Secretary of War, Director of Munitions. United States: U.S. Government Printing Office, 1919. https://archive.org/details/americasmunitio01deptgoog
53. *historian Leonard Levy.* Levy, Leonard Williams. Origins of the Bill of Rights. United Kingdom: Yale University Press, 2001. p. 136
54. *and even silencers.* Cases v. United States, 131 F.2d 916, 922 (1st Cir. 1942), cert. denied, 319 US 770 (1943).
55. *Cases v. US (1943), and others.* United States v. Rybar, 103 F.3d 273 (3d Cir. 1997), cert. denied, 522 US 807 (1997); United States v. Toner, 728 F.2d 115 (2d Cir. 1984); United States v. Warin, 530 F.2d 103 (6th Cir. 1976), cert. denied, 426 US 948 (1976); Cases v. United States, 131 F.2d 916 (1st Cir. 1942), cert. denied, 319 US 770 (1943).
56. *to own guns.* United States v. Verdugo-Urquidez, 494 U.S. 259 (1990) https://supreme.justia.com/cases/federal/us/494/259/
57. *semi-automatic rifles.* Jones, E.D. "District of Columbia's 'Firearms Control Regulations Act of 1975' - The Toughest Handgun Control Law in the United States - Or Is It?" National Criminal Justice Reference Service, 1981, 29. https://www.ncjrs.gov/App/Publications/abstract.aspx?ID=78721.

58. *use in their homes."* District of Columbia v. Heller, 554 U.S. 570 (2008) https://supreme.justia.com/cases/federal/us/554/570/
59. *within the home."* Ibid.

Chapter 9: "You Only Have the Right to Own a Musket" and Other Second Amendment Myths, Debunked

1. *perverted it into tyranny."* Jefferson, Thomas. "A Bill for the More General Diffusion of Knowledge," PTJ, 2:526-35.
2. *the 18th century."* Stephens, John Paul. "Opinion | John Paul Stevens: Repeal the Second Amendment - The New York Times." The New York Times, 2018. https://www.nytimes.com/2018/03/27/opinion/john-paul-stevens-repeal-second-amendment.html.
3. *forty-six percent.* Baumer, Eric P., and Kevin T. Wolff. "Evaluating Contemporary Crime Drop(s) in America, New York City, and Many Other Places." Justice Quarterly 31, no. 1 (2014): 5–38.; Renno Santos, Mateus, and Alexander Testa. "Homicide Is Declining around the World – but Why?" The Conversation, 2019. https://theconversation.com/homicide-is-declining-around-the-world-but-why-125365.
4. *want to own one."* Prothrow-Stith, Deborah, and Michaele Weissman. Deadly Consequences. HarperCollins, 1993, p. 198.
5. *against American citizens.* Lafre, Gary, and Laura Dugan. "78% 22% Terrorist Attacks in the U.S Between 1970 and 2013: Data from the Global Terrorism Database (GTD) Project Investigators," 1970. www.start.umd.edu/. https://www.dhs.gov/sites/default/files/publications/OPSR_TP_TEVUS_Terrorist-Attacks-US_1970-2013_Overview-508.pdf
6. *"It is always there."* Thucydides. History of the Peloponnesian War. United States: Hogan and Thompson, 1836.
7. *be occupied again."* Drews, Robert. The End of the Bronze Age: Changes in Warfare and the Catastrophe ca 1200 B.C. Princeton, New Jersey: Princeton University Press, 1993, p. 8.
8. *blink of an eye.* Fisher, Max, and Amanda Taub. "How Venezuela Went from the Richest Economy in South America to the Brink of Financial Ruin | The Independent | The Independent." Independant, 2017. https://www.independent.co.uk/news/long_reads/how-venezuela-went-richest-economy-south-america-brink-financial-ruin-a7740616.html.
9. *rewrite the constitution.* Neuman, Scott. "Venezuela Agents Arrest

Opposition Leaders In Midnight Raids : The Two-Way : NPR." National Public Radio, 2017. https://www.npr.org/sections/thetwo-way/2017/08/01/540790886/venezuela-agents-arrest-opposition-leaders-in-midnight-raids; Ellsworth, Brian, and Stephanie Nebehay. "U.N. Decries Excessive Force in Venezuela's Crackdown on Protests | World News | US News." US News, 2017. https://www.usnews.com/news/world/articles/2017-08-08/venezuelas-top-court-order-arrest-of-opposition-mayor-muchacho; Casey, Nicholas. "Nicolás Maduro, Venezuela President, Calls for a Rewrite of the Constitution - The New York Times." New York Times, 2017. https://www.nytimes.com/2017/05/01/world/americas/venezuela-nicolas-maduro-constitution.html.

10. *guns in 2009.* "Venezuela Bans Private Gun Ownership - BBC News." Accessed October 15, 2020. https://www.bbc.com/news/world-latin-america-18288430.

11. *the Middle East.* "No Country Is Free from Modern Slavery, but Would You Know It If You Saw It? | Globalization | DW | 25.03.2020." Accessed October 15, 2020. https://www.dw.com/en/why-modern-slavery-and-human-trafficking-still-exist-world/a-52853992.

12. *series of predictable stages.* Podes, Stephan. "POLYBIUS AND HIS THEORY OF 'ANACYCLOSIS' PROBLEMS OF NOT JUST ANCIENT POLITICAL THEORY on JSTOR." History of Political Thought 12, no. 4 (1991): 577–87. https://www.jstor.org/stable/26213908?seq=1.

13. *would be necessary."* Madison, James, The Federalist Papers, No. 51

14. *and oppressing others.* Ervin, Sam J. "SEPARATION OF POWERS: JUDICIAL INDEPENDENCE," n.d.

15. *every respect diabolical."* John Adams to Thomas Jefferson, November 13, 1815. https://founders.archives.gov/documents/Adams/99-02-02-6539

16. *kill a flea."* Adams, Charles Francis., Adams, John. The Works of John Adams, Second President of the United States: With a Life of the Author, Notes and Illustrations. United States: Little, Brown, 1851.

17. *are inevitably ruined."* Speech of Patrick Henry (June 5, 1788) http://www.let.rug.nl/usa/documents/1786-1800/the-anti-federalist-papers/speech-of-patrick-henry-(june-5-1788).php

18. *bombers and tanks."* District of Columbia v. Heller, 554 U.S. 570 (2008) https://supreme.justia.com/cases/federal/us/554/570/

19. *war breaks out."* "Why World War II Matters - Victor Davis Hanson

References

- YouTube." Accessed October 15, 2020. https://www.youtube.com/watch?v=opDuw4OZ3QI&feature=youtu.be&t=2684.

20. *try something stupid.*" "Victor Davis Hanson on Grand Strategy, Immigration, and the 2016 Presidential Election - YouTube." Accessed October 15, 2020. https://www.youtube.com/watch?v=IvEXjW-JoV-Y&feature=youtu.be&t=452.

21. *to live slaves.*" Declaration of the Causes & Necessity of Taking Up Arms. United States: Great Neck Publishing., (n.d.).

22. *of the time.* "Criminal Victimization in the United States, 2008," 2011. https://www.bjs.gov/content/pub/pdf/cvus/current/cv08107.pdf.

23. *wait much longer.* Mell, Howard K., Shannon N. Mumma, Brian Hiestand, Brendan G. Carr, Tara Holland, and Jason Stopyra. "Emergency Medical Services Response Times in Rural, Suburban, and Urban Areas." JAMA Surgery. American Medical Association, October 1, 2017; Sutton, Haley. "See How Your Emergency Response Time Measures Up." Campus Security Report, 2019.

24. *about gun control.* "PoliceOne's 2013 Gun Policy & Law Enforcement Survey Results: Executive Summary." Accessed October 15, 2020. https://www.police1.com/police-products/firearms/accessories/articles/policeones-2013-gun-policy-law-enforcement-survey-results-executive-summary-x02GJHRSJXGbGwH9/.

25. *the United States.* Ludwig, Jens. "Gun Self-Defense and Deterrence." Crime and Justice 27 (January 29, 2000): 363–417.

26. *a lot worse.*" "Man Shot Dead Inside West Philadelphia Barbershop – CBS Philly." Accessed October 15, 2020. https://philadelphia.cbslocal.com/2015/03/22/man-shot-dead-inside-west-philadelphia-barbershop/.

27. *in the crowd.* "Man Slain in Logan Square Was Involved in Early Test of State's Concealed Carry Law in 2015 - Chicago Tribune." Accessed October 15, 2020. https://www.chicagotribune.com/news/breaking/ct-met-murder-victim-shot-by-ccl-holder-20190325-story.html.

28. *in White Settlement, Texas.* "Texas Grand Jury: No Action against Killer of Church Shooter - ABC News." Accessed October 15, 2020. https://abcnews.go.com/US/wireStory/texas-grand-jury-action-killer-church-shooter-73302636.

29. *congregation was armed.* "Stephen Willeford Still Grappling With the Sutherland Springs Mass Murder." Accessed October 15, 2020. https://www.texasmonthly.com/articles/stephen-willeford-sutherland-springs-mass-murder/.

30. *securing the building.* "This Is What Scot Peterson Did during the Parkland School Shooting - CNN." Accessed October 15, 2020. https://www.cnn.com/2019/06/04/us/parkland-scot-peterson-actions/index.html.

31. *negligence, and perjury.* "Parkland Officer Who Stayed Outside During Shooting Faces Criminal Charges - The New York Times." Accessed October 15, 2020. https://www.nytimes.com/2019/06/04/us/parkland-scot-peterson.html.

32. *had already escaped.* "UNPREPARED AND OVERWHELMED | South Florida Sun Sentinel | Sun Sentinel." Accessed October 15, 2020. https://projects.sun-sentinel.com/2018/sfl-parkland-school-shooting-critical-moments/.

33. *to police training.* "Broward Deputies Told to Set up Perimeter around Parkland Shooting | Miami Herald." Accessed October 15, 2020. https://www.miamiherald.com/news/local/community/broward/article203015289.html.

34. *after the shooting.* Nehamas, Nicholas. "After Criticism, BSO Captain in Charge of Parkland Shooting Response Resigns." Miami Herald, 2018. https://www.miamiherald.com/news/local/community/broward/article221975890.html

35. *confront active shooters.* "Parkland Shooting Commission Slams Responding Officers." Accessed October 15, 2020. https://nypost.com/2019/01/03/parkland-shooting-report-backs-arming-teachers-slams-police-response/.

36. *Broward County again.* "Florida Senate Votes To Permanently Remove Former Broward Sheriff Scott Israel – CBS Miami." Accessed October 15, 2020. https://miami.cbslocal.com/2019/10/23/florida-senate-votes-25-15-not-to-reinstate-former-sheriff-scott-israel/.

37. *neglect of duty."* "Florida Governor Replaces Broward Sheriff, Citing 'Incompetence' : NPR." Accessed October 15, 2020. https://www.npr.org/2019/01/11/684652465/florida-governor-replaces-broward-sheriff-citing-incompetence.

38. *calls to police.* "Sheriff Says He Got 23 Calls about Shooter's Family, but Records Show More - CNN." Accessed October 15, 2020. https://www.cnn.com/2018/02/27/us/parkland-shooter-cruz-sheriff-calls-invs/index.html.

39. *on his arms.* Nehamas, Nicholas. "'School Shooter in the Making': All the Times Authorities Were Warned about Nikolas Cruz." Miami Herald, 2018. http://www.miamiherald.com/news/local/

community/broward/article201684874.html

40. *a school shooting.* "F.B.I. Was Warned of Florida Suspect's Desire to Kill but Did Not Act - The New York Times." Accessed October 15, 2020. https://www.nytimes.com/2018/02/16/us/fbi-nikolas-cruz-shooting.html.

41. *up the school.* "UNPREPARED AND OVERWHELMED | South Florida Sun Sentinel | Sun Sentinel." Accessed October 15, 2020. https://projects.sun-sentinel.com/2018/sfl-parkland-school-shooting-critical-moments/.

42. *ignored his advice.* "Retired Secret Service Agent Had Warned Stoneman Douglas about Security Failures - South Florida Sun Sentinel - South Florida Sun-Sentinel." Accessed October 15, 2020. https://www.sun-sentinel.com/local/broward/parkland/florida-school-shooting/fl-sb-douglas-secret-service-steve-wexler-20180605-story.html.

43. *Cynthia Renaud removed.* "Petition · Santa Monica City Council: Remove Santa Monica Police Chief Cynthia Renaud Immediately · Change.Org." Accessed October 15, 2020. https://www.change.org/p/santa-monica-city-council-remove-santa-monica-police-chief-cynthia-renaud-immediately?use_react=false.

44. *16-year old boy.* "1 Teen Killed, 1 Injured after 4th Shooting near Seattle's CHOP | King5.Com." Accessed October 15, 2020. https://www.king5.com/article/news/crime/seattle-shooting-capitol-hill-chop-chaz/281-48392a9e-d760-42f3-9469-c99466ed7a9f.

45. *we don't stay.* "Denver Police Department Lieutenant Ignored 'Retreat Order' during Sunday Clash at Civic Center, Union Leaders Says." Accessed October 15, 2020. https://www.denverpost.com/2020/07/22/denver-police-union-apology-protest-retreat-order/.

46. *assault rifles. Fact.* "(19) Piers Morgan on Twitter: 'The 2nd Amendment Was Devised with Muskets in Mind, Not High-Powered Handguns & Assault Rifles. Fact.' / Twitter." Accessed October 15, 2020. https://twitter.com/piersmorgan/status/275709039235694592?lang=en.

47. *"practical European socialist."* "The 2nd Amendment : For Muskets Only?! - YouTube." Accessed October 15, 2020. https://www.youtube.com/watch?v=CquUBWHU2_s&feature=youtu.be&t=35; "The Sunday Conversation: Lawrence O'Donnell - Los Angeles Times." Accessed October 15, 2020. https://www.latimes.com/entertainment/tv/la-xpm-2013-mar-16-la-et-st-lawrence-odonnell-msnbc-conversation-20130317-story.html.

48. *actor Tom Selleck.* "Tom Selleck on the Rosie O'Donnell Show - Gun Control - YouTube." Accessed October 15, 2020. https://www.youtube.com/watch?v=JwPTUktp0gI.
49. *of the founding.*" Heller, Al V. "SUPREME COURT OF THE UNITED STATES Syllabus DISTRICT OF COLUMBIA ET," 2007.
50. *the late 1600s.* Hoff, Arne. Dutch Firearms. United Kingdom: Sotheby Parke Bernet, 1978.
51. *a test in 1722.* Willbanks, James H.. Machine Guns: An Illustrated History of Their Impact. United Kingdom: ABC-CLIO, 2004.
52. *designs from 1690).* "Flint-Lock Magazine Gun | Cookson, John | V&A Search the Collections." Accessed October 15, 2020. https://collections.vam.ac.uk/item/O77720/flint-lock-magazine-cookson-john/.
53. *shots per minute.* Gilchrist, Marianne McLeod., Macleod, Iseabail. Patrick Ferguson: 'a Man of Some Genius'. United Kingdom: NMS Enterprises, 2003.
54. *rounds per minute.* Peterson, Harold Leslie. Arms and Armor in Colonial America, 1526-1783. United States: Dover Publications, 2000.
55. *rifles too expensive.* Ibid.
56. *the Pacific Coast.* Fletcher, D. T.. Austrian Military Airguns. N.p.: CreateSpace Independent Publishing Platform, 2018; Wier, S K. "The Firearms of the Lewis and Clark Expedition," n.d.
57. *of the trigger.* Kinard, Jeff. Pistols : an illustrated history of their impact. Santa Barbara: ABC-CLIO, 2003.
58. *Second Amendment was written.* "Da Vinci Weapons of War." Accessed October 15, 2020. https://www.italian-renaissance-art.com/Da-Vinci-weapons.html.
59. *his spare time.* "Firearms | Thomas Jefferson's Monticello." Accessed October 15, 2020. https://www.monticello.org/site/research-and-collections/firearms; "Thomas Jefferson's 'Assault Rifle' - The Girardoni Air Rifle." Accessed October 15, 2020. https://thefederalistpapers.org/founders/jefferson/thomas-jeffersons-assault-rifle-the-girardoni-air-rifle.
60. *weapons he captured.* "James Madison Letter of Marque Signed.... Autographs U.S. | Lot #34255 | Heritage Auctions." Accessed October 15, 2020. https://historical.ha.com/itm/autographs/u.s.-presidents/james-madison-letter-of-marque-signed/a/6093-34255.s.
61. "Privateers in the American Revolution." Accessed May 17, 2021. https://www.nps.gov/articles/privateers-in-the-american-revolution.htm.

Chapter 10: 3 Things You Can Do Right Now to Defend Your Second Amendment Rights

1. *need of masters."* Benjamin Franklin to the Abbés Chalut and Arnoux, April 17, 1787. https://franklinpapers.org/framedVolumes.jsp?vol=44&page=605
2. *what you intended."* Cockburn, Patrick. "Saddam Hussein: Deluded and Defiant, a Dictator Awaits His Nemesis | The Independent." Independant, March 6, 2003. https://www.independent.co.uk/news/world/politics/saddam-hussein-deluded-and-defiant-a-dictator-awaits-his-nemesis-121766.html.
3. *Kuwait and Iran, 1979.* "War in Iraq: Not a Humanitarian Intervention | Human Rights Watch," 2004. https://www.hrw.org/news/2004/01/25/war-iraq-not-humanitarian-intervention#.
4. *from Duke University.* Moyer, Melinda Wenner. "More Guns Do Not Stop More Crimes, Evidence Shows - Scientific American." Scientific American, October 1, 2017. https://www.scientificamerican.com/article/more-guns-do-not-stop-more-crimes-evidence-shows/.
5. *in midterm elections.* Bureau, US Census. "Historical Reported Voting Rates." Accessed October 15, 2020. https://www.census.gov/library/visualizations/time-series/demo/voting-historical-time-series.html.
6. *Democrats since 2012.* "Benchmade Knife Co Profile: Recipients • OpenSecrets." Accessed October 15, 2020. https://www.opensecrets.org/orgs/benchmade-knife-co/recipients?id=D000047693.
7. *gun control legislation.* "Daniel Defense's Marty Daniel: I Was Wrong About FixNICS - The Truth About Guns." Accessed October 15, 2020. https://www.thetruthaboutguns.com/daniel-defenses-marty-daniel-changed-mind-fixnics/.

Chapter 11: The Civilian's Guide to Buying (and Safely Using) Guns, Ammo, and Other "Military" Arms

1. *is physical force.* Orwell, George. 'Pacifism and the War' First published: Partisan Review. GB, London. August-September 1942. https://www.orwell.ru/library/articles/pacifism/english/e_patw
2. *disarm it ourselves."* The Political Report of the Central Committee, The Fifteenth Congress of the C.P.S.U.(B.) (7 December 1927). https://www.marxists.org/reference/archive/stalin/works/1927/12/02.htm
3. *his countrymen, 1927.* Wheatcroft, Stephen. "The Scale and Nature of German and Soviet Repression and Mass Killings, 1930-45 1 STEPHEN

WHEATCROFT." Europe-Asia Studies 48, no. 1319–1353 (1996): 8; Ellman, Michael. "The 1947 Soviet Famine and the Entitlement Approach to Famines." Cambridge Journal of Economics 24 (2000): 603–30.

4. *as a thick t-shirt.* "Prosecutor Releases Images from Aurora Theater Shooting - CNN." Accessed October 15, 2020. https://www.cnn.com/2015/09/11/us/colorado-theater-shooting-images/index.html; "Shocking New Photos of James Holmes's Booby-Trapped Apartment - The Washington Post." Accessed October 15, 2020. https://www.washingtonpost.com/; "Before Gunfire in Colorado Theater, Hints of 'Bad News' About James Holmes - The New York Times." Accessed October 15, 2020. https://www.nytimes.com/2012/08/27/us/before-gunfire-in-colorado-theater-hints-of-bad-news-about-james-holmes.html; "Family of Aurora Shooting Victim Sues Ammo, Body Armor Suppliers - Los Angeles Times." Accessed October 16, 2020. https://www.latimes.com/nation/nation-now/la-na-nn-aurora-shooting-guns-20140916-story.html; "Colo. Shooting Jury Examines Weapons, Body Armor." Accessed October 16, 2020. https://www.usatoday.com/story/news/nation/2015/05/07/colo-shooting-jury-examines-holmes-weapons-body-armor/70974806/.

5. *National Institute of Justice (NIJ).* "Ballistic Resistance of Body Armor NIJ Standard-0101.06 | National Institute of Justice." Accessed October 16, 2020. https://nij.ojp.gov/library/publications/ballistic-resistance-body-armor-nij-standard-010106.

Chapter 12: The Fight Ahead

1. *of nature's causes."* von Pufendorf, Samuel (2003). "The Whole Duty of Man According to the Law of Nature". The Whole Duty of Man. Liberty Fund, Inc. Retrieved 13 November 2009.[full citation needed] Note: Translated by Andrew Tooke, editor, Ian Hunter and David Saunders, with Two Discourses and a Commentary by Jean Barbeyrac, translated by David Saunders (Indianapolis: Liberty Fund, 2003).

2. *did not use it."* Thucydides. History of the Peloponnesian War. United States: Hogan and Thompson, 1836.

3. *the same way.* "Global Views of Economic Opportunity and Inequality | Pew Research Center." Accessed October 16, 2020. https://www.pewresearch.org/global/2014/10/09/emerging-and-developing-economies-much-more-optimistic-than-rich-countries-about-the-future/.

4. Glossary: What "They" Don't Want You to Know About Your Second Amendment Rights

References

5. *Guardian of true liberty…"* "From James Madison to George Thompson, 30 June 1825," Founders Online, National Archives, https://founders.archives.gov/documents/Madison/04-03-02-0562. [Original source: The Papers of James Madison, Retirement Series, vol. 3, 1 March 1823–24 February 1826, ed. David B. Mattern, J. C. A. Stagg, Mary Parke Johnson, and Katherine E. Harbury. Charlottesville: University of Virginia Press, 2016, pp. 545–546.]

6. *shoulder thing that goes up."* "What Is a Barrel Shroud? - YouTube." Accessed October 7, 2020. https://www.youtube.com/watch?v=9rGpykAX1fo.

7. *Webster wrote in 1833.* Webster, N. The Webster Bible. Wipf & Stock Publishers, 2016. p. 3

8. *which it was passed."* From Thomas Jefferson to William Johnson, 12 June 1823," Founders Online, National Archives, https://founders.archives.gov/documents/Jefferson/98-01-02-3562.

9. *its modem sense."* James Madison, Selections from the Private Correspondence of James Madison from 1813-1836, J. C. McGuire, editor (Washington, ton, 1853), p. 52, to Henry Lee on June 25, 1824.

10. *illegitimate government."* Williams, David C.. The Mythic Meanings of the Second Amendment: Taming Political Violence in a Constitutional Republic. United Kingdom: Yale University Press, 2003. p. 132

11. *affordability and extreme reliability.* Killicoat, Phillip. "Weaponomics: The Global Market for Assault Rifles by Phillip Killicoat :: SSRN." Accessed October 7, 2020. https://papers.ssrn.com/sol3/papers.cfm?abstract_id=980820.

12. *sport shooting, collecting, and self-defense.* "Calendar No. 426 103D CONGRESS 2D SESSION," n.d. Accessed October 7, 2020. https://www.congress.gov/103/bills/hr4296/BILLS-103hr4296pcs.pdf

13. *kinds of rifles, shotguns, and pistols:* "Senate Bill 23 Assault Weapon Characteristics | State of California - Department of Justice - Office of the Attorney General." Accessed October 7, 2020. https://oag.ca.gov/firearms/regs/genchar2.

14. *assets or collectors items.* "Firearms Commerce in the United States Annual Statistical Update 2018," Bureau of Alcohol, Tobacco, Firearms and Explosives, June 24, 2018, https://www.atf.gov/resource-center/docs/undefined/firearmscommercestatisticalupdate20185087-24-18pdf/download. For more information about what constitutes a "machine gun," see Bureau of Alcohol, Tobacco, Firearms and Explosives, "National Firearms Act Handbook," U.S. Department of Justice (June 2007): 9-15.

Made in the USA
Las Vegas, NV
21 November 2023